Your College Experience: Strategies for Success, Concise 12/e: College Success, Streamlined

John N. Gardner · Betsy O. Barefoot
Student edition: ISBN 978-1-319-02919-7
Loose-leaf version: ISBN 978-1-319-06456-3 (priced about 65% of the traditional text)
e-Books available (priced at approximately 50% of the traditional text)

S0-BRR-603

Written by the leading authorities on the first-year seminar and grounded in research, *Your College Experience* by **John N. Gardner** and **Betsy O. Barefoot** offers today's diverse students the practical help they need to make the transition to college and get the most out of their time there. While maintaining its hallmark theme of goal setting, the Concise Twelfth Edition reflects a focus on practical strategies across all topics of the book to help students be successful from the start. Chapters on Emotional Intelligence and Thinking in College have all been reorganized and thoroughly revised to be more relevant and useful for today's students.

A full package of instructional support materials—including an Instructor's Annotated Edition, Instructor's Manual, Test Bank, lecture slides, videos, and powerful new digital resources—provides new and experienced instructors with the tools they need to engage students in this course and increase retention.

HELPING STUDENTS SUCCEED FROM THE START

Chapter 1 introduces students to the concepts of purpose and goal setting and explores the value of higher education. New content in the chapter includes a summary of high-impact practices, a discussion of the role of peer leaders in the college success course, material on academic planning and working with an academic adviser, and an emphasis on the concept of resilience.

Assess Your Strengths & Set Goals boxes in each chapter ask students to identify their strengths and then set goals around their own objectives for the chapter material.

Getting the Most Out of College: High-Impact Practices

high-impact practices 1–10

Throughout your college experience, you will have the opportunity to participate in activities known as "high-impact practices." High-impact practices are particular activities that research shows have significant positive impact on both your learning and your overall success. One high-impact practice is taking the first-year seminar, which shouldn't surprise you given what you have read in this chapter about the value of this course. Here is a comprehensive list of the ten high-impact practices in which you can participate, listed in the order you are most likely to encounter them. (In this textbook, this icon ⚙ is used to alert you to these opportunities to enrich your learning.):

1. **first-year seminars** The course in which you find yourself now, designed to prepare you for your college experience.
2. **writing-intensive courses** Courses across the curriculum that engage you in multiple forms of writing for different audiences. This textbook offers various writing activities that make your first-year seminar a writing-intensive course.
3. **collaborative assignments** Learning activities in which you work and solve problems with your classmates in this and other courses.
4. **global learning or diversity experiences** Courses and programs in which you explore cultures, life experiences, and worldviews different from your own.
5. **service-learning** Programs or courses in which you engage in required field-based "experiential learning" and reflection while giving back to your community through service.
6. **learning communities** Programs in which you would take two or more "linked" courses with a group of other students and work closely with one another and with your instructors.
7. **campus-wide common intellectual experiences** Programs in which you would take required "common-core" courses, participate in a required learning community, or engage in other shared experiences such as a "common reading."
8. **undergraduate research** A program that gives you the opportunity to participate in systematic investigation and research working one-

assess **your** strengths

Think about the topic of this chapter. Do you already have a good understanding of the benefits of college? Do you have a clear sense of purpose? What personal and career goals do you want to pursue in college? Describe the experience you have with setting goals and reaching them. If you are not quite ready to answer these questions yet, return to them as you read through this chapter.

set **goals**

Think about a challenge you have had in the past with understanding what college is all about or setting personal goals. As you read this chapter, set a goal that relates to chapter material, and be prepared to talk with others in your class about why you selected this goal. For example, you might set a goal to understand the research on the value of a college degree and apply it to your own perso...

New coverage of academic planning and working with an academic adviser highlights for students the value of using these resources from the start.

Working with an Academic Adviser

Before you register for classes next term, sit down for a strategy session with your academic adviser. On most campuses, you'll be assigned an adviser, who is usually an instructor or a staff person in your chosen field of study. Some colleges offer special advisory centers run by professional advisers. A good adviser can help you choose courses, decide on a major, weigh career possibilities, and map out your degree and certificate requirements. Your adviser can also recommend instructors and help you simplify all aspects of your academic life, so it's important to meet with your adviser right away. Here are a few ways to make sure that your first meeting is a valuable experience.

- **Prepare for the meeting by looking at the course catalog, thinking**

ACADEMIC PLANNING

If you have a goal to drive across the United States, you could, in theory, hop in a car that may need an oil change and travel without GPS or an itinerary and without a carefully packed bag or a planned

MOTIVATING STUDENTS TO BE RESILIENT, CONNECT, AND THINK CRITICALLY

Features, all presented through a dynamic new design, help students engage in the course.

Is This You? boxes speak directly to students who are likely taking first-year experience courses. Look for these special messages to first-generation college students, returning students, student athletes, and students encountering common first-year issues such as time-management challenges, difficulty with writing assignments, financial problems, and the clash of new ideas with old beliefs.

is **this** you?

Bouncing Back from a Bad Grade

You bombed a test, and now you are feeling hopeless and unsure about how to do better. First, know that a bad grade is not the end of the world. Almost every student performs poorly at some point in college. Don't let one D or F get you down. Use the opportunity to build your resilience—to become stronger and show your tough spirit. One way to bounce back from disappointment is to take control of the situation. Talk to the course instructor, work to understand what went wrong, and develop a strategy for improvement. That strategy might be finding a tutor, meeting on a regular basis with your instructor, or working with a learning center professional who can help you improve your skills in reading, studying, remembering, and preparing for tests. Your college success instructor can help you decide what first steps you need to take to improve your academic performance.

is **this** you?

Older than Average

Are you an older student, maybe in your thirties or forties, who is back in college? As an adult, you probably have a great deal of life experience in dealing with tough times. You might have real strengths in emotional intelligence that you have developed at work, at home, or with your family, but you may also have some areas that you need to improve. How are you using your skills to stand up for yourself and negotiate with others as you face the challenges of college? Using your existing strengths and skills in college could allow you to be a role model for others. You might want to give some advice to younger students who seem to be struggling with the day-to-day interactions that are part of college life and help those students find ways to be more adaptable, resilient, and assertive.

Your Turn collaborative learning activities foster peer-to-peer communication, collaboration, motivation, good decision making, writing and reflection, and critical thinking. These activities can be used in class, as homework, or as group activities to strengthen the bond between students and their college communities. They are organized into four types based on what students are asked to do: Make Good Choices, Stay Motivated, Work Together, and Write and Reflect.

your **turn** Stay Motivated

Academic Planning

You have probably already met with an academic adviser, but if not, schedule a meeting right away. Think about this meeting and what you accomplished. Then write a short paper or journal entry about something you learned that increased your motivation to take academic planning seriously. Also, describe in writing at least three problems you might encounter when it comes to choosing your major or planning your program of study if you do not take academic planning seriously. How can these possible negative consequences increase your motivation to plan well for your next meeting with your adviser?

your **turn** Write and Reflect

Are You Able to Concentrate?

The next time that you read a textbook, monitor your ability to concentrate. Check your watch when you begin, and check it again when your mind begins to wander. How many minutes did you concentrate on your reading? List some strategies to keep your mind from wandering. Write a journal entry containing ideas you have heard that you think will work well for you.

your **turn** Make Good Choices

Facebook through an Employer's Eyes

Look at your own or a friend's Facebook page. Do you see anything that puts you or your friend in a negative light? Think about how you would alter the content and writing style if this Facebook page were part of a job application. Consider the changes that are needed to give you or your friend a good chance of getting the job. Remember that employers now routinely check Facebook to see what kinds of information potential employees might post. Choose to post only information that you are willing to share with anyone—*especially* a potential employer.

HOW EMOTIONS INFLUENCE SUCCESS

Accentuate the Positive

You probably know people who always find the negative in any situation. Constantly focusing on what's missing or what's not perfect will likely make you the kind of person whom others avoid. Practice looking on the bright side.

marekuliasz/Shutterstock

Emotions are strongly tied to physical and psychological well-being. For example, some studies have suggested that cancer patients who have strong EI live longer than those with weak EI. People who are aware of the needs of others tend to be happier than people who are not. An extensive study done at the University of Pennsylvania found that the best athletes succeed in part because they're extremely optimistic. A number of studies link strong EI skills to college success in particular. Studies indicate that emotionally intelligent students get higher grades. Researchers looked at students' grade point averages at the end of their first year of college. Students who had tested high for intrapersonal skills, stress tolerance, and adaptability when they entered in the fall did better academically than those who had lower overall EI test scores. Here are a few other highlights of those studies:

- **Motivation:** Motivation is one of the most important attributes that college students can have. Figuring out what actually does motivate anyone is complex, but striving to find out and nurture these motivations is the goal.
- **Resilience:** We discussed resilience above—stronger emotional intelligence leads to greater resilience. Students with healthy emotional intelligence might act proactively by asking instructors for feedback on projects, papers, and tests, participating in classroom discussions, and joining study groups. Students with unhealthy EI are likely to struggle academically, panic before taking tests, have trouble concentrating on coursework, and engage in risky behaviors such as alcohol and drug abuse in an effort to cope. Dr. Richard Kadison, a former director of mental health services at Harvard University, noted that "the emotional well-being of students goes hand in hand with their academic development. If they're not doing well emotionally, they are not going to reach their academic potential."[2]

PROVIDING IMPORTANT NEW CONTENT AND UPDATES WITH A FOCUS ON TWO CHAPTERS

The 12/e features revisions from cover to cover, with a focus on the following:

Chapter 3, Emotional Intelligence (EI), has been improved by linking EI concepts to events of daily college life, with elaboration on the concepts of resilience and making good choices. Self-assessments help students evaluate and improve their own EI.

Chapter 5, Thinking in College, gives students a better understanding of what is involved in college-level thinking, with practical strategies on how to achieve it. Students are clearly shown how concepts like fast and slow thinking, problem solving, creativity, and collaboration all relate to college-level thinking. The chapter includes a new critical-thinking assessment, a new application of Bloom's Taxonomy, and a heavily revised Tech Tip shown below.

COLLEGE-LEVEL THINKING: HIGHER AND DEEPER

In college, the level of thinking that your instructors expect from you exceeds that which you did in high school, both in terms of the questions that are asked and the answers that are expected. For instance, if a high school teacher asked, "What are the three branches of the U.S. government?" he or she would ask you to give the one right answer: "legislative, executive, and judicial." A college instructor, on the other hand, might ask, "Under what circumstances might conflicts arise among the three branches of government, and what do the circumstances and the conflicts reveal about the democratic process?" There is no simple, quick, or single acceptable answer to the second question—that's the point of higher education. Questions that suggest complex answers engage you in the process of deep thinking. The shift to this higher or deeper level of thinking can be an adjustment—it might even catch you off guard and cause you some stress.

One step toward deep and critical thinking is becoming comfortable with uncertainty. In college, it's important to challenge assumptions and conclusions, even those presented by so-called experts. Rather than just

Tech Tips in each chapter introduce essential skills related to the moving target that is technology—proper use of e-mail, benefits of e-books, the value of specific programs and apps for good note taking, critically thinking when doing online research, and use of the cloud.

▶ ▶ ▶ ▶

tech**tip**

USE YOUR CRITICAL-THINKING SKILLS IN CONDUCTING RESEARCH

You have probably heard that colleges and universities expect their students to be able to conduct research when they write papers or create projects. In high school or a casual setting, doing research usually means going to a search engine like Google, Yahoo, or Ask.com. Many of us do this so automatically that we say, "Let me 'Google' that." But is a Google search all professors are looking for when they ask you to conduct research? How else could you conduct research?

Internet searches will help you find people basically doing three things: **yelling**, **selling**, or **telling**.

Yelling: Someone has a viewpoint and puts it forward on Blogger or YouTube, but how do you know if they are biased or a member of a fringe or hate group when you use their video in your project?

Selling: Often, people promote products or services in a way that makes them sound like credible sources of information when they are really simply trying to get you to buy something.

Telling: These places and people actually have credible information that you find informative and useful, but how can you verify their credibility?

The Problem

You need to conduct research for a paper, but you're not sure how to evaluate the types of information found on the Internet.

The Fix *Use a critical-thinking system to conduct your research.*

Rommel Canlas/Shutterstock

How to Do It

Start with good questions. If you are researching a topic, such as "marijuana legalization," generate some questions you have about that subject rather than just going to Google and typing "marijuana" into the search box:

- What is the history of marijuana use in the U.S.
- Why was it made illegal in the first place?
- Where has it been legalized and why?
- What have been some of the positive and negative outcomes of making it legal?

Generating questions will save you time by clarifying what you need to know, so you will recognize useful results and ignore the ones that won't help you.

Go to the library. Show the reference librarians your list of questions. They can help you fine-tune them and will recommend good places to find certain kinds of answers.

Use databases. Your school pays for research databases, which collect a variety of credible, scholarly research. When you use research databases, you can be sure that the information is reliable, and you can refine your search terms to produce 20 or 30 returns, as opposed to 20 or 30 million. Most databases are

available online with login information that your college can provide, so you can use them anytime from home or on your laptop.

Use a variety of locations to confirm information. When you see the same information in a variety of credible sources, you can start to trust its accuracy. Remember that there are still good sources of information in print form that are not available online.

Consider the quality of the information. Where did it come from? Who said it and why? How current is it? Has anything major happened in this area since this information was published?

EXTRA STYLE POINTS: Get in the habit of reading (not just watching) a variety of news and information sources. If you get news only from TV or links posted on Facebook, you will miss some important stories. Remember this: Professionals need to be up to date in their own areas of interest and expertise, but they also must be able to understand larger current events happening in the world around them. You must have broad knowledge in order to place your professional knowledge in context.

A COMPLETE PACKAGE OF INSTRUCTOR SUPPORT MATERIALS FOR NEW AND EXPERIENCED INSTRUCTORS.

The **Instructor's Annotated Edition** includes many new, clearly marked Retention Strategies in every chapter—best practices from John Gardner and Betsy Barefoot for keeping students in school. New Peer Leader annotations offer suggestions that peer ▶ ▶ ▶ ▶ leaders (or the instructor of record) can use in designing special activities. New High-Impact Practice (HIP) annotations give tips for incorporating HIP activities. In Class, Outside Class, and FYI annotations are also included.

Research conducted by colleges and universities has found that first-year students are far more likely to be successful if they participate in courses and programs designed to teach them how to succeed in college. This course is designed to help you avoid some of the pitfalls—both academic and personal—that trip up many beginning students.

Although your classmates might not say it out loud, many of them share your concerns, doubts, and fears about being in college. This course will provide a supportive environment in which you can share your successes and your frustrations, get to know others who are beginning college, develop lasting relationships with your instructor and some other students, and begin to think about your plans for life after college.

The Value of Your College Success Textbook

As college professors, researchers, and administrators with many years of experience working with first-year students, we're well aware that starting college can be challenging. We also know that if you apply the ideas in this book to your everyday life, you are likely to enjoy your time in college, graduate, and achieve your life goals.

Your instructor may ask you to read every chapter in this book, but even if you're not required to do so, consider this book a resource to answer questions you might have later this year and throughout your college experience. After this opening chapter, which discusses the value of college, purpose and goal setting, and academic planning, subsequent

ADDITIONAL SUPPORT MATERIALS

The Instructor's Manual and Test Bank includes everything you need to manage your course. New to this edition are sample syllabi for 16-, 12-, and 8-week courses; guidelines for incorporating videos into a college success course; and capstone projects for the end of the course. The Test Bank is also available in a computerized version.

Lecture Slides include complete lecture outlines for each chapter of the book, plus images and figures from the text. Use as is or add your own material to make each presentation your own.

New! *LaunchPad Solo for College Success.* *LaunchPad Solo for College Success* is home to dozens of pre-built assignable digital resources designed to help students engage with key course concepts and prepare for class, including

LearningCurve adaptive quizzing and video activities. Pre-built units are easy to assign or adapt with your own material, such as readings, videos, quizzes, discussion groups, and more. LaunchPad Solo also provides access to a grade book that provides a clear window on performance for your whole class, for individual students and individual assignments. Visit macmillanhighered.com/collegesuccessmedia for more information.

The Academic and Career Excellence System (ACES) is an instrument that measures student strengths in twelve critical areas and prompts students to reflect on their habits, behaviors, attitudes, and skills. Norm-referenced reports indicate whether students are at a high, moderate, or low skill level in particular areas. For more information go to macmillanhighered.com/ACES/catalog.

FOR MORE INFORMATION ON THIS BOOK OR ANY OF ITS SUPPLEMENTS

> Visit macmillanhighered.com/gardner12e

> Speak with your Macmillan sales rep

> View the chart on the inside front cover of the Instructor's Annotated Edition which shows you where to find each asset.

active learning strategies

The following exercises, which do not appear in the student edition, will help your students sharpen their critical skills for college success: writing, critical thinking, learning in groups, planning, reflecting, and taking action.

1 WELCOME TO YOUR COLLEGE EXPERIENCE

WORKING TOGETHER The Many Reasons for College

Using the Your Turn: Make Good Choices, "The Choice to Become a College Student," as a prompt, have your students form small groups to discuss their reasons for attending college. In these groups, have students share the reasons that seem most relevant to them. Each group should compile a list of the most important reasons and share them with the class. Facilitate a discussion of similarities and differences in the lists. Also, discuss with your students which of these reasons they think have changed over time, and why.

EXERCISE 1.1 Solving a Problem

Ask your students to respond to the following questions in class or in an e-mail to you: What has been your biggest unresolved problem in college to date? What steps have you taken to solve it? Respond to students personally, and if they still have questions, invite them to meet with you during office hours.

EXERCISE 1.2 With or Without

This chapter stressed the differences between a high school education and a college education as far as earning power and other outcomes. Ask students to imagine they are still trying to decide whether or not to attend college. Drawing from the material in this chapter as well as from their own ideas, have students make a list of reasons to earn a college degree and a list of reasons not to go to college. For example, pipe fitters earn impressive salaries, while librarians earn much less. How do students justify a college education on those terms?

EXERCISE 1.3 Focusing on Your Concerns

Have students browse the table of contents of this book. Direct them to find one or more chapters that address their most important concerns. Make a list of the chapters your students have chosen, and note how many times students selected particular chapters. You will then be able to see the topics that concern them most and design your class to appeal to their interests.

EXERCISE 1.4 What Are Your Life Goals?

The following list includes some life goals that people set for themselves. This list can help students begin to think about the kinds of goals they might want to set. Ask students to put a check mark next to each of the goals they would like to achieve in their lives. Next, they should review the goals they have checked and circle the five they most want to achieve. Finally, students should review their list of five goals and rank them by priority on a 1-to-5 scale: 1 for most important, 5 for least important. Discuss the choices in class.

____ Supportive friendships

____ Good health

____ Financial security

____ A beautiful home

____ International fame

____ Work you are passionate about

____ A good love relationship

____ A satisfying religious faith

____ A meaningful life

____ Success in my profession

____ A personal contribution to social justice

____ A flexible schedule

____ A satisfying and fulfilling marriage

RETENTION EXERCISE SMART Goal Setting

Ask students to pick a goal—either short-term or long-term—and use the SMART template below to make their goal even more attainable. Students who are skilled at setting and attaining goals are more likely to persist in college.

Write a short-term or long-term personal goal that is related to your college experience. Use the SMART method to further develop your goal.

S: How can you make this goal more **S**pecific?

M: How will you **M**easure whether you have attained this goal at a high level?

A: How do you know that there is a reasonable chance you can **A**ttain this goal?

R: How is this goal **R**elevant to your interests and broader sense of life purpose?

T: What is your **T**ime period for achieving this goal?

For additional practice with the SMART method, refer to Chapter 1 (pages 16–17) which includes Figure 1.2, a blank SMART goal-setting guide for students to fill in with five goals. An example is provided to get them started.

2 TIME MANAGEMENT

WORKING TOGETHER Comparing Class Schedules

In small groups, have your students share their current class schedules. Encourage them to exchange ideas on how to handle time-management problems effectively and to point out the challenges they see in each other's schedules. Discuss ways that students can design more time-efficient schedules for the next term.

EXERCISE 2.1 Goal Setting

Have students complete the following lists:

A. List five goals you would like to set for yourself for the coming decade.
B. List two measurable objectives for achieving each of the goals you set.

EXERCISE 2.2 Your Daily Plan

Have students make a to-do list for the next day. Tell them to list all appointments and activities, noting the hours of the day. Have students label each item with an A, B, or C, with the A's deserving the most attention, and the C's deserving the least. Encourage students to check out the different calendar and personal planner formats, templates, and apps, many of which are available for free online or can be purchased at the campus bookstore.

RETENTION EXERCISE Tracking "Actual Time"

Some students will drop out of college because they are unable to manage their multiple time commitments. Help students become more aware of how they manage their time by using a weekly timetable (see example in Figure 2.2), a planner, or a calendar on their tablets or phones to keep track of how they spend time every hour for an entire week. Ask them to fill in every time slot. At the end of this week, ask students to count how many hours they spent on various activities. What activities merit more time? Which activities should take less time? In what ways did students waste time?

3 EMOTIONAL INTELLIGENCE

WORKING TOGETHER What Would You Have Done?

Share the following scenario with your students.

It's late afternoon on a Thursday, and the only thing between Josh and the weekend is a big biology test at 10:00 a.m. on Friday. There's a lot at stake with this test: It will count for one-third of his final grade. His cell phone rings. It's Susie with an invitation. "A group of us are planning to go out tonight. We thought about an early dinner and a movie. We won't be late," she says. The last time Josh went out on a night before a big test, he came home late. This time he is committed to coming home by 9:00 p.m. to review for the test. Josh goes out with Susie and her friends. He is having a wonderful time, and every time he thinks about going home, he says to himself, "Just a little longer and I will go." Before he knows it, it's 2:00 a.m., and the test is only eight hours away. Josh is exhausted and stressed. He has to decide whether he should sleep a few hours or pull an all-nighter to pass the test. He decides to sleep. He sets the alarm for 4:00 a.m., when he wakes up groggy and out of sorts. Josh starts to study, but his roommate's alarm goes off at 6:00 a.m. His roommate keeps hitting snooze, so the alarm goes off every 15 minutes. Josh is annoyed. He doesn't want to leave the room, but he has to concentrate. He complains, "I'm trying to study. Will you please be quiet!" His stress is getting worse, and now it's 8:30 a.m. His cell phone rings. It's Josh's mother reminding him about his grandmother's birthday. He snaps, "Mom, please don't bother me now. I am studying." He quickly hangs up; he has had it. This is his worst nightmare. He is stressed, on edge, and exhausted, and he feels a big headache coming on.

Divide the class into groups of four or five. Ask the groups to spend 15 or 20 minutes discussing the following questions: If you were in Josh's place, what would you have done? How would you evaluate Josh's emotional intelligence? What could he have done differently? What competencies does he need to improve? Then ask each group to report its responses to the entire class for discussion.

RETENTION EXERCISE Matching Behaviors with EI Competencies

Students who have difficulty managing stress and engage in self-destructive behaviors are often unable to complete a college degree. Have students match the unsuccessful student behaviors in the first column below with the related EI competencies in the second column that would help the student change or overcome the behavior. (Sometimes more than one competency relates to a single behavior.)

4 HOW YOU LEARN

WORKING TOGETHER Multiple Intelligences

After all students have completed the Multiple Intelligences Inventory, ask them to determine their highest point scores. Then, break the class into groups according to those scores. Ask group members to discuss the classes they're now taking and their intended majors. In discussion with the whole class, determine whether students with particular multiple intelligence scores are more likely to engage in certain activities, take certain classes, or select certain majors.

EXERCISE 4.1 Learning Styles Models

In small groups, ask students to discuss the four learning-style models that are presented in this chapter. Which was the easiest to understand? Which was the most difficult? Which of the models did group members like best? Why? Each group should report its opinions to the whole class.

FOR INSTRUCTORS ONLY

Unsuccessful Student Behavior	Related EI Competency
1. Experience stress and do not handle it well	A. Emotional self-awareness
2. Frequently feel overwhelmed	B. Self-regard
3. Don't get along with others	C. Assertiveness
4. Give up easily	D. Independence
5. Engage in destructive behaviors such as binge drinking and drugs	E. Self-actualization
6. Act very impulsively	F. Reality testing
7. Are not able to solve problems	G. Flexibility
8. Are dependent on others	H. Problem solving
9. Show unethical behavior such as stealing or cheating	I. Stress tolerance
10. Have trouble working in teams	J. Impulse control
11. Have very stereotypical views of others and are unaware of their biases and unwilling to change	K. Empathy
12. Are often sad	L. Social responsibility
13. Are not optimistic	M. Interpersonal relationships
14. Have an "I can't" attitude	
15. Blame others for their problems	
16. Think they will get a 4.0 GPA but have missed many classes	
17. Have a hard time making decisions without input from others	

EXERCISE 4.2 Using Your Five Senses to Learn

Have students refer to pages 64–77 in this chapter and decide which mode or modes of learning seem to work best for them: aural, visual, interactive, tactile, or kinesthetic. Ask for suggestions on how they can adapt to other styles. For example, if students are not aural learners, how can they use their preferred ways of learning to master information that is presented in lecture-style courses? Have students brainstorm ways to convert lecture material into a format that is a better match for how they best use their five senses in the learning process.

EXERCISE 4.3 Learning More about Learning Disabilities

Have students use the library or the Internet to find the names of three famous people not mentioned in this chapter who have learning disabilities and how they have dealt with or overcome those disabilities. Ask students to share with the class what they learned from their research.

RETENTION EXERCISE Multiple Intelligences and Success

After students take the short Multiple Intelligences Inventory, divide them into eight groups (one for each intelligence) and ask each group to think of ways that each intelligence (according to Howard Gardner) supports student success and the likelihood that someone will remain in college and graduate. Conversely, ask them to decide whether a specific intelligence makes it difficult for someone to be successful in college.

5 THINKING IN COLLEGE

WORKING TOGETHER Gathering Information for Decision Making

Divide the class into groups of four to six, and have each group choose a major problem on campus, such as binge drinking, cheating, college costs, parking, safety, and sexual assault. Between this class meeting and the next, students should seek information about their group's problem and identify possible solutions by interviewing a campus authority on the topic, searching campus library holdings, and/or conducting a survey of other students. During the next class, ask students to share their findings with other members of their group and cite their sources. Groups should try to reach a consensus on the best

way to solve the problem. If any members of the group are using emotional rather than logical arguments, point that out.

EXERCISE 5.1 Reflecting on Arguments

Review the lists of questions on pages 97–98 of this chapter with students. Are students asking themselves these kinds of questions when they read their textbooks and listen to or take part in discussions? Have students revisit the list each evening for the next week and think about whether they have asked such questions that day and tried to notice whether people were stating their assumptions or conclusions.

RETENTION EXERCISE Learning about a Liberal Education

Students who are enrolled in required general education or liberal arts courses often fail to see the relevance of those courses to their career or life plans. Such students might lose their motivation for academic work and decide to leave college. Discuss with students how a liberal college education is relevant because it teaches them to investigate all sides of an issue and all possible solutions to a problem before they reach a conclusion or decide on a plan of action. Make sure your students understand that the word liberal (from the Latin *libero*, meaning "to free") has no political connotation in this context, but represents the purpose of a college education: to liberate the mind from biases, superstitions, prejudices, and lack of knowledge so that students are in a better position to seek answers to difficult questions. Have students choose one of their instructors whose field is in the humanities (art, literature, languages, history, government, etc.), mathematics, or the sciences (social, biological, or physical). Students should make an appointment to interview the instructor about how a liberal education and the instructor's particular field of study contribute to a fuller life, no matter what a student's major might be.

6 READING TO LEARN

WORKING TOGETHER Thinking Back to High School

Ask students to write down the reading methods that worked best for them in high school. Then, ask them to share these methods with others in the class to initiate a discussion about how reading in college differs from reading in high school.

EXERCISE 6.1 Doing What It Takes to Understand

How far must students go to understand the material in a textbook? Here is one way to find out. Give them the following instructions:

1. Read a brief chapter in your textbook as if you were reading for pleasure.
2. Read it a second time, but pause at the end of each section to mentally review what you just read.
3. Read it a third time, pausing at the end of each section for review. Then go back and highlight important words or sentences.
4. Read it a fourth time, and do all of the above. This time, ask a friend to read with you, and discuss each passage in the chapter before going on to the next. Stop and take notes, write in the margins, and highlight.

Ask students to discuss how this process increased their understanding of the reading.

EXERCISE 6.2 Preparing to Read, Think, and Mark

Direct students to choose a reading assignment from one of their classes. After they preview the material as described earlier in this chapter, have students begin reading until they reach a major heading or have read at least a page or two. They should then stop and write down what they remember from the material. Next, have them go back to the same material and mark what they believe are the main ideas. Suggest that students list four main ideas from the reading so they don't fall into the trap of marking too much.

RETENTION EXERCISE Plan for Active Reading

Students who are poor readers will have great difficulty in college and, unless they improve their skills, are likely to drop out or flunk out. To help students improve their reading skills, ask them to bring a textbook from another course to your next class. During class, ask them to consider the four-step "Plan for Active Reading" on page 107. Ask them which step is the hardest and which is the easiest. The easiest may be "marking." Ask students to check their textbooks to see if any have too much highlighting or too many marks. The

hardest stage may be "reading with concentration." Ask students to get in small groups and develop a list of ideas for "concentrating while reading." Do any of the steps seem unnecessary to your students? Discuss the importance of each step.

7 GETTING THE MOST FROM CLASS

WORKING TOGETHER Comparing Notes

Present a small lecture to students on any topic of your choosing. The lecture can be related to the text or presented on another topic. Have students take notes on your lecture. Then ask students to pair up with others to explain their note-taking systems and share their notes. Ask them whether or not they agreed on what was important during the lecture. Give students your notes on the lecture so that they can compare and contrast their notes with yours. You might want to collect the students' notes and review them to make sure that they have taken notes on the most important points in the lecture.

EXERCISE 7.1 Encouraging Students to Speak Up in Class

Managing class participation is often a challenge for any first-year seminar instructor. Some students tend to monopolize group discussion while others seem reluctant to say anything. A way to help shy students feel more comfortable about speaking in front of the class is the "think, pair, share" technique. Pose an open-ended question to your students; give them a chance to think about how they would respond, and then ask them to discuss their response with one other person. Then, ask one or both students from each pair to share their response with the whole class. You may not have time to solicit a response from each pair of students. If time is limited, do this exercise over a few successive class periods on different topics to make sure that every student has a chance to speak for his or her pair.

EXERCISE 7.2 What System of Note Taking Works for You?

Have students pick one of their lecture courses and implement each of the methods of note taking described in this chapter over the next four or five class periods: Cornell, outline, paragraph, and list formats, or a combination. Ask students to decide which method seems to work best for them. Which method will be easiest to review when studying for tests?

EXERCISE 7.3 Using a Recall Column to Memorize

Have students refer to Figure 7.1 on page 138, and study the material provided in the right-hand column until they think they know it well enough to be tested on it. Cover the right-hand column and using the recall column, ask students to try to recite, in their own words, the main ideas from these sample notes. Allow them to uncover the right-hand column when they need to refer to it. Ask students whether this system seems to work. If not, why not?

RETENTION EXERCISE Engagement

Research finds that engagement can be linked to retention, particularly for students often considered at risk—first-generation students or historically underserved populations. Ask students working in small groups, either during class or out of class, to discuss the term *engagement* and what it means to them. Why do they think college and university educators focus so much on getting students engaged? Why do older students tend to be more engaged in learning than students just out of high school? Ask them to consider whether within their peer group it's cool to be "engaged in learning." Have groups share their ideas with the whole class.

8 STUDYING

WORKING TOGETHER The Name Game

Sitting in a circle, have students state their first names preceded by a descriptive adjective (for example, Sophisticated Susan, Tall Tom, and Jolly Jennifer). Proceed around the circle, having each student state his or her name and descriptor, followed by the names and descriptors of all preceding students. Students can help each other when someone's memory fails. After all students have had a turn, discuss what the class learned from the exercise.

EXERCISE 8.1 Getting the Big Picture

Select a concept from this book, and have students respond to the four questions under the heading "Improving Your Memory," listed on pages 159–60. Have students share their work in

small groups. Then ask one person in the group to share with the entire class.

EXERCISE 8.2 Using Memory Strategies

Have students practice using association, visualization, and flash cards to improve their memories. Ask them to try the following strategies with a week's lessons from one of their courses:

1. Visualization. Close your eyes and "see" your notes or textbook assignments in action. Break your notes into chunks, and create a visual image for each chunk.
2. Association. Associate a chunk of information with something familiar. For example, if you want to remember that the word *always* usually signifies a wrong answer on multiple-choice or true/false quizzes, associate *always* with a concept such as "always wrong."
3. Flash cards. Write a key word or phrase from the material on one side of a card, and put the details on the other side. An example might be as follows: Write the words "Ways to Remember" on one side; on the other side, write, "Go over it again. Use all senses. Organize it. Mnemonics."

After students have tried all three methods, ask which method worked best for them.

EXERCISE 8.3 How Accurate Is Your Memory?

This exercise demonstrates how difficult it can be to remember things accurately. One student whispers the name of an object (e.g., lamp, bike, hamburger) to another student. The second student then whispers the word to a third student and adds a second word. The third student whispers both words to another student, adding still another word, and so forth. Each student who adds a word should write it down. When the final student recites the list, students whose words were left out or changed should speak up. The class should then discuss what strategies they were using to remember the list and why they forgot certain items.

RETENTION EXERCISE Creating an Acrostic

Memory is an essential study and test-taking skill that predicts success in college. To help students develop one memory strategy, divide the class into small groups, and have students select a list of words that someone in the group needs to remember. For instance, a group member might select the original thirteen colonies in the United States or famous composers of the Romantic period. Have each group create a sentence that everyone can remember, using the first letters of each word in the list. For instance, the composers Liszt, Chopin, Berlioz, Weber, Schumann, and Wagner could be remembered by using the sentence "Let's Call Brother While Sister Waits."

9 TEST TAKING

WORKING TOGETHER Forming a Study Group

Have students form a study group for a course. Students should think about their strengths and weaknesses in a learning or studying situation. Then have each study group brainstorm how each strength can help everyone in the group prepare for tests and exams. What helpful strengths will each student look for in another group member? How can their own strengths help others? Students should create a study plan for their study groups. They should review the test schedule for the course and set times for future meetings. What will each member of the group do in preparation for the next meeting?

EXERCISE 9.1 Designing an Exam Plan

Use the following guidelines to have students design an exam plan for one of their courses:

1. What type of exam will be used?
2. What material will be covered? Is the exam cumulative?
3. What types of questions will the exam contain?
4. How many questions do you think there will be?
5. What approach will you use to study for the exam?
6. How many study sessions—and how much time—will you need?

Now, ask students to list all material to be covered and create a study schedule for the week before the exam, allowing as many 1-hour blocks as they will need.

EXERCISE 9.2 Creating Your Own Peaceful Scene

To help students deal with test-taking anxiety, have them think about the most peaceful place they can imagine, real or imaginary. It might be a place they

remember fondly from childhood, a special family vacation spot, a place where they always feel safe, a place they have always wanted to visit, or a place from a favorite book or movie. Now, have them think about what they would hear, see, smell, taste, and feel if they were there right now. Do not just have them think about how relaxed they would feel; ask them to be specific about what they would experience: the warmth of a fire, a gentle breeze, the sand between their toes, rain on the roof. Have students use all five senses to take themselves to their peaceful places. Practice this technique regularly with students, and they will be able to re-create peaceful scenes with ease when they need to relax.

RETENTION EXERCISE Test Taking

The connection between grades and retention is significant. As you approach the midterm, ask your students to think back on the tests they've taken so far. In small groups, ask them to identify their worst and best grades. Then, ask them to discuss with each other what factors might have affected their performance, especially factors they can control (such as amount and timing of preparation, sleep, exercise, diet, management of distractions, etc.).

10 INFORMATION LITERACY AND COMMUNICATION

WORKING TOGETHER Conducting a Group Search at the Library

Have students plan a library visit in groups of three. Before they go, one member of the group should call a librarian and ask for a brief meeting. When they arrive, they should ask the librarian to show them where to find reference books, periodicals, and scholarly journals. Students should also ask how to use online databases on the library computers to aid their searches. Decide which database each student will search, and have students search for a topic of their choosing. Students should print their findings and share them with the class. What did they learn?

WORKING TOGETHER Write, Pair, Write, Share

Direct your students to do this exercise in small groups of five or six. Use the following instructions:

1. Write. For about 10 minutes, use the freewriting technique to write about something that is on your mind. Remember, don't stop to think; just keep writing.

2. Pair. When you are told to stop writing, pair off with another student in your group, and share what you have written by talking about it. Listen to what the other person in your minigroup has to say about what you told her or him. Take notes if you wish.
3. Write. When you are next told to write, reflect on the interaction in your minigroup, but do it individually, on paper. How has the discussion reinforced, modified, or changed your original thoughts on the subject? Write this down.
4. Share. At the given signal, return to your small group of five or six. Appoint a leader, a recorder, and a reporter. Share your thoughts with the entire group. Listen to what group members have to say. Present your report to the group at large. Reflect on what learning has taken place and what the next steps should be. How might you apply this process to one of your other classes?

EXERCISE 10.1 Getting Oriented to Periodicals

To encourage students to get familiar with the periodicals in the library, have them complete the following tasks and answer these questions:

1. Find out how your library arranges periodicals (magazines, journals, newspapers). It probably isn't obvious, so don't hesitate to ask. Why do you think the periodicals are organized in this way?
2. Select an important event that was in the news the year you were born. To find out what was happening then, you might want to consult an almanac or ask a reference librarian to recommend a chronology. Find a contemporary (written at the time of the event) news report as well as a scholarly article that analyzes the event in a journal. Describe the event. Why was it significant? Note some of the differences you found between the news report and the scholarly article.

EXERCISE 10.2 Tempted to Take Shortcuts

Ask your students to read this scenario and identify all the ethical and practical problems with Jack's strategy. What suggestions would your students have for Jack?

At the end of history class on Monday, Jack's instructor told the students, "As you're finalizing the paper that is due on Friday, let me know if you have any questions about how to cite your sources. Remember to submit your paper at my office no later than 5:00 p.m." Jack panicked. He had completely forgotten about this paper and hadn't even begun working on it, much less thinking about how to cite sources. He raced out of class and went back to his room where his roommate was just waking up. Jack's roommate had the solution: "Just pick a topic that a lot of people have written about—something like World War II—go to Wikipedia, and copy all the information. Wikipedia even has all the sources listed." Jack had never used Wikipedia before, but he thought "borrowing" the Wikipedia write-up was a good last-minute solution.

EXERCISE 10.3 Using the Guidelines for Successful Speaking

An important objective of first-year seminars is to help students become more comfortable in giving oral presentations. Student presentations in first-year seminars are usually brief and can be focused on an assigned topic or a topic chosen by the students themselves. Be sure to direct your students to the Guidelines for Successful Speaking in this chapter before they give their presentations. Let them know that they will be evaluated (either formally or informally) on the degree to which they have followed these guidelines.

EXERCISE 10.4 Getting Comfortable in Your Library

To encourage students to get familiar with the library, have them complete the following activity:

Unobtrusively observe what goes on around the information services or reference area (not the circulation desk where you check out books). Watch at least five transactions. Watch the people who ask questions, and watch the staff people who answer them. Does it appear to you that the "customers" receive friendly, competent help? Do the staff members sit and point, or are they on their feet? Do they sometimes accompany inquirers to stack areas or work with them at the computer stations? How might what you observe influence your strategy for getting help if and when you need it?

RETENTION EXERCISE Getting Involved

Students who are involved on campus will be more likely to persist with their college careers. This exercise links involvement with strategies to increase learning and skill building.

Make a list of offices, centers, or activities on your campus in which students can become involved and can practice their writing and speaking skills. (Examples could include the campus radio station, a newspaper or literary magazine, student government or other leadership activity, a Greek organization, a tutoring center, a writing center, etc.) Divide students into pairs or small teams of three or four and have each group visit one of these offices to learn more about its focus and requirements for student involvement. Have each group make a brief presentation to the class about what group members learned, and especially what writing or speaking experience students could gain by becoming involved with these activities.

11 DIVERSITY

WORKING TOGETHER Reflecting on Identity

1. Have students form groups of four to six people. Have them identify areas in which they all share similarities, and keep a written record of those areas. Group members must all agree with an item before it can be added to the list. Next, ask students to create a list of differences.
2. Have students respond to the following questions: How easy or difficult was it to come up with similarities and to agree on them? To what level of depth do the group similarities go? (For example, "We all have hair" versus "We are all religious people.") Was it easy or hard to identify differences? Which list was longer?

EXERCISE 11.1 Examining the Curriculum

At this point, students might have identified some majors that interest them. Have students use your campus's course catalog to identify courses in majors that focus on the topics of multicultural-ism and diversity. Why do they think academic departments have included these subjects in the curriculum? How would studying diversity and multiculturalism help students to prepare for their fields of choice?

EXERCISE 11.2 Appreciating Your Gender

Have students read the following four questions pertaining to gender and create a list of answers:

1. What aspects do you like about being your gender?
2. What are the best things that have happened to you because you are that gender?

3. What are some things that have happened because of your gender that you do not want to experience again?
4. What would you like other people to know about your gender?

RETENTION EXERCISE Diversity

Students who feel marginalized at your institution because of their race, gender, sexual orientation, economic status, or other characteristics will be at risk for dropout. Ask your students to take the perspective of someone different from them, and write a short essay on whether the institutional environment is or is not supportive of that individual. Examples would be white men or women, students of color, students of different religions, students with different sexual orientations, students of different ages.

12 MONEY

WORKING TOGETHER Financial Advice

Divide the class into groups of four or five, and have each group appoint a discussion note-taker. Ask members in each group to share any financial advice they have received from friends or family. Bring the class together, and ask each note-taker to report on what group members shared. Ask students to comment on the kinds of advice they're receiving and the overall challenges of money management.

EXERCISE 12.1 Calculating Interest Charges

Ask students to select a recent credit card bill and note on a piece of paper the amount spent that month. Then have them assume they charged the same amount in each of the next eleven months and paid only the minimum payment each month. Now have them calculate the balance they will have in one year, including interest charges. To help them complete this assignment, refer them to online interest rate calculators, such as the one at **bankrate.com/brm/calc/minpayment.asp.** If they're not sure of some amounts, have them use 15.99 percent as their APR and 31.99 percent as the APR default rate.

EXERCISE 12.2 Debit or Credit?

By a show of hands, ask how many students have at least one credit card. Then ask how many have debit cards. Ask students who have at least one of each which they use the most and why. Ask students who have credit cards but no debit card to explain why they don't feel they need the latter. Underscore the difference between debit cards and credit cards.

RETENTION EXERCISE Being Financially True to Yourself

Assign a paper asking students to share any concerns they have about their current financial situation. Have them include any improvements they have made in keeping track of their money, as well as any areas they feel are getting out of hand. After reading the papers, share the positives and negatives with the class without identifying student contributors.

YOUR COLLEGE EXPERIENCE

Strategies for Success

brief contents

contents

PART ONE   FOUNDATIONS

David Shaffer/Getty Images

1   WELCOME TO YOUR COLLEGE EXPERIENCE   3

Michael Krinke/Getty Images

2   TIME MANAGEMENT   23

 Indicates sections that refer to high-impact practices. See page 9 for more information.

wavebreakmedia/Shutterstock

3 EMOTIONAL INTELLIGENCE 45

Student Profile 46

wavebreakmedia/Shutterstock

4 HOW YOU LEARN 61

Student Profile 62

Phase4Studios/Shutterstock

PART TWO   PREPARING TO LEARN

5 THINKING IN COLLEGE 87

Chris Schmidt/Getty Images

6 READING TO LEARN 105

⌖ Indicates sections that refer to high-impact practices. See page 9 for more information.

wavebreakmedia/Shutterstock

⊙ Indicates sections that refer to high-impact practices. See page 9 for more information.

Blend Images-Hill Street
Studios/Getty Images

PART THREE PREPARING FOR LIFE

Blend Images-Andersen
Ross/Getty Images

Image Source/Getty Images

Indicates sections that refer to high-impact practices. See page 9 for more information.

instructor's annotations is denoted with the heading "HIGH-IMPACT PRACTICE." Also, a special icon ⊙ identifies content in the features and narrative of the student edition that relates to HIPs. For instance, readers will see the HIP icon adjacent to the Your Turn: Work Together and Your Turn: Write and Reflect activities, and with content coverage related to writing, collaboration, diversity, global learning, or service learning. Furthermore, icons placed within the table of contents and the list of Your Turn features show you where to find HIP material.

2. **An emphasis on motivation and the importance of the choices students make.** Through the narrative and special features, the new edition helps students see how good choices bring them closer to their goals, guides them in understanding how being resilient involves bouncing back from poor choices and making increasingly smarter ones, and motivates them to make these smarter decisions. Each chapter includes a Your Turn: Stay Motivated feature, a Your Turn: Make Good Choices feature, and an ending exercise that invites students to Reflect on Choices through writing. Collegiate success is often determined by both large and small choices that students make in the first term of college, and we want students to be aware of how their choices can dramatically change the outcomes of their college experience.

3. **Updates across all chapters, with extensive revisions to fundamental coverage in one chapter in each major part.** In Chapter 3, Emotional Intelligence, we present strong links between emotional intelligence concepts and the daily events of college life. In Chapter 5, Thinking in College, students explore what college-level thinking involves. See more information about changes in each chapter on pages xxi–xxiii.

4. **Assistance for using peer leaders in college success courses.** As many colleges and universities now recognize the importance of upper-level students as coteachers or peer leaders for the first-year seminar, the Instructor's Annotated Edition now includes special annotations for and about them. Each chapter includes suggestions that peer leaders (or the instructor of record) can use in designing special activities that can be led by peer leaders. The Use Your Resources section includes peer leaders as valuable sources for student support.

5. **An increased focus on four-year higher education.** With the publication of a new edition of *Your College Experience* specifically developed for students attending two-year and community colleges, the Concise Twelfth Edition now focuses more intentionally on the particular issues of students in baccalaureate colleges and universities. Given that students attending open-enrollment institutions are becoming increasingly broad and diverse, the Concise Twelfth Edition provides support, information, and guidance appropriate for students at all higher education institutions.

The Concise Twelfth Edition continues the Gardner and Barefoot tradition of helping students self-assess their strengths, practice goal setting, focus on purpose and motivation, and maintain their engagement in this course. A section on goal setting in Chapter 1 gets students thinking immediately about this important skill. Assess Your Strengths and Set Goals boxes early in each chapter ask students to set goals, and Reflect on Choices and Apply

What You Have Learned exercises at the end of each chapter ask students to think back on how the chapter relates to choices they make and to apply what they have learned in the chapter to current and future academic work.

The following features appear in the Concise Twelfth Edition:

Chapter-opening profiles help students see themselves in the text. Each chapter of the text opens with the story of a recent first-year student who has used the strategies presented in the chapter to succeed in college. The profiled students come from diverse backgrounds and attend diverse colleges and universities around the country.

Thought-provoking photographs and cartoons in every chapter—many of them new to this edition—with carefully written titles and captions reinforce concepts in the narrative and encourage critical thinking. For instance, in the Time Management chapter, a captioned photo of NFL coach Pete Carroll and his players encourages students to "Set Priorities like the Pros." In the communication chapter, a new photo of Ellen DeGeneres hosting the Academy Awards provides a great example of audience interaction, and its caption discusses how the comedy icon used to be scared to speak before an audience.

Your Turn **collaborative learning activities foster peer-to-peer communication, collaboration, and critical thinking.** These activities can be used in class, as homework, or as group activities to strengthen the bond between students and their college communities. They are organized into four types based on what students are asked to do or to consider: Work Together, Write and Reflect, Make Good Choices, and Stay Motivated. A complete list of all Your Turn activities, organized by type and with page numbers included to make it easy for instructors to assign them, can be found on p. xvi.

Is This You? **boxes speak directly to students in circumstances that are commonly found among students taking first-year experience courses.** Look for these special messages to first-generation college students, returning students, veterans, students with children, and student athletes. They also cover common first-year issues that many students encounter, such as being disappointed in a class, financial problems, and the clash of new ideas with old beliefs. The feature directs students to specific content within the chapter.

Coverage of technology and learning. The link between technology and learning is highlighted in every chapter of the twelfth edition with a Tech Tip feature. These features introduce critical technology skills that span the classroom and real life. All Tech Tip features have been extensively revised for the new edition, with titles such as Get Digitally Organized (Chapter 2); Use Blogs and Twitter (Chapter 3); Correlate Online Learning with Your Learning Style (Chapter 4); Take Better Notes in Better Ways (Chapter 7); Use the Cloud (Chapter 8); Conduct Effective Searches (Chapter 10); and Go Beyond the Filter (new, Chapter 11). **Models** (including **digital models**) let students see principles in action. Because many students learn best by example, full-size models—more than in any competing book—show realistic examples of strategies for academic success such as using time-management tools, annotating a textbook, using mind maps, and taking notes in various formats. Digital models are included to reflect the tools today's students use in their everyday lives.

Expanded examples from across the curriculum. The text now includes more concrete scenarios, pages, exercises, and problems from STEM, humanities, and social science courses.

Use Your Resources **boxes connect students to their campus, faculty, and other students.** To help students take more control of their own success, every chapter includes a quick overview of additional resources for support, including learning-assistance centers, books, Web sites, and fellow students—with a prompt for students to add their own ideas.

Skills-based practice exercises provide hands-on, point-of-use reinforcement of major concepts. Students use these exercises to practice skills that they can then apply to other academic courses. For instance, the Time Management chapter includes a tool for students to conduct a Procrastination Self-Assessment, and the test-taking chapter includes a new Test Anxiety Quiz.

Retention Strategies in every chapter of the Instructor's Annotated Edition offer best practices from John Gardner and Betsy Barefoot to help students persist in the first year. In addition, a 16-page insert at the beginning of the Instructor's Annotated Edition includes chapter-specific exercises and activities designed as retention strategies to support writing, critical thinking, working in groups, planning, reflecting, and taking action.

Key Chapter-by-Chapter Revisions

In addition to new features that appear across all chapters of the book, each chapter also features key new and updated content:

Chapter 1, Welcome to Your College Experience, introduces students to the concepts of purpose and goal setting and explores the value of higher education. New to this reorganized chapter is a summary of high-impact practices that are featured throughout the book, an introduction to the role of peer leaders in the college success course, and new material on academic planning and working with an academic adviser. In addition, the authors introduce students to the concept of resilience, a topic that is addressed throughout the new edition.

Chapter 2, Time Management, addresses the tools today's students use to stay organized. This chapter includes information about the relationship between locus of control and one's ability to manage time. Students are guided in using time-management tools and understanding how to avoid procrastination. The chapter includes a new procrastination self-assessment and a valuable tool for measuring the impact of distractions.

Chapter 3, Emotional Intelligence, has been improved by linking emotional intelligence concepts to the daily events of college life, with additional explanation on the concepts of resilience and making good choices. The chapter also includes self-assessments that help students evaluate and improve their own level of emotional intelligence.

Chapter 4, How You Learn, introduces students to learning styles and learning preferences. The chapter includes the VARK Inventory, which can be used in class. Also, three other learning-styles theories are described in the chapter: David Kolb's Experiential Learning Theory, the Myers-Briggs Type Indicator, and Howard Gardner's Theory of Multiple Intelligences. A brief version of the Multiple Intelligences Inventory is included. The chapter ends with coverage of learning disabilities to help students know how and when to seek help for themselves or other students.

Chapter 5, Thinking in College, has been heavily revised and reorganized to give students a better understanding of what is involved in college-level thinking and practical strategies on how to achieve that high level of thinking. Students are clearly shown how concepts like fast and slow thinking, problem solving, creativity, and collaboration all relate to critical thinking. The chapter includes a critical-thinking assessment that is new to this edition, as well as a new application of Bloom's Taxonomy.

Chapter 6, Reading to Learn, helps students meet the particular challenges of reading college textbooks across the various disciplines. It introduces them to the steps involved in active reading and explains how to use strategies such as outlining and mapping to understand and retain important content for tests and exams. Strategies for reading with concentration, reading improvement, and monitoring are provided. New visuals include a sample organizer, several new photos, and sample textbook pages from an economics and chemistry textbook, which reflect the text's increased attention to the STEM fields.

Chapter 7, Getting the Most from Class, covers topics such as preparing for class, listening, taking notes, and participating. The chapter introduces students to various note-taking methods, particularly the Cornell method. The chapter's Tech Tip presents helpful note-taking apps. Students are encouraged to overcome any reluctance they might have about asking a question in class or participating out loud in a group discussion.

Chapter 8, Studying, includes an essential focus on the basics—how to study and how to remember. Students are warned about the pitfalls of multitasking and the downsides of trying to study in an environment that is full of distractions. The chapter opens with a new assessment that asks students to determine their willingness to make tough choices to improve their study habits and includes a new figure showing a sample mind map.

Chapter 9, Test Taking, helps students learn how to prepare for tests and exams, understand and deal with test anxiety, and appreciate the value of maintaining academic integrity. The chapter covers different types of tests and different test environments, including online testing. A major theme in the chapter is the importance of being resilient—not allowing a poor grade on a test to negatively affect a student's motivation. A new visual showing a sample page from a math textbook reinforces the value of working practice problems as a great way to study for tests.

Chapter 10, Information Literacy and Communication, connects writing and speaking to the important topic of information literacy. The chapter now more clearly walks students through the steps of the writing process. The chapter emphasizes doing good research and getting comfortable using the resources at the campus library. Students are also introduced to ways to evaluate and cite sources and recognize bias.

Chapter 11, Diversity, takes a broad view of diversity and considers the many advantages of a diverse campus environment that includes differences in gender, race, ethnic group, sexuality, age, economic status, religion, and learning and physical abilities. The chapter advises students to refrain from stereotyping and instead get to know others as individuals before drawing conclusions about an entire group.

Chapter 12, Money, emphasizes the importance of budgeting and gives students a template for designing their own budget. The chapter also explores responsible use of credit and debit cards, and ways for students to obtain and maintain financial aid.

Extensive Resources for Instructors

- **LaunchPadSolo for College Success.** *LaunchPad Solo for College Success* is home to dozens of assignable and assessable digital resources, including LearningCurve adaptive quizzing and video activities. Pre-built units are easy to assign or adapt with your own material, such as readings, videos, quizzes, discussion groups, and more. LaunchPad Solo also provides access to a grade book that provides a clear window on performance for your whole class, for individual students and individual assignments.

  - **Unique to LaunchPad Solo: *LearningCurve for College Success.*** *LearningCurve for College Success* is an online, adaptive, self-quizzing program that quickly learns what students already know and helps them practice what they haven't yet mastered. An updated version of LearningCurve available with *LaunchPad Solo for College Success* features a larger question pool with new multiple-choice questions.

  - **Ordering information.** LaunchPad Solo is available to package at a significant discount with select College Success titles. Please contact your Macmillan Learning representative for more information. To order *LaunchPad Solo for College Success* standalone, use ISBN 978-1-319-06478-5.

- **The Academic and Career Excellence System (ACES).** This instrument measures student strengths in twelve critical areas and prompts students to reflect on their habits, behaviors, attitudes, and skills. Norm-referenced reports indicate whether students are at a high, moderate, or low skill level in particular areas. For more information, go to **macmillanhighered.com/ACES/catalog**.

- **Instructor's Annotated Edition.** A valuable tool for new and experienced instructors alike, the Instructor's Annotated Edition includes the full text of the student edition with abundant marginal annotations, chapter-specific exercises, and helpful suggestions for teaching, fully updated and revised by the authors. In this edition are numerous retention strategies and high-impact practice tips and exercises to help you help your students succeed and stay in school.

- **Instructor's Manual.** The Instructor's Manual includes chapter objectives, teaching suggestions, an introduction to the first-year experience course, a sample lesson plan for each chapter, sample syllabi, final projects for the end of the course, and various case studies that are relevant to the topics covered in the text. The Instructor's Manual is available online.

- **Computerized Test Bank.** The Computerized Test Bank contains more than 600 multiple-choice, true/false, short-answer, and essay questions designed to assess students' understanding of key concepts. This edition features more challenging scenario-based questions that ask students to apply their understanding to concepts in the text. An answer key is included. A digital text file is also available.

- **Lecture Slides.** Available online for download, lecture slides accompany each chapter of the book and include key concepts and art from the text. Use the slides as provided to structure your lectures, or customize them as desired to fit your course's needs.

- *French Fries Are Not Vegetables.* This comprehensive instructional DVD features multiple resources for class and professional use. Also available online on *LaunchPad Solo for College Success.* ISBN 978-0-312-65073-5.

- **Curriculum Solutions.** Our new Curriculum Solutions group brings together the quality and reputation of Bedford/St. Martin's content with Hayden-McNeil's expertise in publishing original custom print and digital products. With our new capabilities, we are excited to deliver customized course solutions at an affordable price. Make *Your College Experience*, Concise Twelfth Edition fit your course and goals by integrating your own institutional materials, including only the parts of the text you intend to use in your course, or both. Please contact your local Macmillan Learning sales representative for more information and to see samples.

- **CS Select custom database.** The CS Select database allows you to create a textbook for your College Success course that reflects your course objectives and uses just the content you need. Start with one of our core texts, and then rearrange chapters, delete chapters, and add additional content—including your own original content—to create just the book you're looking for. Get started by visiting **macmillanhighered.com/csSelect**.

- **TradeUp.** Bring more value and choice to your students' first-year experience by packaging *Your College Experience*, Concise Twelfth Edition, with one of a thousand titles from Macmillan publishers at a 50 percent discount from the regular price. Contact your Macmillan Learning sales representative for more information.

Student Resources

- *LaunchPad Solo for College Success.* LaunchPad Solo is an online course solution that offers our acclaimed content including videos, LearningCurve adaptive quizzes, and more. For more information, see the Resources for Instructors section.

- **E-book options.** E-books offer an affordable alternative for students. You can find PDF versions of our books when you shop online at our publishing partners' sites. Learn more at **macmillanhighered.com/ebooks**.

- *The Bedford/St. Martin's Planner* includes everything that students need to plan and use their time effectively, with advice on preparing schedules and to-do lists, along with blank schedules and monthly and weekly calendars for planning. Integrated into the planner are tips and advice on fixing common grammar errors, taking notes, and succeeding on tests; an address book; and an annotated list of useful Web sites. The planner fits easily into a backpack or purse, so students can take it anywhere. To order the planner standalone, use ISBN 978-0-312-57447-5. To package the planner, please contact your Macmillan Learning sales representative.

- *Bedford/St. Martin's Insider's Guides.* These concise and student-friendly booklets on topics that are critical to college success are a perfect complement to your textbook and course. One Insider's Guide can be packaged with *any* Bedford/St. Martin's textbook. Additional Insider's Guides can also be packaged for additional cost. Topics include:
  - New! *Insider's Guide for Adult Learners*
  - New! *Insider's Guide to College Etiquette,* 2e
  - New! *Insider's Guide for Returning Veterans*
  - New! *Insider's Guide to Transferring*
  - *Insider's Guide to Academic Planning*
  - *Insider's Guide to Beating Test Anxiety*
  - *Insider's Guide to Building Confidence*
  - *Insider's Guide to Career Services*
  - *Insider's Guide to College Ethics and Personal Responsibility*
  - *Insider's Guide to Community College*
  - *Insider's Guide to Credit Cards,* 2e
  - *Insider's Guide to Getting Involved on Campus*
  - *Insider's Guide to Global Citizenship*
  - *Insider's Guide to Time Management,* 2e

For more information on ordering one of these guides with the text, go to **macmillanhighered.com/collegesuccess**.

- *Journal Writing: A Beginning.* Designed to give students an opportunity to use writing as a way to explore their thoughts and feelings, this writing journal includes a generous supply of inspirational quotes placed throughout the pages, tips for journaling, and suggested journal topics. To order the journal standalone, use ISBN 978-0-312-59027-7.

Acknowledgments

Special thanks to the reviewers of this edition, whose wisdom and suggestions guided the creation of the twelfth edition of the text:

Donna Dabney, Norfolk State University
Maria Flynn, West Kentucky Community and Technical College
DeLandra Hunter, Clayton State University
Hector Menchaca, Tarrant County College—Trinity River Campus
Darrah Mugrauer, Delaware Valley College

Amy Nemmetz, University of Wisconsin—Platteville
Heather Ortiz, Ranger College
Jennifer Palcich, University of North Texas
Carolyn Sanders, University of Alabama in Huntsville
Deborah Stephens, East Tennessee State University

We also thank those who reviewed the Instructor's Manual and Test Bank so thoroughly: Margaret Garroway, Howard Community College; Greta Henglein, Martin Methodist College; Patti Richter, Northwestern State University of Louisiana; Mary Kay Skrabalak, University of Alabama; Brenda Tuberville, Rogers State University. We would also like to continue to thank our reviewers from the eleventh, tenth, and ninth editions, as they helped to shape the text you see today.

Eleventh Edition: Chris Benson, Madonna University; Andrea Berta, University of Texas at El Paso; Margaret Garroway, Howard Community College; Court Merrigan, Eastern Wyoming College; Cyndee Moore, National College; Donna Musselman, Santa Fe College; Alan Pappas, Santa Fe College.

Tenth Edition: Nichelle DeNeen Acrum, Augusta State University; Peter Conrath, Professional Business College; Stella Fox, Nassau Community College; Lauren Grimes, Lorain County Community College; Elizabeth Hammett, College of the Mainland; Alice Lanning, University of Oklahoma; Rajone A. Lyman, Houston Community College; Judith A. Lynch, Kansas State University; Gail Malone, South Plains College; Court Merrigan, Eastern Wyoming College; Louise Mitchum, Louisburg College; Carolyn Poole, San Jacinto College Central; Rajan M. Shore, Blue Ridge Community College; Kerri Sleeman, Michigan Technological University; Jim West, St. Philip's College; Robert Whitley, Caldwell Community College and Technical Institute.

Ninth Edition: Darby Johnsen, Oklahoma City Community College; Deborah Lanza, Sussez County Community College; Miranda Miller, Gillette College; SusAnn Key, Midwestern State University; Pamela R. Moss, Midwestern State University.

Eighth Edition: Rachel A. Beech, Arizona State University-Polytechnic; Paula Bradberry, Arkansas State University; Khalida I. Haqq, Mercer County Community College; Elizabeth Hicks, Central Connecticut State University; Debra Olsen, Madison Area Technical College.

As we look to the future, we are excited about the numerous improvements to this text that our creative Bedford/St. Martin's team has made and will continue to make. Special thanks to Edwin Hill, Vice President, Editorial, Macmillan Learning Humanities; Erika Gutierrez, Publisher; Susan McLaughlin, Development Manager; Simon Glick, Senior Executive Editor for College Success; Bethany Gordon, Associate Editor; Mary Jane Chen, Editorial Assistant; Kayti Corfield, Marketing Manager; and Greg Erb, Senior Production Editor.

Most of all, we thank you, the users of our book, for you are the true inspirations for our work.

Contributors

Although this text speaks with the voices of its two authors, it represents contributions from many other people. We gratefully acknowledge those contributions and thank these individuals, whose special expertise has made it possible to introduce new students to their college experience through the holistic approach we deeply believe in.

Amber Manning-Oullette of Southern Illinois University provided guidance on revising the Emotional Intelligence and Thinking in College chapters. Amber is the Director of Enrollment Management for the SIU College of Business, focusing on recruitment and retention strategies for under-graduate students. She holds a B.S. in Psychology and an M.S. in Counselor Education and received her Doctorate in Educational Administration and Higher Education from SIU in May 2015.

Amber enjoys working with first-year students. In her previous position, she coordinated more than one hundred sections of student success courses, designed curricula, implemented faculty training, and assisted in assessment through a University College model. She was also instrumental in the implementation of the First-Year Experience program for incoming SIU students. One of her passions is coordinating a first-year women's leadership course and living learning community to empower her students. Her academic research interests surround first-year student early interventions, at-risk student development programs, sex education, sexual assault, women's leadership, women's cognitive development, and retention initiatives. She is active in the First-Year Experience movement and continues to present and publish her research at national, regional, and institutional conferences.

Given the nature of technology as a moving target, we relied on the work of Mark Hendrix of Palm Beach State College to update the Tech Tips for the Concise Twelfth Edition. Mark heavily revised or rewrote the Tech Tips, providing new themes in several cases, with the goal of providing students with information to increase their productivity when using the apps, software, or hardware described.

Mark has been an educator for over twenty-five years. He taught in adult and community education before earning a master's degree in education from the University of St. Thomas in St. Paul, Minnesota. He has worked as a teacher or program director in a variety of adult and vocational programs and alternative high school programming, in addition to teaching at community colleges and universities in Minnesota, Kansas, and Florida. He has served on numerous boards of community organizations and has helped them creatively and enthusiastically embrace challenges and thrive in a changing environment. Currently, he is an Associate Professor at Palm Beach State College in Palm Beach County, Florida. He has been recognized for his dynamic teaching strategies, use of technology in the classroom, and his ability to work effectively across departments and outside organizations.

Lea Susan Engle rewrote and updated the chapter on information literacy for the previous edition, helping to incorporate the topics of writing and speaking. Lea is a former instructor and first-year experience librarian at Texas A&M University and currently serves as Training Coordinator for the Canvas learning management system at The University of Texas at Austin. Lea earned a B.A. in Women's Studies from the University of Maryland, College Park and holds an M.S. in Information Studies and an M.A. in Women's and Gender Studies from the University of Texas at Austin.

Her professional interests include educational technology, the first-year experience, creative outreach methods, feminist pedagogy, library service to GLBTQ users, formative assessment, taking risks, and fostering cross-campus collaborations. She is a library evangelist, fulfilling her dream of strategically positioning librarians in all areas of academia.

Casey Reid vastly updated the chapter on Time Management to reflect the needs of today's students. Casey graduated in 2002 from Missouri State University with a B.A. in Anthropology and Professional Writing, and in 2004 she received an M.A. in Writing from the same institution. From 2004 through 2011, she worked on the English faculty at Metropolitan Community College (MCC) in Kansas City. From 2011–2014, she was MCC's College Orientation Coordinator, initiating and directing a mandatory first-year seminar class for 6,000–7,000 new students each year. In 2014, she became the Director of Developmental Education Programs at East Central College, where she implements first-year seminars and programs for students in developmental education classes. When she isn't working, she adds balance to her life by running, biking, hiking, reading, spending time with her three rescued dogs, and hanging out with friends and family.

Chris Gurrie is an Assistant Professor and Director of the Speech Communication Program at the University of Tampa. He also teaches first-year experience seminars and advises undergraduate students. He holds a doctorate from Nova Southeastern University, and when he is not teaching he speaks about the concept of immediacy and student-instructor connections. He has published other articles about communication among the Millennial Generation. He contributed the first generation of Tech Tips, which were introduced in the tenth edition, and wrote the *Guide to Teaching with YouTube*, which is available online and as part of the Instructor's Manual.

We would also like to acknowledge and thank the numerous colleagues who have contributed to this book in its previous editions:

Chapters 2, 6, 7, 8, 9: Jeanne L. Higbee, University of Minnesota
Chapter 3: Catherine Andersen, University of Baltimore
Chapters 4: Tom Carskadon, Mississippi State University
Chapter 7: Mary Ellen O'Leary, University of South Carolina
Chapter 10: Charles Curran, Distinguished Professor Emeritus, University of South Carolina at Columbia
Chapter 12: Natala Kleather (Tally) Hart, founding head of the Economic Access Initiative at The Ohio State University; and Kate Trombitas, Director of Development at The Ohio State University College of Nursing

PART ONE
FOUNDATIONS

David Shaffer/Getty Images

1 WELCOME TO YOUR COLLEGE EXPERIENCE

Student Goals

- Understand the importance of this course and this textbook
- Explore the outcomes of the college experience
- Set goals for attending college
- Adjust to college life
- Understand the basics of academic planning

Michael Krinke/Getty Images

2 TIME MANAGEMENT

Student Goals

- Gain strategies and tools to manage your time
- Understand how setting priorities leads to having more balance in your life
- Learn how to combat procrastination and avoid distractions
- Appreciate the value of time and how to use it wisely and budget it properly

wavebreakmedia/
Shutterstock

3 EMOTIONAL INTELLIGENCE

Student Goals

- Learn what emotional intelligence is
- Explore emotional intelligence in everyday life: motivation, resilience, establishing balance, prioritizing, and anger management
- Develop emotional intelligence in college
- Examine how emotions influence success
- Understand ways to improve your emotional intelligence

wavebreakmedia/
Shutterstock

4 HOW YOU LEARN

Student Goals

- Discover your learning style
- Learn how to handle a mismatch between how you learn best and how you are being taught
- Understand and recognize a learning disability

1
WELCOME TO YOUR COLLEGE EXPERIENCE

YOU WILL EXPLORE

The value of a college education, the college success course, and this textbook

What the college experience is about

The importance of exploring your purpose and setting goals for attending college

The value of academic planning and working with an academic adviser to choose a major and build a program of study

What high-impact practices are and the positive impact they can have on your learning and overall success

Rontavius Jamal Snipes, 23

Biology major
Clayton State University, Georgia

> **Working twenty-two hours while taking sixteen credits means that I rarely get enough sleep because I have to stay up late studying. So my biggest goal for now is to find a way to better manage my time.**

Setting both long- and short-term goals has always been important to Rontavius Snipes. After high school, when he found himself living in Atlanta and working at a dead-end job, he set his sights on going to college and enrolled at Clayton State University. Now that he's in college, he's majoring in biology with the goal of attending dental school after graduation, and he knows that getting good grades and staying involved on campus will help him achieve that ultimate goal.

Like many students, Rontavius also needs to balance working (he works at a pharmacy 30 miles from campus) with attending and participating in school, so many of his goals have involved small steps. "I am currently the president of the pre-dental student association," he explains. "The group is small, but this semester I plan to attend a leadership seminar to get some extra motivation to be able to lead a successful student organization." He also gets involved on campus in smaller ways by promoting concerts and plays, which helps him stay connected with other students. He acknowledges, however, that working while

attending school does have its challenges, which he is still trying to solve. "Working twenty-two hours while taking sixteen credits means that I rarely get enough sleep because I have to stay up late studying. Finding a social life away from my roommates and my girlfriend can be difficult too, so my biggest goal for now is to find a way to better manage my time." Still, Rontavius knows that the hard work will pay off. "Prior to attending college, I never thought about things deeply and took everything at face value. I have greater intuition now and definitely feel that the price I pay for education is well worth it," he says.

In the future, Rontavius hopes to travel the world tackling issues such as poverty, cultural barriers, and the economic glass ceiling that many people face, and his favorite class so far, Sociology 1101, plays nicely into those goals. "That class pushes my life message," he says, "that we should try to understand other cultures and not be so close-minded. I have been the subject of negative stereotypes, and I just love how this class shows how these ways of thinking came about."

To access LearningCurve and more, go to LaunchPad for *Your College Experience* at macmillanhighered.com /gardner12e. For the Concise edition, go to macmillanhighered.com /collegesuccessmedia.

Rontavius knows how important a college education is to his future economic status, but he also knows that going to college presents him with many learning opportunities that he couldn't access any other way. He has already discovered how important it is to think deeply and has recognized that he has leadership skills. Rontavius is also encountering challenges, primarily in time management. He has to work and also wants a satisfying personal life. Therefore, he wants strategies to help him better manage his limited time and maintain good grades.

This book is designed to help you both overcome the struggles that face you and explore all that college has to offer. As you read this book, you will discover your own strengths, learn to be a good thinker, and become skilled at making good choices. You will develop an appreciation of the power you have to direct the aspects of your life, such as managing relationships with your friends, instructors, and family, selecting out-of-class opportunities to pursue, and allocating your time to school, work, and leisure activities. But the most important skill you will need to learn in college is how to keep learning throughout your life. As you're settling into your new college routine, we want to welcome you to the demanding and rewarding world of higher education and equip you with a set of strategies you can use to do your best.

THE VALUE OF A COLLEGE EDUCATION

American society values higher education, which explains why the United States currently has more than 4,400 colleges and universities. College is the primary way that people achieve upward social mobility or the ability to attain a higher standard of living. That might accurately describe your purpose for being in college: to attain a higher standard of living. In earlier centuries, a high standard of living was almost always a function of family background. Either you were born into power and money or you spent your life working for others who had power and money. In most countries today, however, receiving a college degree helps level the playing field for everyone. A college degree can minimize or eliminate the restrictions to achievement that stem from differences in background, race, ethnicity, family income level, national origin, immigration status, family lineage, and personal connections. Simply put, college participation is about ensuring that more people have the opportunity to be evaluated on the basis of merit rather than family status, money, or other forms of privilege. It makes achieving the American dream possible.

In 1900, fewer than 2 percent of Americans of traditional college age attended college. Today, new technologies and the information explosion are changing the workplace so drastically that to support themselves and their families adequately, most people will need some education beyond high school. In spite of the fact that today more than 67 percent of high school graduates (approximately 18 million students) are attending

IN CLASS ❯ We highly recommend some activities for getting acquainted on the first day of class to lay the foundation for active learning. If a peer leader is working in your class, you might want to assign him or her responsibility for this get-acquainted activity. Ask the students to pair up and interview a classmate they do not know. The interview should take roughly 5 to 8 minutes, and the topics for the interview might include name, hometown, college major, career thoughts, and something the individual is proud of. Have the members of each pair introduce each other to the rest of the class. Ask for anonymous feedback at the end of the first class, including thoughts on what each student hopes to learn.

IN CLASS ❯ Ask your students what college means to them. What thoughts come to mind? The discussion might explore the expectations they had before they came to college.

IN CLASS ❯ This is an opportune time to ask students what they might have heard about the differences between their high school and this particular college or university. Remind them that being successful in college is likely to take much more time than being successful in high school.

college, we are seeing a wave of questions in the media about whether or not college is really worth it.

Rontavius, the student profiled at the beginning of this chapter, likely would answer that yes, college is really worth it, but what do the data say? A *New York Times* analysis of data from the Economic Institute (**epi.com**) finds that the answer is "yes." Dramatic differences exist between the earning power of students with a high school diploma and those with a four-year college degree. In 2013, four-year college graduates earned about twice as much per hour as high school graduates. While there are concerns about the cost of college today, the cost of not attending college is even more dramatic. David Autor, an economist from the Massachusetts Institute of Technology, reported that not going to college will, over your lifetime, cost you about half a million dollars.[1]

You can also take a look at Figure 1.1 to see how earning a college degree will improve your earning potential. This figure breaks down unemployment rates and weekly earnings according to education level. The more education you have, the more likely you are to be employed, and the higher your earnings will be.

Beyond the financial benefits that earning a college degree gives to an individual, society benefits as a whole when people earn college degrees. College is an established process designed to further formal education so that students who attend and graduate will be prepared for certain roles in society. Today, for many, those roles are found predominantly in what has become known as the "information economy," which means that most college graduates will earn their living by creating,

---

[1]David Leonhardt, "Is College Worth It? Clearly, New Data Say," *The New York Times*, May 27, 2014, www.nytimes.com/2014/05/27/upshot/is-college-worth-it-clearly-new-data-say. html?_r=0, accessed August 7, 2014.

FIGURE 1.1 ❯ Education Pays

Earning a college degree will improve your earning potential. This figure breaks down unemployment rates and weekly earnings according to education level. Use this information as motivation to make the most of college. The more education you have, the more likely you are to be employed, and the higher your earnings will be.

Source: U.S. Department of Labor, Bureau of Labor Statistics, *Current Population Survey*, 2013.

managing, and using information. For others, college is a crucial way for students to prepare for leadership roles in their communities, companies, professions, or military units.

Another reason students get a four-year college degree is to prepare them to continue their education in a graduate or professional school. If you want to become a medical doctor, dentist, lawyer, or college professor, a four-year college degree is just the beginning, but it is a required step on the path to such professions. Let's say you aspire to be a pharmacist and are planning to get a bachelor's degree in chemistry. Your primary purpose for your degree in chemistry is to gain admittance to pharmacy school. Perhaps you have also considered that if your plans should change, having a degree in chemistry will get your foot in the door in several different industries, so another purpose for your degree is having an edge in the job market upon graduation.

The Value of Your College Success Course

Since you are reading this textbook, it is likely that you are enrolled in a first-year seminar, first-year experience, or "college success" course. In this book we use all three names. The course—possibly the most important course you will take—and this textbook—possibly the most important textbook you will read—are all about improving your chances for success in college and beyond. Before you start reading, though, you probably have some questions.

Research conducted by colleges and universities has found that first-year students are far more likely to be successful if they participate in courses and programs designed to teach them how to succeed in college. This course is designed to help you avoid some of the pitfalls—both academic and personal—that trip up many beginning students.

Although your classmates might not say it out loud, many of them share your concerns, doubts, and fears about being in college. This course will provide a supportive environment in which you can share your successes and your frustrations, get to know others who are beginning college, develop lasting relationships with your instructor and some other students, and begin to think about your plans for life after college.

The Value of Your College Success Textbook

As college professors, researchers, and administrators with many years of experience working with first-year students, we're well aware that starting college can be challenging. We also know that if you apply the ideas in this book to your everyday life, you are likely to enjoy your time in college, graduate, and achieve your life goals.

Your instructor may ask you to read every chapter in this book, but even if you're not required to do so, consider this book a resource to answer questions you might have later this year and throughout your college experience. After this opening chapter, which discusses the value of college, purpose and goal setting, and academic planning, subsequent chapters cover topics such as managing your time, discovering your personal learning style, and understanding how your emotions affect your learning and interactions with others. The next chapters focus on what happens in class and cover topics such as thinking, listening, taking notes, reading, taking tests, writing and speaking, and developing information literacy skills. The concluding chapters address issues that are relevant both to college and to life beyond college, and will teach you important life skills such as money management and understanding diversity.

Though some of the textbook's content may seem like common sense, much of it is based on research and the experiences of thousands of college students and educators. And although some topics in this book might have been presented in high school, we find that many college success strategies cannot be properly understood until students are actually in college and have an immediate "need to know."

THE COLLEGE EXPERIENCE

What is the college experience? Depending on who you are, your life circumstances, and why you decided to enroll, college can mean different things. College is often portrayed in books and movies as a place where young people live away from home in ivy-covered residence halls. We frequently see college depicted with a major focus on big-time sports, heavy drinking, and partying. Yes, you'll find some of that at some colleges, but most students today don't move away from home, don't live on campus, and don't see much ivy. College is far more than any single image you might carry around in your head. And college students today come from more walks of life than ever before.

Why College Is Important for You

College is about thinking, and it will help you understand how to become a careful and critical thinker, someone who doesn't believe everything that he or she hears or reads but instead looks for evidence before forming an opinion. Developing solid thinking skills will empower you to make sound decisions throughout your life.

Although college is often thought of as a time when traditional-age students become young adults, we realize that on today's college campuses, many students are already adults. Whatever your age, college can be a time when you take risks, learn new things, and meet new and different people, all in a relatively safe environment. It's OK to experiment in college, within limits, because that's what college is designed for.

College will provide you with numerous opportunities to develop a variety of formal and informal social networks. These networks will help you make friends and develop alliances with faculty members and fellow students who share your interests and goals. Social networking sites such as Facebook and Twitter provide a way to enrich your real-life social networks in college.

College definitely can and should be fun, and we hope it will be for you. You will meet new people, go to athletic events and parties, build camaraderie with new friends, and feel a sense of school spirit. Many college graduates relive memories of college days throughout their lives, fanatically root for their institution's athletic teams, return for homecoming and class reunions, and encourage their own children to attend their alma mater. In fact, you might be a legacy student, someone whose parents or grandparents attended the same institution that you do.

In addition to being fun, college is a lot of work. Being a college student means spending many hours studying each week, staying up late at night, taking high-stakes exams, and possibly working harder than you ever have before. For many students, college becomes much like a job, with defined duties, expectations, and obligations. Most important is that college will be a set of experiences that will help you to further define your goals and achieve your own purpose.

Getting the Most Out of College: High-Impact Practices

high-impact practices 1–10

Throughout your college experience, you will have the opportunity to participate in activities known as "high-impact practices." High-impact practices are particular activities that research shows have significant positive impact on both your learning and your overall success. One high-impact practice is taking the first-year seminar, which shouldn't surprise you given what you have read in this chapter about the value of this course. Here is a comprehensive list of the ten high-impact practices in which you can participate, listed in the order you are most likely to encounter them. (In this textbook, this icon is used to alert you to these opportunities to enrich your learning.):

1. **first-year seminars** The course in which you find yourself now, designed to prepare you for your college experience.
2. **writing-intensive courses** Courses across the curriculum that engage you in multiple forms of writing for different audiences. This textbook offers various writing activities that make your first-year seminar a writing-intensive course.
3. **collaborative assignments** Learning activities in which you work and solve problems with your classmates in this and other courses.
4. **global learning or diversity experiences** Courses and programs in which you explore cultures, life experiences, and worldviews different from your own.
5. **service-learning** Programs or courses in which you engage in required field-based "experiential learning" and reflection while giving back to your community through service.
6. **learning communities** Programs in which you would take two or more "linked" courses with a group of other students and work closely with one another and with your instructors.
7. **campus-wide common intellectual experiences** Programs in which you would take required "common-core" courses, participate in a required learning community, or engage in other shared experiences such as a "common reading."
8. **undergraduate research** A program that gives you the opportunity to participate in systematic investigation and research working one-to-one with a faculty member.
9. **internships** Direct experience with service-learning or in a work setting often related to your career interests.
10. **capstone courses and projects** Courses or experiences that would require you in the senior year to reflect on what you have learned in all your courses and create a project of some sort that integrates and applies your knowledge.

Does College Seem Like a Strange Land?

Are you a student who has recently come to the United States from another country? Perhaps you have immigrated with family members or on your own. Whatever the situation, learning the unique language, culture, and expectations that exist at a U.S. college can be a challenge. Do instructors' expectations and students' behaviors seem different than what you experienced in your home country? Seek out English as a second language (ESL) courses or programs if you need help you with your English skills. Also, visit the international student counselors to find out how you can continue to increase your understanding of life in the United States, both on and off campus.

Blend Images/Arial Skelley/Getty Images

Some high-impact practices may be activities or courses that are mandatory to fulfill general education or major requirements, but others will be optional. It's a good idea to seek out as many of these practices as you can manage, because doing so will result in heightened learning and greater success for you.

---

your turn   Make Good Choices

The Decision to Become a College Student

Write five reasons that you chose to go to college at this time in your life. Share what you wrote with a classmate and see how many of your reasons are the same or different.

Traditional Students: Making the Transition

If you are a traditional student, meaning that you just graduated from high school, the transition you are making means that you have to adjust to some distinct differences between high school and college. For instance,

Getting Started with Goal Setting

Think about how you define success. Is success about money, friendship, or power? Is it about achieving excellence in college and beyond, or is it about finding a sense of purpose in your life? For most people, success is a combination of all these factors and more. Although luck or "who you know" may play a role, first and foremost your success will be the result of intentional steps you take. So, in your quest for success, where do you start?

Identify Your Personal Strengths. Do you like to talk, deal with conflict, and stand up for yourself? Are you a good reader? If your answers to these questions are "yes," you may want to consider a career in the legal profession. Are you a good science student, and do you enjoy working with your hands? If so, you might want to think about dentistry. Your campus career center can help you discover your unique strengths—and weaknesses—which can influence your direction as you explore career choices.

Ask Yourself Tough Questions. Am I here to find out who I am and to study a subject that I am truly passionate about, regardless of whether it leads to a career? Am I here to engage in an academic program that provides an array of possibilities when I graduate? Am I here to prepare myself for a graduate program or for immediate employment? Am I here to obtain specific training in a field that I am committed to? Am I here to gain specific skills for a job I already have?

RETENTION STRATEGY ❯ These questions are very important for solidifying the connection between a student's sense of purpose for being in college and his or her career choice. Purposeful students are more likely to persist in college than students who lack a sense of purpose.

Establish Goals for Today, This Week, This Year, and Beyond. Although some students prefer to "go with the flow" and let life happen to them, those students are more likely to flounder and less likely to achieve success in college or in a career. So, instead of "going with the flow" and simply reacting to what college and life present, think instead about how you can take more control over the decisions and choices you make now, because these decisions and choices will lay the foundation for the achievement of future life goals. It is easy to make vague plans for the future, but you must determine which short-term steps are necessary if those plans are to become a reality.

College is an ideal time to begin setting and fulfilling short- and long-term goals. A short-term goal might be to read twenty pages from your history text twice a week to prepare for an exam that will cover the first hundred pages of the book. A long-term goal might be to begin predicting which elective college courses you could choose that would help you attain your career goals.

Thinking about a career might seem unrelated to some of the general education courses you are required to take in your first year. Sometimes it's hard to see the connection between a history or literature course and what you want to do with the rest of your life. If you're open to learning, however, you may discover potential areas of interest that you have never considered before, and these areas of interest may lead you to discover a new career path.

Setting SMART Goals

Follow these guidelines to set some short-term goals and consider how they fall within the framework of setting goals that are *specific, measurable, attainable, relevant,* and achievable within a given *time* (SMART).[2] (Figure 1.2 gives you a chance to practice.)

1. Be specific about what you want to achieve and when.
2. State your goal in measurable terms.
3. Be sure that the goal is attainable. If you don't have the necessary skills, strengths, and resources to achieve your goal, change it to one that is more appropriate for you. Be sure that you really want to reach the goal. Don't set out to work toward something only because you want to please others.
4. Know how the goal is relevant to your life and why the goal matters. Be sure that your goal helps your larger life plan and gives you a sense of moving forward.
5. Consider the time frame and whether the goal is achievable within the period you desire. Allow yourself enough time to pursue it considering any difficulties you might have. Plan for ways you might deal with problems. Decide which goal comes next. How will you begin? Create steps and a time line for reaching your next goal.

For instance, let's assume that after you graduate, you think that you might want to work in an underdeveloped country, perhaps spending some time in the Peace Corps. What are some short-term goals that would help you reach this long-term objective? One goal might be to take courses focused on different countries or cultures, but that goal isn't very specific and doesn't state a particular time period. A much more specific goal would be to take one course each year that helps you build a body of knowledge about other countries and cultures. An even more specific goal would be to review the course catalog, identify the courses you want to take, and list them on a personal time line.

Before working toward any long-term goal, it's important to be realistic and honest with yourself. Is it truly *your* goal—one that you yourself value and desire to pursue—or is it a goal that a parent or friend argued was right for you? Given your abilities and interests, is the goal realistic? Remember that dreaming up long-term goals is the easy part. To reach your goals, you need to be specific and systematic about the steps you will take today, this week, and throughout your college experience.

RETENTION STRATEGY ❯ Retention and degree attainment are more likely when students have a strongly developed sense of purpose and the ability to set short-term and long-term goals.

ACADEMIC PLANNING

If you have a goal to drive across the United States, you could, in theory, hop in a car that may need an oil change and travel without GPS or an itinerary and without a carefully packed bag or a planned

---

[2]T. Doran, "There's a S.M.A.R.T. Way to Write Management's Goals and Objectives," *Management Review* 70, no. 11 (1981): 35–36.

FIGURE 1.2 ❯ Practice Setting SMART Goals

Using this chart, try to set one goal in each of the areas listed: academic, career, personal, and financial. Follow the goal through time, from immediate to long term. An example is provided for you.

IN CLASS ❯ Figure 1.2 gives students a chance to practice goal setting by walking through the SMART model.

Types of Goals	Immediate (this week)	Short Term (this term)	Long Term (this year)
Example: Academic	I will list all of my tests and project due dates on my academic calendar.	I will keep a file with my own test and exam grades in case of a discrepancy with my final grades.	I will research graduate programs in my field to determine if I have the grades and scores to be admitted.
Academic			
Career			
Personal			
Financial			

budget. You could simply follow the stars and road signs and hope for the best with weather, lodging, money, and the condition of the car. You might make it to your destination—which you didn't even narrow down beyond getting to the opposite coast—but what is likely to go wrong? How would some planning have improved the journey? Planning your college education is no different. Some preparation, a navigation system, and a clear destination will help you reach your goals, and smoothly.

Academic planning is a vital step in your college career, and it should be an ongoing process that starts on day one. Once you lay a foundation for your studies, you'll save time and money, avoid missing credits, and take ownership of your curriculum. You'll also stay motivated with a clear sense of how each step in your academic plan contributes to your overall purpose for being in college. It's no coincidence that students who engage in academic planning are more likely to stay in school. They are the people who know where they're going and how to get there. They have set their goals, and they know what it takes to achieve them.

Choosing a Major

Even before you have figured out your purpose for going to college, you might be required to select a program of study also referred to as a major,

RETENTION STRATEGY ❯ Although being undecided can have a negative correlation with retention, that is not always the case. Make sure that you do not reinforce any stigma for students who are "undecided." Instead, urge them to think of themselves more positively as "exploratory." It is very important to get such students to use your career center early in the first year to influence their direction and commitment. Tell them that this course will deal with major, career, and course selection.

IN CLASS ❯ Take a poll to determine how many students are undecided and how many have already selected a major. Assure the students that both are perfectly acceptable places to be when they first come to college. Explain that it is important for students to keep an open mind in their studies and use this time to explore their options.

an area of study like psychology, engineering, education, or nursing. Selecting a major is one step in academic planning. In every major, students take a variety of courses; some are directly related to the area of study, whereas others are general education and elective courses. For example, all students should take college-level math and English courses as part of general education, but they can choose electives depending on their interests.

Many students change majors as they better understand their strengths and weaknesses, learn more about career options, and become interested in different areas of study. Some colleges and universities allow you to be undecided for a while or to select liberal arts as your major until you make a decision about what to study.

Although it's OK to be undecided, planning your major and your college curriculum as soon as possible saves valuable time and resources. Even if you're on financial aid, you're not going to have an unlimited amount of cash. If you randomly take courses without a specific goal in mind, your tuition funds could dry up before your plan takes shape. Therefore, it's essential to have a strategy for your program of study. Start by building a solid base of general courses that could qualify you for a few different majors, but leave time in your schedule to explore other subjects that grab your interest. Do you like math? Try an accounting or economics class. Love *CSI*? Sign up for Criminology 101 or the equivalent. An academic adviser or counselor can provide you with proper information and guidance to make a decision about your major.

Working with an Academic Adviser

IN CLASS ❯ Make sure that your students know who their academic adviser is, and that they have an appointment to see their adviser before the end of the term.

Before you register for classes next term, sit down for a strategy session with your academic adviser. On most campuses, you'll be assigned an adviser, who is usually an instructor or a staff person in your chosen field of study. Some colleges offer special advisory centers run by professional advisers. A good adviser can help you choose courses, decide on a major, weigh career possibilities, and map out your degree and certificate requirements. Your adviser can also recommend instructors and help you simplify all aspects of your academic life, so it's important to meet with your adviser right away. Here are a few ways to make sure that your first meeting is a valuable experience.

- **Prepare for the meeting by looking at the course catalog, thinking about available majors, and familiarizing yourself with campus resources.** If you haven't decided on a major, investigate opportunities for taking an aptitude test or self-assessment to help you narrow down your options; ask your adviser about these tests during your meeting. (You will read more about self-assessments and self-exploration.) The early days of college are critical; once classes start, you might not have time for in-depth research.
- **Prepare materials to bring to the meeting.** Even if you submitted one with your application, take along a copy of your academic transcript.

The transcript, which contains your complete high school record, is an important tool. It shows your academic adviser where you've been, what your academic strengths are, and where your interests lie.

- **Make a list of majors that appeal to you.** Academic advisers love it when students come prepared. It shows that you're passionate and serious about your future.
- **Map out your time frame and goals.** Do you plan to enroll full-time or part-time? If you're at a four-year college or university, when do you plan to graduate and with what degree? Are you planning to go to graduate school to finish your studies? If you are at a two-year college, do you want an associate's degree or a certificate? Do you plan to transfer to a four-year institution?
- **Know the right questions to ask.** Once you've chosen a major, you'll need to understand how to move forward in your academic program to meet the necessary requirements. Fortunately, the process is straight-forward. You will have prerequisites, which are the core courses that you need to take before you can enroll in upper-level classes in your major. Your major may also have corequisites, courses that you have to take in conjunction with other courses during the same term, such as a chemistry lab alongside your chemistry class. With this knowledge under your belt, here is what you need to find out:
    1. How many credits must I take each term to graduate on time? (Note: If you are on financial aid, doing a work-study program, or are a college athlete, you may have to take a minimum number of credits per term to maintain your benefits.)
    2. What are the prerequisites for my major? Corequisites?
    3. If I've taken any advanced placement credits or exams, can I use them to fulfill some of my major's requirements?
    4. What career opportunities will I have once I graduate? What will the salary potential look like?
- **Know what to take away from your meeting.** By the end of the meeting, you should have a printout of your current course schedule and plans for classes that you might take in the next term and beyond. At many institutions, you and your adviser will set up a five- to seven-term plan online.
- **Know these rules of thumb about selecting your classes:**
    1. Most full-time students take four to six courses a term. Most classes don't meet every day. With that in mind, decide which classes you want to take, find out which days and times they meet, and make sure they don't overlap.
    2. To get the classes you want, make sure to register as early as possible, either in person or online.
    3. Resist the temptation to cram all your classes into one or two days. It's better to aim for a manageable workload, so spread your classes over the week.
    4. Go for a mix of hard and easy classes. Especially at the beginning, you might not realize how challenging college classes can be or how much outside work they entail. If you load up on organic chemistry, Russian 101, and advanced thermodynamics, your grades and general well-being could suffer.

IN CLASS ❯ After the fall advising period, ask your students to reflect in class on their advising interactions by responding to questions such as these: Did they get the help they needed? Did they feel comfortable with their advisers? Are they still confused about courses and schedules? Be alert for continuing advising issues that you may need to address either in class or one-on-one with some students.

- **Know what to do if your academic adviser isn't very helpful.** If you think that you and your adviser are not a good match, talk to your college success course instructor about what you need to do to be assigned to a different adviser. Alternately, drop by the campus counseling center for assistance. But whatever you do, be resilient. Don't throw in the towel. Academic planning is so critical to your success in college that it's worth persevering until you find an adviser with whom you feel comfortable.
- **Set up subsequent meetings with your academic adviser.** Touch base with your adviser at least once a term, if not more. It's important to stay connected and make sure that you're on a positive track. Programs change requirements occasionally, so it's smart to touch base to make any necessary adjustments. Here are some questions to ask your adviser as you check in:

1. Have there been any changes to my program of study?
2. If I want to officially withdraw from a class, will I be penalized at a later time?
3. Am I still taking classes in the right order?
4. What courses do I need to take to satisfy the major requirements at the institution where I plan to transfer?
5. For those students who are considering graduate school: Am I meeting the criteria for graduate school, and will my grades qualify me for the program I'm interested in?

high-impact practice 2

HIGH-IMPACT PRACTICE ❯ This "Your Turn" exercise suggests that students write briefly about their academic advising experience. This short writing assignment can be part of an ongoing student journal or a separate short paper. Although this is not an English composition class, use these early writing assignments to become aware of any writing problems your students have so that you can refer them for assistance either now or later in the term.

your turn   Stay Motivated

Academic Planning

You have probably already met with an academic adviser, but if not, schedule a meeting right away. Think about this meeting and what you accomplished. Then write a short paper or journal entry about something you learned that increased your motivation to take academic planning seriously. Also, describe in writing at least three problems you might encounter when it comes to choosing your major or planning your program of study if you do not take academic planning seriously. How can these possible negative consequences increase your motivation to plan well for your next meeting with your adviser?

assess your strengths

Time management is challenging for almost all college students. What time-management tools are you already using to manage your time? How do you set and manage your priorities? As you begin to read this chapter, consider the strengths you have in this area.

set goals

Think about challenges you have had in the past with managing your time. Use this chapter to help you understand some strategies and develop goals that relate to time management, such as developing an hour-by-hour record this week of how you spend your time.

MANAGING YOUR TIME

People approach the concept of time differently based on their personalities and backgrounds. Some people are always punctual, while others are almost always late. Some students enter all due dates for assignments on a calendar as soon as they receive the syllabus for each class. Other students take a more laid-back approach and prefer to go with the flow rather than follow a daily or weekly schedule. These students might deal well with the unexpected, but they might also leave everything to the last minute and be less successful than if they managed their time more effectively. Even if you prefer to go with the flow, improving your organizational skills can help you do better in college, work, and life. Think of it this way: If *you* were hiring someone for a job, wouldn't you choose an organized person who gets things done on time?

Taking Control of Your Time

The first step to effective time management is recognizing that you can be in control. Psychologists use the term *locus of control*—*locus* means "place"—to refer to a person's beliefs about how much control they have over the events that affect them. Being in control means that you make your own decisions and accept responsibility for the outcomes of those decisions.

Some people believe that their locus of control is internal, or within themselves; others believe that it is external, or beyond their power. If you frequently find yourself saying "I don't have time," you likely have an external locus of control. The next time you find yourself saying this, stop and ask yourself whether it is actually true. Do you *really* not have time, or have you made a choice not to make time for a particular task or activity? When we say we don't have time, we imply that we don't have a choice. We do have a choice because we have control over how we use our time and how many commitments and small decisions we choose to make every day. For example, we have control over when we get up in the morning; how much sleep we get; and how much time we spend studying, working, and exercising. All of these small decisions have a big impact on our success in college and in life.

PEER LEADER > As a peer leader, you can help your students make the right choices about time management by sharing both your strategies and your challenges in managing your own time. Contribute to the class discussion on this issue or talk one-on-one with the students in your classroom.

RETENTION STRATEGY > Relate the concept of *locus of control* to wise choices in time management. Students who learn to take responsibility for their own choices increase their chances of persisting and graduating.

Your Memory Cannot Be Your Only Planner

How you manage your time reflects what you value—what is most important to you and what consequences you are willing to accept when you make

IN CLASS ▶ Students might question the value of spending so much time to save time. Ask them to be patient; there may be a learning curve, and time spent on the front end will save more time later. Research indicates that college students who know how to plan their time can produce good work and have fun as well.

certain choices. For instance, if you value time with friends above everything else, your academic work likely takes a backseat to social activities. How you manage your time also corresponds to how successful you will be in college and throughout life. Almost all successful people use some sort of calendar or planner to help them keep up with their appointments, assignments, tasks, and other important activities. Using your memory as your only planner—trying to remember everything you have to do without recording it anywhere—means that you will probably forget important events and deadlines.

---

yourturn Make Good Choices

Does Your Planner Work for You?

What kind of planner do you currently use, if any? Do you use a paper planner or mark the calendar on your phone? Do you think you have chosen the best kind of planner for you? Why or why not? Can you think of a different planner that might work even better?

USING TIME-MANAGEMENT TOOLS

Getting a bird's-eye view—or big picture—of each college term will allow you to plan ahead effectively. An **academic calendar** is a calendar that shows all the important dates that are specific to your campus: financial aid, registration, and add/drop deadlines; midterm and final exam dates; holidays; graduation deadlines; and so forth. You may have received an academic calendar when you registered for classes, or your campus bookstore may have one for sale.

Knowing your big-picture academic deadlines will be helpful as you add deadlines for specific assignments, papers, and exams into your calendar. It is important to refer to your college's academic calendar to add important dates and deadlines, such as when the registration period starts and ends and when you need to pay your tuition or file your application for financial aid or scholarships. Remember, also, that you have to keep track of important dates, not only in your own life, but also in the lives of those close to you—birthdays, doctor's appointments, work schedules, travel, visits from out-of-town guests, and so on. Different aspects of your life have different sorts of time requirements, and the goal is to stay on top of all of them.

You might prefer to use an electronic calendar on your phone, tablet, laptop, or desktop. (See the Tech Tip in this chapter for different options.) Regardless of whether you prefer a paper or electronic calendar, it's a good idea to begin the academic term by reviewing the syllabus for each of your courses and then completing a preview (Figure 2.1), recording all of your commitments for each day, and using different colors for each category:

- Classes
- Study time for each class you're taking
- Tests and assignment due dates
- Personal obligations such as work, family, friends
- Scheduled social events (including phone numbers in case you need to cancel)

FIGURE 2.1 > Monthly Calendar

Using the course syllabi provided by your instructors, create your own monthly calendars for your entire term. Provide details such as the number of hours you anticipate spending on each assignment or task.

MONTH: SEPTEMBER

MONDAY	TUESDAY	WEDNESDAY	THURSDAY	FRIDAY	SATURDAY	SUNDAY
					1	2
3 9–12 Work	4 First Day of Classes 9–12 Psychology 2–5 Work 8–9 Psychology: Read Ch. 1	5 9–12 Work 1–4 Math 8–10 Math HW1	6 10–1 English 2–5 Work 8–10 English: Read Ch. 1	7 10–12 Work 9–10 Psychology: Review Notes	8 10–4 Work 8–9 Math HW 1 9–10 English: Read Ch. 1	9 2–4 Review Math Notes 6–10 Party at Susan's
10 9–12 Work 1–5 Biology	11 9–12 Psychology 2–5 Work 8–10 Biology: Read Ch. 1	12 9–12 Work 1–4 Math 8–10 Psychology: Read Ch. 2	13 10–1 English 2–5 Work 7–8 Math HW 2 9–11 Biology: Read Ch. 1	14 10–12 Work 1–3 Lunch with Mary 6–7 Start English Summary Paper	15 10–4 Work 4–6 Shopping 9–10 Finish English Summary Paper	16 10–1 Study for Psychology Test 6–8 Review Math notes for Quiz 1
17 9–12 Work 1–5 Biology 7–10 Study for Psychology Test	18 9–12 Psychology Psychology Test 1 2–5 Work 8–9 Review Math notes for Quiz 1	19 Work 9–12 Math 1–4 Math Quiz 1 8–9 Revise English Summary Paper	20 10–1 English English Summary Paper due 2–5 Work 8–10 Biology: Read Ch. 2	21 10–12 Work 1–2 Attend Student Club Meeting 6–9 Math HW 3	22 10–4 Work 5–7 Psychology: Read Ch. 3 9–10 English: Read Ch. 2	23 10–12 Biology: Read Ch. 2 9–10 Biology: Lab Report 1
24 9–12 Work 1–5 Biology 6–8 Math Tutoring 10–11 Math HW 3	25 9–12 Psychology 2–5 Work 8–10 Biology: Read Ch. 3 10–11 Math HW 3	26 9–12 Work 1–4 Math 8–9 Psychology: Read Ch. 4 9–10 Prepare English Paper Outline	27 10–1 English 2–5 Work 7–9 Math HW 9–10 Review Biology Notes	28 10–12 Work 1–3 Meet with Biology Study Group 8–9 Biology: Lab report 2 9–11 English: Read Ch. 3	29 10–4 Work 8–9 English: Read Ch. 3	30 4–8 Nina's Birthday

Recording your daily commitments allows you to examine your toughest weeks during each month and each term. If research paper deadlines and test dates fall during the same week, find time to finish some assignments early to free up study time. If you use an electronic calendar, set reminders for these important deadlines and dates.

Overall, you should create monthly (Figure 2.1), weekly (Figure 2.2), and daily (Figure 2.3) views of your calendar. All three views are available

FIGURE 2.2 > Weekly Timetable

Using your term calendar, create your own weekly timetable using a conventional template or one that uses an app such as LifeTopix. At the beginning of each term, track all of your activities for a full week by entering everything you do and how much time each task requires into your schedule. Use this record to help you estimate the time you will need for similar activities in the future.

SEPTEMBER

Time	MONDAY 3	TUESDAY 4 First Day of Classes	WEDNESDAY 5	THURSDAY 6	FRIDAY 7	SATURDAY 8	SUNDAY 9
5 am							
6 am							
7 am							
8 am							
9 am	Work	Psychology	Work				
10 am				English	Work	Work	
11 am							
12 pm							
1 pm			Math				
2 pm		Work		Work	Mom's Doctor's Appointment		Review Math Notes
3 pm							
4 pm							
5 pm							
6 pm							Party at Susan's
7 pm							
8 pm		Psychology: Read Ch. 1	Math HW 1	English: Read Ch. 1		Math HW 1	
9 pm					Psychology: Review Notes	English: Read Ch. 1	
10 pm							
11 pm							
12 am							

FIGURE 2.3 > Daily Planner
Notice how college, work, and personal activities are noted on this daily planner.

IN CLASS > A student's schedule controls how each day and each week is structured. Discuss how a class schedule and commuting to class are factors in time management.

	FRIDAY, SEPTEMBER 14
5 am	
6 am	
7 am	
8 am	
9 am	
10 am	*Work*
11 am	
12 pm	
1 pm	*Lunch with Mary*
2 pm	
3 pm	
4 pm	
5 pm	
6 pm	*Start English Summary Paper*
7 pm	
8 pm	

in an electronic planner, but you can also create monthly, weekly, and daily calendars with paper planners.

Once you complete your monthly templates, you can put them together to preview your entire academic term. Remember to provide details such as the number of hours you anticipate spending on each assignment or task.

As you create your schedule, try to reserve study time for each class and for each assignment. Not all assignments will take an equal amount of time to complete. Estimate how much time you will need for each one, and begin your work well before the assignment is due. A good time manager frequently allows for emergencies by finishing assignments before actual due dates. If you are also working on or off campus, reconsider how many hours per week it will be reasonable for you to work on top of your academic commitments, and whether you need to reduce your credit load to ensure that you have enough time for both work and school.

Remember that managing your time effectively requires practice. You may have to rearrange your schedule a few times, rethink some priorities, and try to use your time differently. The more you apply time-management skills, the more time you can save.

Being a good student does not necessarily mean studying day and night and doing little else. Scheduling time for work and pleasure is important, too. After all, most students have to juggle a *lot* of responsibilities. You might have to work to help pay for college, and you probably want to

IN CLASS ❯ Tell students that when researchers do focus groups of high-performing students and ask them what their most important success strategy is, the students report "time management."

spend time with family or friends to recharge your battery. And most people also need time to relax and unwind; that time can include getting some exercise, reading a book for pleasure, or seeing a movie. Note that the daily planner (Figure 2.3 on the previous page) includes time for other activities as well as time for classes and studying.

When using an electronic calendar, it's a good idea to print a backup copy in case you lose your phone, cannot access the Internet, experience a computer crash, or leave your charger at home or in your residence hall. Carry your calendar with you in a place where you're not likely to lose it. Checking your calendar regularly helps you keep track of commitments and maintain control of your schedule. This practice will become invaluable to you in your career. Check your calendar daily for both the current week and the coming week. It takes just a moment to be certain that you aren't forgetting something important, and it helps relieve stress. Consider setting regular times to check your calendar every day, perhaps right after eating breakfast and then again in the evening, to see what's coming in the days and weeks ahead.

Keep the following points in mind as you organize your day:

IN CLASS ❯ Caution students to be specific when filling in their planners. For instance, "Read Chapter 8 in history" is preferable to "Study history," which is still better than simply "Study." Remind them to use the time between classes to review material from the previous class and prepare for the next class.

- **Set realistic goals for your study time.** Assess how long it takes to read a chapter in your different textbooks and how long it takes you to review your notes from different instructors.
- **Use waiting, commuting, and travel time to review.** Allow time to review your notes as soon as you can after class. You can review your notes if you have a break between classes or while you're waiting for or riding the bus or train. Consider formally budgeting this commuting time in your planner. If you have a long drive, consider listening to recorded notes or asking those riding with you to quiz you. Make a habit of using waiting time wisely, and it will become bonus study time to help compensate for unexpected events that might pop up in your day and throw off your schedule.
- **Limit distracting and time-consuming communications.** Check your phone, tablet, or computer for messages or updates at a set time, not whenever you're tempted to do so. Constant texting, browsing, or posting can keep you from achieving your academic goals. Remember that when time has passed, you cannot get it back.
- **Avoid multitasking.** Doing more than one thing at a time, referred to as multitasking, requires that you divide your attention among tasks. You might think that you are good at multitasking. However, the reality is (and research shows) that you can get tasks done faster and more accurately if you concentrate on one at a time.[1] Don't take our word for it: Try setting up your schedule to focus on one important task at a time. You'll probably find you do a better job on your assignment, test, or project.
- **Be flexible.** You cannot anticipate every disruption to your plans. Build extra time into your schedule so that unexpected events do not prevent you from meeting your goals.
- **Schedule breaks.** Relax, catch up with friends and family, or spend time in the cafeteria or student center.

RETENTION STRATEGY ❯ Because we know that the influence of students on other students is such an important factor in student success, this would be good time to invite a small number of outstanding students to class to share their time-management strategies.

---

[1] E. Ophir, C. Nass, and A. Wagner, "Cognitive Control in Media Multitaskers," *Proceedings of The National Academy of Sciences* 106, no. 37 (2009).

- Break big jobs into smaller steps. Tackle short, easy-to-accomplish tasks first.
- Avoid doing other things that might seem more fun, and promise yourself a reward for finishing the task, such as watching your favorite TV show or going out with friends. For completing larger tasks and assignments, give yourself bigger and better rewards.
- Find a place to study that's comfortable and doesn't allow for distractions and interruptions.
- Say *no* to friends and family members who want your attention; agree to spend time with them later, and schedule that time.
- Shut off and put away all electronic devices during planned study sessions. If you *need* to use an electronic device for studying, turn off all social media and any other applications that are not part of your studying—and *keep* them off.
- Consider asking those living with you to help keep you on track. If they see that you are not studying when you should be, ask them to remind you to get back to the books. If you study in your room, close your door.

IN CLASS ❯ Ask students to think about distractions and report the kinds of distractions they have in their environments. How are distractions a problem?

IN CLASS ❯ Time management often requires the use of the word *no*. Ask students to discuss how saying no relates to the way they manage their time.

Dealing with Distractions

Overcoming procrastination and planning your time effectively are closely associated with achieving your goals. What you do on a daily basis affects your outcomes for that week, that month, that year, and so on. Distractions may push you off course and away from your intended goals. A good first step is becoming aware of what distractions trip you up and considering how much control you have over them.

Table 2.1 lists possible distractions that may or may not be a problem for you. Choose Yes (a problem) or No (not a problem) for each one. Then note whether the distraction is controllable or uncontrollable and write down possible solutions.

IN CLASS ❯ Ask students to discuss how much time they spend on the Internet each day. How much on social networking sites? Is this a time-management problem? For some students, time spent on social networks is a problem that can rise to the level of addiction. Consider inviting someone from your counseling center to speak about this issue.

TABLE 2.1

Distraction	Yes (Y) No (N)	Controllable (C) Uncontrollable (U)	Solutions
Texting/Messaging			
Social media			
Gaming/Videos/Music			
Sports/Hobbies			
Television/Streaming			
Lack of sleep			
Relationships			
Meals/Snacking			
Daydreaming			
Perfectionism			
Errands/Shopping			
Lost items			

(continued)

TABLE 2.1 *(continued)*

Distraction	Yes (Y) No (N)	Controllable (C) Uncontrollable (U)	Solutions
Worries/Stress			
Family			
Socializing/Friends			
Multitasking			
Illness, self or others			
Work schedule			
Pleasure reading			

What did you learn about yourself, the distractions that get in your way, and some ideas for taking control? What choices are you willing to make to maximize your time?

SETTING PRIORITIES

As you work to overcome procrastination and limit distractions, think about how to **prioritize**, which means putting your tasks, goals, and values in order of importance. (Below, we'll discuss strategies to avoid becoming overextended, which goes hand in hand with setting priorities.) Ask yourself which goals are most important, but also which ones are most urgent. For example, studying in order to get a good grade on tomorrow's test might have to take priority over attending a job fair today, or completing an assignment that is due tomorrow might have to take priority over driving your friend somewhere.

However, don't ignore long-term goals in order to meet short-term goals. With good time management, you can study during the week prior to the test so that you can attend the job fair, too. Skilled time managers often establish priorities by maintaining a term calendar and to-do lists on which they rank the items in order of importance to determine schedules and deadlines for each task.

From the beginning of the term, plan your work on term papers and major projects that might not be due for several weeks or even months. Consult with a tutor or a more experienced student to help you break large assignments down into smaller steps, such as choosing a topic, doing research, creating an outline, or writing a first draft. Once you have entered your future commitments in a term planner and

is**this**you?

Time Flies

Do you find yourself wondering where your time has gone at the end of a long day? Are you aware of how you spend your time when you're not in class, or does this time just seem to vanish? Of all the time-management strategies presented in this chapter, developing an awareness of how you spend your time might be the most important. Using a day planner or your smart phone, develop an "ideal" hour-by-hour schedule that covers the next week. At the end of each day, go back and check to see if you used your time as planned. If not, make sure your projections were realistic, adjust them if necessary, and then try some of the strategies presented in this chapter to improve your ability to control the way you spend your time.

Set Priorities Like the Pros

Professional coaches help their teams thrive by setting effective priorities, whether it's making a plan for the next play, for the whole game, or for an entire season. In setting your own priorities, take a lesson from these coaches: Prioritize your long-term plans while making sensible play-by-play decisions every day.

Jeff Gross/Getty Images

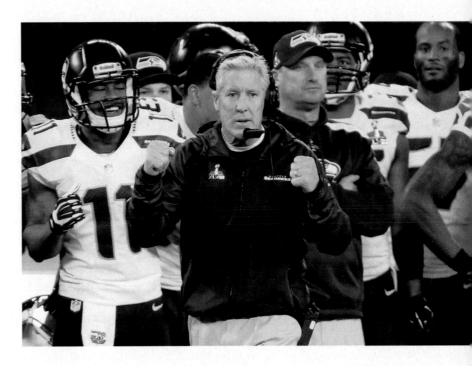

decided how your time will be spent each week, create your to-do list, which is especially handy for last-minute reminders. A to-do list helps you keep track of errands to run, appointments to make, and anything else you might forget. You can keep this list on your cell phone or tablet, in a notebook, or on a bulletin board in your room. Use your to-do list to keep track of all the tasks you need to remember, not just academics. Consider developing a system for prioritizing the items on your list: using different colors of ink for different groups of tasks; highlighting the most important assignments; marking items with one, two, or three stars; or adding letters A, B, C, and so on to indicate which tasks are most important (Figure 2.4).

IN CLASS > Ask students to discuss the importance of a to-do list. Why is a list important in time management? What experiences have students had with to-do lists? You can share your own experiences with such lists.

FIGURE 2.4 > To-Do List

You can keep a to-do list on a mobile device, in a notebook, or on a bulletin board. Use it to keep track of all the tasks you need to remember, not just academics. Consider adding Saturday and Sunday as these are productive days for many busy people. As you complete a task, cross it off your list. Enjoy the satisfaction of each accomplishment.

THIS WEEK	COLLEGE	WORK	PERSONAL
Monday	Schedule a math tutoring session	Meet with the department chair about my schedule	Make a haircut appointment
Tuesday	Make appointment with Prof. Velez to discuss paper topic		Order birthday gift for dad
Wednesday	Meet my history study group at 4:00 p.m.	Work in department, 9:00 a.m.–noon	
Thursday	Finish English essay		Pick up dry cleaning
Friday		Work in department, 9:00 a.m.–noon	Make eye appointment

Find a Balance

RETENTION STRATEGY > A leading theory about retention is known as *academic and social integration*. When you get students doing both academic work and socializing together, they stay in college longer. Get them to think about how they can and should do this.

Another aspect of setting priorities while in college is finding a way to balance your academic schedule with the rest of your life. Social and extracurricular activities (for instance, participating in a club, writing for the college newspaper, attending special lectures, concerts, athletic events, or theater performances) are important parts of the college experience. Time spent alone and time spent thinking are also essential to your overall well-being.

Don't Overextend Yourself

IN CLASS > Ask students to discuss how they know when they are overextended and what they can do if they feel stressed. Then ask whether they need to relinquish any commitments. Will any negative consequences result from giving up these commitments? What commitments are realistic to maintain while attending school full-time? Part-time?

Being **overextended**, or having too much to do given the resources available to you, is a primary source of stress for college students. Determine what a realistic workload is for you, but note that this can vary significantly from one person to another, and only you can determine what is realistic. Although being involved in social and family life is very important, don't allow your academic work to take a backseat to other time commitments. Take on only what you can handle. Learn to say *no,* as this is an effective time-management strategy! Say no to requests that will prevent you from meeting your academic goals. Remember that even if you can find the time for extra tasks, you may not be able to find the energy.

IN CLASS > Ask students whether they are constantly juggling one deadline to meet another or skipping one class to finish an assignment for another class. Assure them that although they will need to work on both time and stress management, most other students are facing the same challenges, and most will learn to handle them successfully.

If you are feeling stressed, assess your time commitments and let go of one or more. If you choose to drop a course, make sure you do so before the drop deadline so that you won't have a low grade on your permanent record. If you receive financial aid, keep in mind that you must be registered for a minimum number of credit hours to maintain your current level of financial aid. Read more about financial aid in the chapter on managing money.

Hang On

It's important to find a balance between your studies, work, family, exercise, and other responsibilities so you do not overextend yourself. Keep your goals and priorities in mind, and avoid an event like this one the day before an exam!

© Jessica Rinaldi/Reuters/Corbis

Stay Focused

Many students of all ages question their decision to attend college and sometimes feel overwhelmed by the additional responsibilities it brings. Some first-year students, especially recent high school graduates, might temporarily forget their main purposes for coming to college and spend their first term of college engaging in a wide array of new experiences.

Allowing yourself a little time to adjust to college is OK within limits, but you don't want to spend the next four or five years trying to make up for poor decisions made early in your college career, such as skipping class and not taking your assignments seriously. Such decisions can lead to a low grade point average (GPA) and the threat of academic probation or, worse, academic dismissal.

A great way to focus and to keep your priorities on track is to finish what *needs* to be done before you move from work to pleasure. From time to time, you will have competing responsibilities; for example, you might have to work additional hours at your job when you need additional time to study

IN CLASS > Have pairs of students discuss their "perfect life" ten years from now. What goals do they need to set now to achieve their dreams?

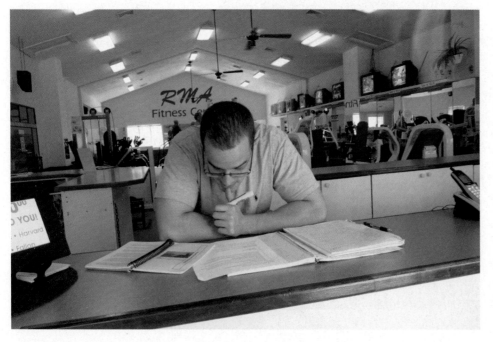

Work Study

Did you know that the majority of college students have jobs? If you need to work, try to find a job that is flexible and allows you to study during down-time. Use every available minute to stay up to date with your classwork.
Courtesy of Sue McDermott Barlow

for an exam. In cases like these, talk to the people involved, including your instructors and your employer, to see how you can manage the conflict.

high-impact practice 2

HIGH-IMPACT PRACTICE ❯ This Your Turn exercise combines the important high-impact practice of writing with helping your students clarify what they value most and will prioritize in college.

your turn   Write and Reflect

What Are Your Priorities?

List your current priorities, and assign a value to each on a scale of 1–5 with 1 as most important and 5 as least important. Write a short paper about why you consider some things more important than others. Think about whether your personal priorities support your goals for college success.

_____   _____
_____   _____
_____   _____
_____   _____
_____   _____

APPRECIATING THE VALUE OF TIME

Time is a valuable resource, perhaps your most valuable resource. You've likely heard the expression "Time is money." Just as you don't want to waste your money, you shouldn't waste your time or the time of others. Did you ever make an appointment with someone who either forgot the

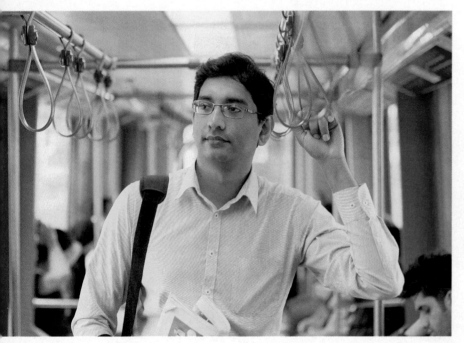

Getting from Here to There
College students have the responsibility to get themselves to class on time and must plan transportation carefully, whether walking, driving, bicycling, ride-sharing, taking public transportation, or using another method of getting from place to place. If you have an emergency situation that causes you to run late, talk to your instructor. He or she will understand a real emergency and help you make up work you missed.
wong yu liang/Shutterstock

appointment entirely or was very late? How did you feel? Were you upset or disappointed because the person wasted your time? Most of us have experienced the frustration of having someone else disrespect our time. In college, if you repeatedly arrive late for class or leave early, you are breaking the basic rules of politeness and showing a lack of respect for your instructors and your classmates.

Punctuality, or being on time, is expected in college, work, and elsewhere in our society. Being strictly on time may be a difficult adjustment for you if you grew up in a home or culture that is more flexible in its approach to time, but it is important to recognize the value of punctuality. Although you should not have to alter your cultural identity to succeed in college, you must be aware of the expectations that instructors typically have for students.

Here are a few basic guidelines for respectful behavior in class and in other interactions with instructors:

- Get to class on time. This means you need to get enough sleep at night so that you can wake up at a time that allows you to arrive in class early enough to take off your coat, shuffle through your backpack, and have your completed assignments and notebooks ready to go by the time the class starts.
- Be on time for scheduled appointments, such as during office hours.
- Avoid behaviors that show a lack of respect for both the instructor and other students, such as leaving class to answer your cell phone. Similarly, texting, doing homework for another class, falling asleep, or talking (even whispering) during a lecture are all considered rude.
- Make transportation plans in advance, and have a backup plan.

Not only is time management important for you, but it is also a way in which you show respect for your coworkers, friends, family, college instructors, and yourself. Can you think of the number of times you may have been late (one of the symptoms of procrastination) this week alone? Think back and then take the quiz shown here in Table 2.2:

TABLE 2.2

Situation	Number of Times This Week
How many times were you late to class?	
How many times were you late for appointments/dates?	
How many times were you late for work, a carpool, or another job and/or responsibility?	
How many times were you so late returning an e-mail, phone call, or text that a problem resulted from this lateness?	
How many times were you late paying a bill or mailing any important document?	
How many times were you late getting to bed or waking up?	
TOTAL	

Did the total number of times you were late surprise you? Two to five incidences of being late in a week is fairly normal. Everyone is late sometimes. Being late more than eight times this week might indicate that you are avoiding situations and tasks that are unpleasant for you. Or maybe you find it difficult to wait for other people, and so you would rather have others wait for you. Try and think of lateness from the other person's perspective. Getting more organized might help if you find that you don't have enough hours in the day to get everything done the way you think it should be. Position yourself for success and develop a reputation for being dependable!

Creating a Workable Class Schedule

Building your class schedule so that it works for you is part of using your valuable time wisely. If you live on campus, you might want to create a schedule that situates you near a dining hall at mealtimes or allows you to spend breaks between classes at the library. Alternatively, you might need breaks in your schedule for relaxation, catching up with friends, or spending time in a student lounge, college union, or campus center. You might want to avoid returning to your residence hall to take a nap between classes if the result is that you could feel lethargic or oversleep and miss later classes. Also, if you attend a large university, be sure to allow adequate time to get from one class to another.

Scheduling Your Classes in Blocks

One option for building a class schedule is using blocks of time when you can schedule several classes in a row, back-to-back, without any breaks. If you're a commuter student or if you must carry a heavy workload to afford going to school, you might prefer block scheduling, which allows you to cut travel time by attending school one or two days a week. Block scheduling might also provide more flexibility if you have to schedule a job or family commitments.

Scheduling classes in blocks, however, can also have significant drawbacks. When all your classes are scheduled in a block of time, you run several risks. If you become ill on a class day, you could fall behind in all your classes. You might also become fatigued from sitting in class after class. When one class immediately follows another, it will be difficult for you to have a last-minute study period immediately before a test because you will be attending another class and are likely to have no more than a 15-minute break in between. Finally, remember that if you take back-to-back classes, you might have several exams scheduled for the same day. Scheduling classes in blocks might work better if you have the option of attending lectures at alternative times in case you are absent, if you alternate classes with free periods, and if you seek out instructors who are flexible with due dates for assignments.

If your classes are offered at more than one time of day or more than one day a week, you will find it easier to design a schedule that works best for you. Often, however, you will be forced to take a class at an inconvenient time because that's the only time the class is offered. Remember that any schedule you develop will have pros and cons, but with advance planning, you can make the most of your in-class and out-of-class time.

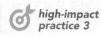
your turn Work Together

Scheduling Your Classes

In a small group or with a partner, share your current schedule and explain what you like or dislike about it. If your current schedule is not working well, discuss why that might be and identify changes you can make for the next term.

checklist for success

Time Management

- [ ] **Make sure that you set clear priorities for the way you spend your time.** All your time doesn't have to be spent studying, but remember that your instructors will expect you to study two hours out of class for each hour in class.

- [ ] **Get organized by using a calendar or planner.** Choose either an electronic or a paper calendar. Your campus bookstore will have a campus-specific version. Your calendar can help you allocate time in the present for completing large assignments that are due in the future.

- [ ] **Create and use daily paper or electronic to-do lists.** Crossing off those tasks you have completed will give you a real sense of satisfaction.

- [ ] **Quickly identify and address common time-management problems you are having before they spiral out of control.** Be aware of problems with procrastination, distractions, overscheduling, and motivation. As you notice them happening, take stock and make changes. If any of these issues becomes a serious problem, seek help from your campus counseling center.

- [ ] **Remember the relationship between time and respect.** Be aware of how others might perceive your behavior. If you disregard formal or informal appointments or if you are consistently late for class, you are showing a lack of respect for others even if that's not your intent.

- [ ] **Think about your course schedule.** As you plan for next term, try to schedule your classes in a way that works best for you, given your other obligations.

2 build your experience

REFLECT ON CHOICES

high-impact practice 2 College presents you with choices. One of them is whether you are going to pay close attention to how you spend your time. If you choose to neglect the issue of time management, you will risk losing a resource that you can never recover and sabotaging your chances for success in college. Did any of the time-management tips in this chapter appeal to you? If so, which ones? Do you still have questions about time management? If so, what are they? Write about these choices and questions in a journal entry or readily accessible file. Revisit these questions throughout your first-year experience.

APPLY WHAT YOU'VE LEARNED

Now that you have read and discussed this chapter, consider how you can apply what you have learned to your academic and personal life. The following prompts will help you reflect on chapter material and its relevance to you both now and in the future.

1. Review the procrastination section of this chapter. Think of one upcoming assignment in any of your current classes and describe how you can avoid waiting until the last minute to get it done. Break down the assignment and list each step it will take to complete the assignment. Give yourself a due date for each step and a due date for completing the assignment.

2. After reading about effective time-management strategies, consider how you manage your own time. If you were grading your current set of time-management skills, what grade (A, B, C, or lower) would you give yourself? Why? What is your biggest impediment to becoming a more effective time manager?

USE YOUR RESOURCES

> **Academic Skills Center** Your campus academic skills center offers more than just assistance in studying for exams. Head here for time-management advice specific to you. For instance, if you are struggling with managing the process of writing a paper, talk with a writing tutor about how to break the process into manageable steps, and create a timetable for those steps so you can meet course deadlines. If you are an online student, communicate with your instructors and other online students about how to manage time in an online environment.

> **Counseling Center** Make an appointment at your campus counseling office if your time-management problems involve emotional issues.

> **Your Academic Adviser or Counselor** If you have a good relationship with your academic adviser, ask him or her for time-management advice or for a referral to another person on campus.

> **Office for Commuter Students** If you commute back and forth to campus, visit the office for commuter students to see what kinds of suggestions they offer about transportation to and from campus. You may be able to reduce the amount of time you spend in transit.

> **Your Peer Leader** Peer leaders in college success classes are selected for their wisdom and experience. Talk to your peer leader about how he or she has developed time-management strategies.

> **A Fellow Student** Don't overlook your closest resources! If you feel your time slipping away, ask a friend who is a good student for advice.

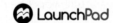 LaunchPad

LaunchPad is a great resource! For *Your College Experience*, go to macmillanhighered.com/gardner12e. For the Concise edition, go to macmillanhighered.com/collegesuccessmedia.

wavebreakmedia/Shutterstock

3
EMOTIONAL INTELLIGENCE

YOU WILL EXPLORE

What emotional intelligence is all about

Emotional intelligence in everyday life: motivation, resilience, establishing balance, prioritizing, and anger management

Developing emotional intelligence in college

How emotions influence success

Ways to improve your emotional intelligence

⚹ High-impact practices 2 (writing) and 3 (collaboration)

Gustavo Mejia, 20
Business Administration major
South Texas College

> " Going to college is not only about enjoying success and accomplishments, but also about persevering when things get difficult or go wrong. "

When he was growing up in Turmero, Venezuela, Gus Mejia's family always encouraged him to attend college. "I see college as the path to the future," he says, "one that will help me build a better life for my family." Gus began college at Sinclair Community College in Dayton, Ohio, where he took classes full-time while working two days a week at his uncle's restaurant. He quickly learned a few things that helped him succeed. "As an international student, I left important parts of my life behind when I made the decision to go to college, such as family and my country. Being alone for almost a year taught me how important it is to have a positive attitude and an optimistic spirit."

This realization didn't come without hard work and practice. One of the most important things Gus had to learn during his first year of college was how to deal with the stress of managing college, work, and living in a new environment, and Gus figured out that having a good sense of his own emotional intelligence helped. Being aware of how these stresses affected him emotionally helped him better understand how to deal with difficult situations and kept him from reacting negatively during times of stress. Emotional intelligence has also played a big role in Gus's favorite class (so far): organizational behavior, where he had to learn how to work with other students, no matter what their customs and beliefs. "I liked this class not only because it related directly to my major," he says, "but also because it taught me to communicate with others. Being able to work efficiently with different people from different backgrounds is very valuable."

Gus decided to begin the transfer process last year. Transferring to South Texas College represented a new beginning for him, one that came with its own fair share of challenges that he had to face with a clear head. Some of the credits for his classes—such as English literature, as well as courses on Microsoft Excel and PowerPoint—did not transfer because they weren't part of the business curriculum at his new college. Gus had to learn all the requirements for transferring, including admission tests, and be sure to meet them to make the transition as smooth as possible. His one piece of advice for other first-year students: Don't give up. "Going to college is not only about enjoying success and accomplishments, but also about persevering when things get difficult or go wrong," he says.

Gus had the ability to understand himself and others and to get along with people in a new environment. He was also able to manage time well, get things done, and anticipate potential problems before they occurred. Gus's problems with transferring to a new college are not uncommon, but he was able to deal with them without letting them become a barrier to his success. Why do some individuals struggle to handle stressful situations while others, like Gus, seem to handle them with ease? Although we tend to think of these abilities as inborn personality traits that can't be changed, social skills and stress-management skills really can be learned and improved.

P articularly in the first year of college, some students who have the ability to succeed academically can have difficulty establishing positive relationships with others, dealing with pressure, or making wise decisions. Other students exude optimism and happiness and seem to adapt to their new environment without any trouble. The difference between the two types of students lies not in their academic talent but in their emotional intelligence (EI), or their ability to recognize and manage moods, feelings, and attitudes. A growing body of evidence shows a clear connection between students' EI and whether they stay in college.

As you read this chapter, you will develop an understanding of EI, and you will learn how to use it to become a more successful student and person. You will begin to look at yourself and others through an EI lens, observe the behaviors that help people succeed, get to know yourself better, and learn to examine your feelings before you act. Then, as you read each subsequent chapter in this book, try to apply what you have learned about EI and think about how it might relate to the behaviors of successful college students. You can't always control the challenges and frustrations of life, but with practice, you *can* control how you respond to them.

WHAT IS EMOTIONAL INTELLIGENCE?

Emotional intelligence is the ability to recognize, understand, use, and manage emotions—moods, feelings, and attitudes. There are many competing theories about EI, some of them complex. While experts vary in their definitions and models, all agree that emotions are real, can be changed for the better, and have a profound impact on whether a person is successful.

 LaunchPad

To access LearningCurve and more, go to LaunchPad for *Your College Experience* at **macmillanhighered.com /gardner12e**. For the Concise edition, go to **macmillanhighered.com /collegesuccessmedia**.

There are many competing theories and assessment tools for EI. Four basic models are the most widely used: the Mayer-Salovey-Caruso Emotional Intelligence Test (MSCEIT) developed by John Mayer, Peter Salovey, and David Caruso; Daniel Goleman and Richard Boyatzis's Emotional Competence Inventory; Esther Orioli and Robert Cooper's EQ Map; and the Emotional Quotient Inventory (EQ-i) and the EQ 360, developed by Reuven Bar-On. Because the EQ-i was the first validated tool for college-age students and because most of the research in college has been done using this instrument, we use this tool and model as the focus of this chapter.

RETENTION STRATEGY >
Emotions can be distractions and disruptions, or they can be supporters and enablers of college success and retention. Ask students to discuss how their emotions help them engage in their coursework.

In the simplest terms, emotional intelligence consists of two general abilities:

1. *Understanding emotions* involves the capacity to monitor and label your feelings accurately (nervousness, happiness, anger, relief, and so forth) and to determine why you feel the way you do. It also involves predicting how others might feel in a given situation. Emotions contain information, and the ability to understand and think about that information plays an important role in behavior.

2. *Managing emotions* involves the ability to modify and even improve feelings. At times, you need to stay open to your feelings, learn from them, and use them to take appropriate action. At other times, it is better to disengage from an emotion and return to it later. Anger, for example, can lead you to act in negative or antisocial ways; used positively, however, anger can help you overcome adversity, bias, and injustice.

The first key step in learning to control your emotions and use them in productive ways is to understand that you and your emotions are not one

Emotional Intelligence Questionnaire

Your daily life gives you many opportunities to take a hard look at how you handle emotions. Here are some questions that can help you begin thinking about your own EI.

1. What do you do when you are under stress?
   a. I tend to deal with it calmly and rationally.
   b. I get upset, but it usually blows over quickly.
   c. I get upset but keep it to myself.

2. My friends would say that:
   a. I play, but only after I get my work done.
   b. I am ready for fun anytime.
   c. I hardly ever go out.

3. When something changes at the last minute:
   a. I easily adapt.
   b. I get frustrated.
   c. I don't care, since I don't really expect things to happen according to plan.

4. My friends would say that:
   a. I am sensitive to their concerns.
   b. I spend too much time worrying about other people's needs.
   c. I don't like to deal with other people's petty problems.

5. When I have a problem to solve, such as having too many assignments due at the end of the week:
   a. I write down a list of the tasks I must complete, come up with a plan indicating specifically what I can accomplish and what I cannot, and follow my plan.
   b. I am very optimistic about getting things done and just dig right in and get to work.
   c. I get a little frazzled. Usually I get a number of things done and then push aside the things I can't do.

Review your responses. a responses indicate that you probably have a good basis for strong EI. **b** responses indicate that you may have some strengths and some challenges in your EI. **c** responses indicate that your success in life and in school could be negatively affected by your EI.

and the same. You can stand apart from and observe your emotions; you are separate from them. Whatever your emotions at any given moment, you might be using them to filter your perception of a situation by magnifying all the negative details and filtering out all positive aspects—without realizing that you're doing this. You might even pick out a single pleasant or unpleasant detail and dwell on it exclusively so that your vision of reality becomes distorted. If you are feeling sad, you might view the world in a certain way, while if you are feeling happy, you are likely to interpret the same events differently.

Another important step in becoming more emotionally intelligent is developing an awareness of how your emotions affect you. When you start paying attention to emotions instead of ignoring them, you will have a better emotional understanding of different situations, and therefore be able to respond to these situations more appropriately. You can learn not only how to cope with life's pressures and demands, but also how to harness your knowledge of the way you feel, which can lead to more effective problem solving, reasoning, decision making, and creative endeavors.

A number of sophisticated tools can be used to assess emotional intelligence, or you can take the short questionnaire on the previous page to begin thinking about it. Even without a formal test, you can take a number of steps to get in touch with your own EI. You'll have to dig deep inside yourself and be willing to be honest about how you really think and how you really behave. This process can take time, and that's fine. Think of your EI as a work in progress.

your turn Stay Motivated

Overcoming Tough Challenges

Think about a challenge you have experienced in college that made you want to throw in the towel. How did that challenge affect your overall motivation for doing well in college? What lessons did you learn from the experience, and how can you use those lessons in the future to maintain your motivation?

EMOTIONAL INTELLIGENCE IN EVERYDAY LIFE

You have already used your emotional intelligence in your life experiences. For example, you graduated from high school and are making the transition to college. The decision to attend college might have involved evaluating the reputation and characteristics of different colleges or universities and the opportunities they offered. But if you had been planning to attend a particular college your whole life, you might have filtered your college-choice experience through your emotional attachment to one place. If you made campus visits, how did you react to hearing information that concerned or excited you, exploring the different buildings, or meeting staff, faculty, or other students? What impact did your emotions have on your final decision?

Naming and labeling emotions, in addition to focusing on related experiences, strengthens emotional intelligence skills. For instance, new college students often face the fear of social rejection. You might feel ignored or rejected by students you have met before. The feeling of rejection can even cause a physical reaction—your face might feel hot and you might even feel slightly sick to your stomach. If you can acknowledge and name what you are feeling, you will be less likely to be controlled by it. You will be in a better place to confront the fear by walking up to the students, introducing yourself again, and perhaps asking to join them.

Hearing something emotional often triggers our own emotional reaction. For instance, how would you react if a close friend said she had been sexually assaulted? Could you be empathetic and helpful, or would your own emotional reaction cause you to barrage her with questions about where she had been, what she had been wearing, and whether she had been drinking? These accusations could impede your friend's recovery and make her even more vulnerable. As you work to develop your emotional intelligence, you'll need to consider how to use logic rather than your own emotional reactions to evaluate a situation and be helpful to others.

Motivation

Most college students have many responsibilities, and it can be hard to stay motivated when you have too much to do. Positive feedback can help, and it's important to realize that this can come from within—motivating yourself is a big part of being emotionally intelligent. Draw from past positive experiences to propel yourself through a current challenge. Consider how conquering a challenge provides an example to others. What positive outcomes will result? Being emotionally intelligent also means knowing

"The key to stress management is knowing how to vent your frustration."

Don't Blow Your Top

There are good ways and bad ways to vent frustration. Having it out with another person or eating a gallon of ice cream are poor strategies. Going for a walk or run, doing yoga, or "talking it out" with someone you trust, however, will help you deal with the frustrations that are common to college life without making things worse.

© Randy Glasbergen

Overall Mood. It might sound sappy, but having a positive attitude really does improve your chances of doing well. Bar-On emphasizes the importance of two emotions in particular:

- **Optimism.** Looking on the bright side of any problem or difficulty and being confident that things will work out for the best.
- **Happiness.** Being satisfied with yourself, with others, and with your situation in general. It makes sense: If you feel good about yourself and manage your emotions, you can expect to get along with others and enjoy a happy, successful life.

Knowledge of self is strongly connected to respect for others and their way of life. If you don't understand yourself and why you do the things you do, it can be difficult for you to understand others. What's more, if you don't like yourself, you can hardly expect others to like you.

HIGH-IMPACT PRACTICE ❯ Ask students to write down their top ten stressors. Then break students into small groups and have them reach a consensus on the top stressors for first-year college students. Finally, have each group share its list with the rest of the class. How different are the lists? How similar are they? What does that suggest?

---

yourturn Make Good Choices

Act Instead of React

Your emotional reactions, whether positive or negative, affect your interactions with other people. Pretend that you are your own therapist. In what kinds of situations have you had "knee-jerk" reactions when you've reacted with defensiveness, anger, sadness, annoyance, resentment, or humiliation? Take a step back and "process" these reactions. Think about what you said or did in response to your feelings, and why. Then talk with a trusted friend or classmate about how you reacted and whether you could have chosen to act differently. What can you do to take control and make good choices the next time you are faced with a potentially volatile situation?

Accentuate the Positive

You probably know people who always find the negative in any situation. Constantly focusing on what's missing or what's not perfect will likely make you the kind of person whom others avoid. Practice looking on the bright side.

marekuliasz/Shutterstock

HOW EMOTIONS INFLUENCE SUCCESS

Emotions are strongly tied to physical and psychological well-being. For example, some studies have suggested that cancer patients who have strong EI live longer than those with weak EI. People who are aware of the needs of others tend to be happier than people who are not. An extensive study done at the University of Pennsylvania found that the best athletes succeed in part because they're extremely optimistic. A number of studies link strong EI skills to college success in particular. Studies indicate that emotionally intelligent students get higher grades. Researchers looked at students' grade point averages at the end of their first year of college. Students who had tested high for intrapersonal skills, stress tolerance, and adaptability when they entered in the fall did better academically than those who had lower overall EI test scores. Here are a few other highlights of those studies:

- **Motivation:** Motivation is one of the most important attributes that college students can have. Figuring out what actually does motivate anyone is complex, but striving to find out and nurture these motivations is the goal.
- **Resilience:** We discussed resilience above—stronger emotional intelligence leads to greater resilience. Students with healthy emotional intelligence might act proactively by asking instructors for feedback on projects, papers, and tests, participating in classroom discussions, and joining study groups. Students with unhealthy EI are likely to struggle academically, panic before taking tests, have trouble concentrating on coursework, and engage in risky behaviors such as alcohol and drug abuse in an effort to cope. Dr. Richard Kadison, a former director of mental health services at Harvard University, noted that "the emotional well-being of students goes hand in hand with their academic development. If they're not doing well emotionally, they are not going to reach their academic potential."[2]
- **Persistence:** Some college students develop persistence in spite of the obstacles and challenges during their college experience. Persistent students make forward progress through challenging situations, even if progress is slow.
- **Delaying gratification:** Research has shown that students who can delay gratification tend to do better overall. Impulse control leads to achievement. A study conducted in the 1970s looked at the case of willpower in children. It is referred to as the Stanford Marshmallow Study.[3] The study observed children's behavior when they were left alone at a table with a marshmallow. They were told that they could have a second marshmallow if they waited 15 minutes before eating

IN CLASS > A component of "impulse control" is "delaying gratification." Divide the class into small groups and ask them to discuss this concept and how it relates to children, college students, and adults in today's society. When is it OK for us to get what we want immediately? When are we better off practicing delayed gratification?

---

[2]Richard Kadison and Theresa Foy DiGeronimo, *College of the Overwhelmed: The Campus Mental Health Crisis and What to Do about It* (San Francisco: Jossey-Bass, 2004), 156.

[3]Walter Mischel, et al., "Delay of Gratification in Children," *Science*, 244, no. 4907 (1989): 933–38.

the first one. Fourteen years later, the children who had immediately eaten their marshmallow were more likely to experience significant stress, irritability, and an inability to focus on goals. The children who had waited to eat their marshmallow scored an average of 210 points higher on the SAT; had more confidence, better concentration, and reliability; held better-paying jobs; and reported being more satisfied with life.

Healthy EI and the First-Year Seminar

Healthy EI contributes to overall academic success, positive professional and romantic relationships, and overall career development and satisfaction. EI skills can be enhanced in a first-year seminar. In one study conducted in Australia and another conducted separately in the United States, researchers found that college students enrolled in a first-year seminar who demonstrated good EI skills were more likely to do better in college than students who did not exhibit those skills.

You can get by in college without strong EI, but you might miss out on the full range and depth of competencies and skills that can help you succeed in your chosen field and have a fulfilling and meaningful life.

IN CLASS ❯ Ask students to think about this course, its content, and its in-class activities. What have they been doing in this class—and what could they do more of—that might help them develop their EI skills?

RETENTION STRATEGY ❯ Students who are easily frustrated and make impulsive decisions may give up on college. Encourage any student who expresses the wish to drop out or transfer to have a one-on-one discussion with you or a counselor before taking that step.

HOW TO IMPROVE YOUR EMOTIONAL INTELLIGENCE

Developing your EI is an important step toward getting the full benefit of a college education. Think about how you cope with emotional stress. Do you often give up because something is just too hard or because you can't figure it out? Do you take responsibility for what you do, or do you blame others if you fail? How can you communicate effectively if you are not assertive or if you are overly aggressive? If you're inflexible, how can you solve problems, get along with coworkers and family members, or learn from other people's points of view?

The good news is that you *can* improve your EI. It might not be easy—old habits are hard to change—but it can definitely be done. Here are some suggestions:

1. **Identify your strengths and weaknesses.** Take a hard look at yourself, and consider how you respond to situations. Most people have trouble evaluating their own behaviors realistically, so ask someone you trust and respect for insight.
2. **Set realistic goals.** As you identify areas of emotional intelligence that you would like to improve, be as specific as possible. Instead of deciding to be more assertive, for example, focus on a specific issue that is giving you trouble.
3. **Formulate a plan.** With a particular goal in mind, identify a series of steps you could take to achieve the goal, and define the results that would indicate success.
4. **Check your progress on a regular basis.** Continually re-evaluate whether or not you have met your goals, and adjust your strategy as needed.

techtip

USE BLOGS AND TWITTER

Everyone is an expert at something. Web sites like WordPress, Twitter, and Blogger give people space to write about or otherwise produce information that they know something about. Many of the most frequently used news Web sites and social networking sites get information that is sent—or "fed"—to them from someone's blog.

Twitter is a microblogging site. It's called "microblogging" because you can only write a maximum of 140 characters per message, or "tweet." Get off the sidelines and into the world of microblogging. It doesn't take much time to post to Twitter because of its 140-character limit. Twitter also allows you to follow the tweets of people, events, and organizations that interest you.

The Problem

You've heard people talk about blogs and Twitter, but you don't know why you'd join or what you'd do with them.

The Fix   *Dive in!*

How to Do It

Research areas that you find interesting on blogging sites like wordpress.com, blogger.com, technorati.com, or alltop.com, or create a Twitter account.

Add the WordPress, Blogger, or Twitter app to your phone or tablet. This will allow you to keep up-to-date on information you find interesting and will get you in the habit of commenting, liking, responding, and posting so that you develop your "digital self" as a professional.

Participate in a network of people who share your interests. While you are in college, connect with people who are experts in your professional or personal areas of interest. Follow their posts to get advice and understand what people are talking about. You can also create a blog yourself and have other people follow your journey.

Sports/Entertainment: You can use Twitter or a blog to keep up with your favorite actors, bands, and sports teams. Some tweet about projects they're working on, some tweet political commentary, and others just share great jokes.

Education: Authors tweet or blog about their books and often engage in conversations with their readers.

Professionals and scholars in many fields share links to news articles, book reviews, Web sites, and videos related to their careers and areas of study.

Job-hunting: Many career Web sites have Twitter accounts and blogs. Following the official Twitter feed of a company you want to work for can lead to instant notifications of new job opportunities and give you the chance to get your résumé ready.

Community involvement: One amazing feature of Twitter is that it allows for real-time global conversations on important issues. Twitter was a key component in the Arab Spring of 2011–2012, a period that saw dozens of political demonstrations and revolutionary movements across the Arab world.

EXTRA STYLE POINTS: Create an online professional self that shows how fun or interesting or creative or compassionate you really are. A word of caution: Think about what you reveal about your emotional intelligence by what you post, and think about what you can tell about others' emotional intelligence by their posts.

☐ b. talk with people who know about the program.

☐ c. use the controls or keyboard.

☐ d. follow the diagrams in the book that came with it.

10. You like Web sites that have:

☐ a. things you can click on, shift, or try.

☐ b. interesting design and visual features.

☐ c. interesting written descriptions, lists, and explanations.

☐ d. audio channels where you can hear music, radio programs, or interviews.

11. Other than price, what would most influence your decision to buy a new nonfiction book?

☐ a. the way it looks is appealing

☐ b. quickly reading parts of it

☐ c. a friend talks about it and recommends it

☐ d. it has real-life stories, experiences, and examples

12. You are using a book, CD, or Web site to learn how to take photos with your new digital camera. You would like to have:

☐ a. a chance to ask questions and talk about the camera and its features.

☐ b. clear written instructions with lists and bullet points about what to do.

☐ c. diagrams showing the camera and what each part does.

☐ d. many examples of good and poor photos and how to improve them.

13. You prefer a teacher or a presenter who uses:

☐ a. demonstrations, models, or practical sessions.

☐ b. questions and answers, talk, group discussion, or guest speakers.

☐ c. handouts, books, or readings.

☐ d. diagrams, charts, or graphs.

14. You have finished a competition or test and would like some feedback:

☐ a. using examples from what you have done.

☐ b. using a written description of your results.

☐ c. from somebody who talks it through with you.

☐ d. using graphs showing what you achieved.

15. You are going to order food at a restaurant or café. You would:

☐ a. choose something that you have had there before.

☐ b. listen to the waiter or ask friends to recommend choices.

☐ c. choose from the descriptions in the menu.

☐ d. look at what others are eating or look at pictures of each dish.

16. You have to make an important speech at a conference or special occasion. You would:

☐ a. make diagrams or get graphs to help explain things.

☐ b. write a few key words and practice saying your speech over and over.

☐ c. write out your speech and learn from reading it over several times.

☐ d. gather many examples and stories to make the talk real and practical.

Scoring the VARK. Now you will match up each one of the boxes you selected with a category from the VARK Questionnaire using the following scoring chart. Circle the letter (V, A, R, or K) that corresponds to each one of your responses (A, B, C, or D). For example, if you marked both B and C for question 3, circle both the V and R in the third row.

Responses to Question 3:	A	B	C	D
VARK letter	K	(V)	(R)	A

Count the number of each of the VARK letters you have circled to get your score for each VARK.

Scoring Chart

Question	A Category	B Category	C Category	D Category
1	K	A	R	V
2	V	A	R	K
3	K	V	R	A
4	K	A	V	R
5	A	V	K	R
6	K	R	V	A
7	K	A	V	R
8	R	K	A	V
9	R	A	K	V
10	K	V	R	A
11	V	R	A	K
12	A	R	V	K
13	K	A	R	V
14	K	R	A	V
15	K	A	R	V
16	V	A	R	K

Total number of **V**s circled = _____   Total number of **A**s circled = _____
Total number of **R**s circled = _____   Total number of **K**s circled = _____

Because you could choose more than one answer for each question, the scoring is not a simple matter of counting. It's like four stepping stones across water. Enter your scores **from highest to lowest** on the stones in the figure, with their V, A, R, and K labels.

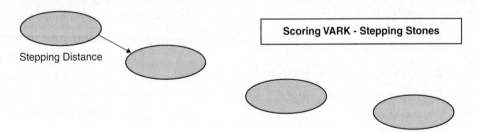

Stepping Distance

Scoring VARK - Stepping Stones

Your stepping distance comes from this table:

The total of my four VARK scores is	My stepping distance is
16–21	1
22–27	2
28–32	3
More than 32	4

Follow these steps to establish your preferences:

1. Your first preference is always your highest score. Check that first stone as one of your preferences.

2. Now subtract your second highest score from your first. If that figure is larger than your stepping distance, you have a single preference. Otherwise, check this stone as another preference and continue with step 3.

3. Subtract your third score from your second one. If that figure is larger than your stepping distance, you have a strong preference for two learning styles (bimodal). If not, check your third stone as a preference and continue with step 4.

4. Last, subtract your fourth score from your third one. If that figure is larger than your stepping distance, you have a strong preference for three learning styles (trimodal). Otherwise, check your fourth stone as a preference, and you have all four modes as your preferences! You may also find that you prefer the four learning styles equally.

Note: If you are bimodal or trimodal or you have checked all four modes as your preferences, you are *multimodal* in your VARK preferences.

IN CLASS > After the students have completed the VARK inventory, discuss the model. Take a poll to determine the variety of learning styles among the class. What does this variety mean for the dynamics of the class?

HIGH-IMPACT PRACTICE > Ask students to write a short paper on what they learned after completing and scoring the VARK Questionnaire. This brief writing assignment will help students reflect on the value of understanding their own learning preferences.

---

your turn   Work Together

Sharing Different Approaches to Learning

Did you know what type of learner you were before taking the VARK? Find one or two other students in your class with different learning styles. Share thoughts on strategies you are using to study in all your classes, referring to the examples in Table 4.1. What strategies are working for everyone in the group?

high-impact practice 3

HIGH-IMPACT PRACTICE > This collaborative exercise can help students share study strategies across multiple learning styles. Collaboration will help them remember and apply what they learn.

Use VARK Results to Study More Effectively

How can knowing your VARK score help you do better in your college classes? The following table offers suggestions for using learning styles to

TABLE 4.1 > Study Strategies by Learning Style

Visual	Aural	Read/Write	Kinesthetic
Underline or highlight your notes.	Talk with others to verify the accuracy of your lecture notes.	Write and rewrite your notes.	Use all your senses in learning: sight, touch, taste, smell, and hearing.
Use symbols, charts, or graphs to display your notes.	Put your notes on audio-tape, or audiotape class lectures.	Read your notes silently.	Supplement your notes with real-world examples.
Use color to highlight important concepts.	Read your notes out loud; ask yourself questions and speak your answers.	Organize diagrams or flowcharts into statements.	Move and gesture while you are reading or speaking your notes.
Create a graphic representation of your notes (e.g., a mind map) and redraw it from memory.		Write imaginary exam questions and respond in writing.	

develop your own study strategies. Consider also how online course management systems (see this chapter's Tech Tip) provide opportunities for different types of learners to connect with the material they are studying.

The Kolb Inventory of Learning Styles

RETENTION STRATEGY >
Consider telling your students about research that shows that the learning-style preferences of most students do *not* align with the learning/teaching-style preferences of most faculty members. Specifically, students tend to prefer hands-on experiential learning, while some instructors tend to prefer teaching through lectures. By explaining this reality, you can get your students thinking about how they can adapt to these differences. If students can adjust, they are more likely to be successful, and hence retained.

The Kolb Inventory of Learning Styles is a widely used and referenced learning model that is more complex than the VARK Inventory. While the VARK Inventory investigates how learners prefer to use their senses in learning, the Kolb Inventory focuses on the abilities we need to develop so we can learn. This inventory, developed in the 1980s by David Kolb, is based on a four-stage cycle of learning (see Figure 4.1 below).

According to Kolb, effective learners need four kinds of abilities:

1. *Concrete experience* abilities, which allow them to be receptive to others and open to other people's feelings and specific experiences. An example of this type of ability is learning from and empathizing with others.
2. *Reflective observation* abilities, which help learners reflect on their experiences from many perspectives. An example of this type of ability is remaining impartial while considering a situation from a number of different points of view.
3. *Abstract conceptualization* abilities, which help learners integrate observations into logically sound theories. An example of this type of ability is analyzing ideas intellectually and systematically.
4. *Active experimentation* abilities, which enable learners to make decisions, solve problems, and test what they have learned in new situations. An example of this type of ability is being ready to move quickly from thinking to action.

Kolb's Inventory of Learning Styles measures differences along two basic dimensions that represent opposite styles of learning. The first dimension is *abstract-concrete*, and the second is *active-reflective*. See Figure 4.1 below to visualize how these opposing characteristics combine to create four discrete groups of learners: *divergers, assimilators, convergers,* and *accommodators.*

Doing well in college will require you to adopt some behaviors that are characteristic of each of these four learning styles. Some of them might be uncomfortable for you, but that discomfort will indicate that

FIGURE 4.1 > Kolb's Four-Stage Cycle of Learning

you're growing, stretching, and not relying on the learning style that might be easiest or most natural for you.

If you are a diverger, you are adept at reflecting on situations from many viewpoints. You excel at brainstorming, and you're imaginative, people-oriented, and sometimes emotional. On the downside, you sometimes have difficulty making decisions. Divergers tend to major in the humanities or social sciences.

If you are an assimilator, you like to think about abstract concepts. You are comfortable in classes where the instructor lectures about theoretical ideas without relating the lectures to real-world situations. Assimilators often major in math, physics, or chemistry.

If you are a converger, you like the world of ideas and theories, but you are also good at thinking about how to apply those theories to real-world, practical situations. You differ from divergers in your preference for tasks and problems rather than social and interpersonal issues. Convergers tend to choose health-related and engineering majors.

If you are an accommodator, you prefer hands-on learning. You are skilled at making things happen, and you rely on your intuition. You like people, but you can be pushy and impatient at times, and you might use trial and error, rather than logic, to solve problems. Accommodators often major in business, especially in marketing or sales.[1]

---

your turn   Stay Motivated

Where Are You on the Cycle of Learning?

On the basis of the descriptions we have provided here, where do you see yourself in the Kolb Inventory? Are you more like a diverger, assimilator, converger, or accommodator? Do you sometimes feel forced to engage in behaviors that are uncomfortable for you? Is it hard to be motivated when you want hands-on experience but find that some courses require you to consider abstract theories, or when you want to use your imagination but find you must come up with concrete answers? Choose to adopt behaviors that are characteristic of each of Kolb's learning styles. Don't let some initial discomfort hamper your motivation.

The Myers-Briggs Type Indicator

One of the best-known and most widely used personality inventories that can also be used to describe learning styles is the Myers-Briggs Type Indicator, or MBTI.[2] Whereas the VARK measures your preferences for using your senses to learn and the Kolb Inventory focuses on learning abilities, the MBTI investigates basic personality characteristics and how they relate to human interaction and learning. The MBTI was created by Isabel Briggs Myers and her mother, Katharine Cook Briggs. The inventory identifies and measures psychological types as developed in the personality theory

An online bibliography listing almost eight thousand known studies on the MBTI is available at **capt.org.** For instructors in any academic specialty, workshops (including online workshops) to train and qualify you to give the MBTI are available from several reputable organizations listed on the Myers & Briggs Foundation Web site (**myersbriggs.org**).

IN CLASS > Ask students their thoughts about an inventory that claims to measure personality types. Ask for student volunteers to do an Internet search on the Myers-Briggs Type Inventory and share their findings in class.

---

[1]Republished with permission of John Wiley & Sons, Inc., from "The Experimental Learning Model," from *The Modern American College: Responding to the New Realities of Diverse Students and a Changing Society*/Chickering. Copyright © 1981 Jossey-Bass; permission conveyed through Copyright Clearance Center, Inc.

[2]Isabel Briggs Myers, *Introduction to Type*, 6th ed. (Mountain View, CA: CPP, 1998).

Take a Time-Out

Do you find that you need some occasional time by yourself? Although introverts are more likely to enjoy time alone, even extraverts can benefit from private time to relax or escape from the hustle and bustle of daily life.

Jonathan Stark

IN CLASS ❯ Develop a lesson on the Myers-Briggs types. Explain how the letters are used. Ask someone on campus who has experience with the Myers-Briggs assessment to assist you or come talk to your class.

of Carl Gustav Jung, the great twentieth-century psychoanalyst. The MBTI is given to several million people around the world each year. Employers often use this test to give employees insight into how they perceive the world, make decisions, and get along with other people. Many first-year seminar or college success courses also include a focus on the MBTI because it provides a good way to begin a dialogue about human interaction and how personality types affect learning.

All the psychological types described by the MBTI are normal and healthy. There is no good or bad or right or wrong; people are simply different. When you complete the MBTI, your score represents your "psychological type," or the combination of your preferences on four different scales. These scales measure how you take in information and how you then make decisions or come to conclusions about that information. Each preference has a one-letter abbreviation. The four letters together make up your type. Although this book doesn't include the actual survey, you will find a description of the basic MBTI types below. Based on these scales, you can be any combination of these eight types.

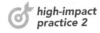

high-impact practice 2

HIGH-IMPACT PRACTICE ❯ If you require students in your class to make frequent entries in a journal, you are providing them with an intensive, but nonthreatening, writing experience. Be sure to provide some feedback on the content of these journal entries.

yourturn Write and Reflect

Discerning the Extraverts from the Introverts in Your Life

Read the following descriptions of extraverts and introverts. Make a list of your friends and family members, and indicate with an "E" or an "I" which are extraverts and which are introverts. How about you? Which type describes you best? Would you like to be different from the way you are? Reflect on these questions in a journal entry.

Extraversion (E) versus Introversion (I): The Inner or Outer World. The E-I preference indicates whether you direct your energy and attention primarily toward the outer world of people, events, and things or the inner world of thoughts, feelings, and reflections. Personality characteristics of extraverts and introverts are summarized here:

Extraverts	Introverts
Outgoing, gregarious, talkative (may talk too much)	Shy, reflective; careful listeners
People of action (may act before they think)	Consider actions deeply (may think too long before acting or neglect to act at all)
Energized by people and activity	Refreshed by quiet and privacy
Good communicators and leaders	Less likely to voice their opinions; often viewed as unaware of people and situations around them

Sensing (S) versus Intuition (N): Facts or Ideas.

The S-N preference indicates how you perceive the world and take in information: directly, through your five senses, or indirectly, by using your intuition. Personality characteristics of sensing and intuitive types are summarized here:

Sensing Types	Intuitive Types
Interested above all in the facts, what they can be sure of; dislike unnecessary complication; prefer practicing skills they already know	Fascinated by concepts and big ideas; prefer learning new skills over those already mastered
Relatively traditional and conventional	Original, creative, and nontraditional
Practical, factual, realistic, and down-to-earth	Innovative but sometimes impractical; need inspiration and meaning; prefer to look to the future rather than at the present
Accurate, precise, and effective with routine and details; sometimes miss the "forest" for the "trees"	May exaggerate facts unknowingly; dislike routine and details; work in bursts of energy

Thinking (T) versus Feeling (F): Logic or Values.

The T-F preference indicates how you prefer to make your decisions: through logical, rational analysis or through your subjective values, likes, and dislikes. Personality characteristics of thinking types and feeling types are summarized here:

Thinking Types	Feeling Types
Logical, rational, analytical, and critical	Warm, empathetic, and sympathetic
Relatively impersonal and objective in making decisions, less swayed by feelings and emotions; sometimes surprised and puzzled by others' feelings	Need and value harmony; often distressed or distracted by argument and conflict; reluctant to tackle unpleasant interpersonal tasks
Need and value fairness; can deal with interpersonal disharmony	Need and value kindness and harmony
Fair, logical, and just; firm and assertive	Facilitate cooperation and goodwill in others; sometimes unable to be assertive when appropriate
May seem cold, insensitive, and overly blunt and hurtful in their criticisms	Occasionally illogical, emotionally demanding, and unaffected by objective reason and evidence

It is inappropriate, unethical, and illegal to use the MBTI as a screening device to decide whether or not to hire an applicant for a job or admit someone to an educational program. The proper use of the MBTI is to help people identify satisfying career specialties for themselves.

PEER LEADERS > As a peer leader, you have probably had some introduction to the Myers-Briggs Type Indicator. If not, visit your counseling or career center for a quick introduction. Facilitate a class discussion on the advantages or disadvantages of being one type or another. Stress how all types include characteristics that are valuable in college and in the workplace. Students will quickly be able to "assign" types to themselves, their friends, and family members. Remind them that all types have value both in and after college.

IN CLASS > If your students have taken the MBTI, arrange the chairs or desks in a circle or square, beginning with the most "sensing" students and progressing to the most "intuitive" students as you circle around the group. Arrange students by MBTI type as much as possible so that students are next to people with whom they feel naturally comfortable and can quickly make friends. Note that they are sitting opposite, and are thus most likely to speak and listen to, people whose viewpoints are quite different from theirs. It might sound odd, but it really works!

FYI > Myers's *Introduction to Type* is the only full-length book on psychological type. It is richly informative and requires no prior training in psychology. Our favorite brief discussion is *Introduction to Type in Organizations*, 3rd ed., by Sandra Krebs Hirsh and Jean M. Kummerow (Mountain View, CA: CPP, 2012).

Judging (J) versus Perceiving (P): Organization or Adaptability. The J-P preference indicates how you characteristically approach the outside world: by making decisions and judgments or by observing and perceiving instead. Personality characteristics of judging and perceiving types are summarized here:

Judging Types	Perceiving Types
Orderly, organized, punctual, and tidy	Spontaneous and flexible
In control of their own world and sphere of influence	Adapt to their world rather than try to control it; comfortable dealing with changes and unexpected developments
Quick decision makers; like to make and follow plans	Slow to make decisions; prefer a wait-and-see approach
Sometimes judgmental and prone to jump to conclusions or make decisions without enough information; have trouble changing plans	Tendency toward serious procrastination and juggling too many things at once without finishing anything; sometimes messy and disorganized

To learn more about these personality types and to access a questionnaire to find out more about your type, visit the Myers & Briggs Foundation at **myersbriggs.org/my-mbti-personality-type/take-the-mbti-instrument.** Remember that while some Myers-Briggs personality types may be particularly advantageous in certain situations, no one type is inherently superior to another. Be alert to both the positive and negative effects your type might have on your success in college.

Multiple Intelligences

IN CLASS > Present students with some criticisms and some praise of Howard Gardner's work. Then organize a debate on the topic of multiple intelligences.

Another way of measuring how we learn is the theory of **multiple intelligences,** which suggests that all human beings have at least eight different types of intelligence. This theory was developed in 1983 by Dr. Howard Gardner, a professor of education at Harvard University. Gardner's theory is based on the idea that the traditional definition of human intelligence is very limited. Gardner argues that students should be encouraged to develop the abilities they have, and that evaluation should measure all forms of intelligence.

high-impact practice 2

HIGH-IMPACT PRACTICE > The ongoing debate about Howard Gardner's theory can be an opportunity for your students to write a longer paper (up to five pages) in which they take a position for or against Gardner's theory and use existing scholarship or research to support their views.

your turn   Write and Reflect

Is There Really More than One Type of Intelligence?

Do a Google search for the phrase *multiple intelligences debate.* Write a one-page paper that describes different opinions about Howard Gardner's theory. Do you agree with the theory? Why or why not?

Gardner's work is controversial because it questions our traditional definitions of intelligence. According to Gardner's theory,

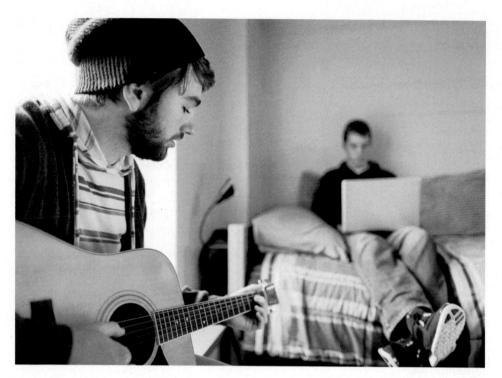

all human beings have at least eight different types of intelligence, as follows:

1. A **verbal/linguistic** learner likes to read, write, and tell stories, and is good at memorizing information.
2. A **logical/mathematical** learner likes to work with numbers and is good at problem solving and logical processes.
3. A **visual/spatial** learner likes to draw and play with machines and is good at puzzles and reading maps and charts.
4. A **bodily/kinesthetic** learner likes to move around and is good at sports, dance, and acting.
5. A **musical/rhythmic** learner likes to sing and play an instrument and is good at remembering melodies and noticing pitches and rhythms.
6. An **interpersonal** learner likes to have many friends and is good at understanding people, leading others, and mediating conflicts.
7. **Intrapersonal** learners like to work alone, understand themselves well, and are original thinkers.
8. A **naturalistic** learner likes to be outside and is good at preservation, conservation, and organizing a living area.

Where do you think you see yourself? In your opinion, which of these eight intelligences best describes you? As you think of your friends and family, what kinds of intelligences do you think they have? Verify your assumptions about the intelligences of friends and family members by taking the Multiple Intelligences Inventory together. Were there any surprises or were your assumptions confirmed?

Multiple Intelligences Inventory

Put a check mark next to all the items within each intelligence that apply to you.

Verbal/Linguistic Intelligence

_____ I enjoy telling stories and jokes.

_____ I enjoy word games (e.g., Scrabble and puzzles).

_____ I am a good speller (most of the time).

_____ I like talking and writing about my ideas.

_____ If something breaks and won't work, I read the instruction book before I try to fix it.

_____ When I work with others in a group presentation, I prefer to do the writing and library research.

Logical/Mathematical Intelligence

_____ I really enjoy my math class.

_____ I like to find out how things work.

_____ I enjoy computer and math games.

_____ I love playing chess, checkers, or Monopoly.

_____ If something breaks and won't work, I look at the pieces and try to figure out how it works.

Visual/Spatial Intelligence

_____ I prefer a map to written directions.

_____ I enjoy hobbies such as photography.

_____ I like to doodle on paper whenever I can.

_____ In a magazine, I prefer looking at the pictures rather than reading the text.

_____ If something breaks and won't work, I tend to study the diagram of how it works.

Bodily/Kinesthetic Intelligence

_____ My favorite class is gym because I like sports.

_____ When looking at things, I like touching them.

_____ I use a lot of body movements when talking.

_____ I tend to tap my fingers or play with my pencil during class.

_____ If something breaks and won't work, I tend to play with the pieces to try to fit them together.

Musical/Rhythmic Intelligence

_____ I enjoy listening to CDs and the radio.

_____ I like to sing.

_____ I like to have music playing when doing homework or studying.

_____ I can remember the melodies of many songs.

_____ If something breaks and won't work, I tend to tap my fingers to a beat while I figure it out.

Interpersonal Intelligence

_____ I get along well with others.

_____ I have several very close friends.

_____ I like working with others in groups.

_____ Friends ask my advice because I seem to be a natural leader.

_____ If something breaks and won't work, I try to find someone who can help me.

Intrapersonal Intelligence

_____ I like to work alone without anyone bothering me.

_____ I don't like crowds.

_____ I know my own strengths and weaknesses.

_____ I find that I am strong-willed, independent, and don't follow the crowd.

_____ If something breaks and won't work, I wonder whether it's worth fixing.

Naturalist Intelligence

_____ I am keenly aware of my surroundings and of what goes on around me.

_____ I like to collect things like rocks, sports cards, and stamps.

_____ I like to get away from the city and enjoy nature.

_____ I enjoy learning the names of living things in the environment, such as flowers and trees.

If you have trouble paying attention or getting organized, you won't really know whether you have ADD or ADHD until you are evaluated. Check out resources on campus or in the community. After you have been evaluated, follow the advice you get, which might or might not mean taking medication. If you receive a prescription for medication, be sure to take it according to your physician's directions. You can also improve your focus through your own behavioral choices, whether or not you have an attention disorder. The Web site for the National Institute of Mental Health offers the following suggestions for adults with attention disorders:

> A professional counselor or therapist can help an adult with ADHD learn how to organize his or her life with tools such as a large calendar or date book, lists, reminder notes, and by assigning a special place for keys, bills, and paperwork. Large tasks can be broken down into smaller, more manageable steps so that completing each part of the task provides a sense of accomplishment.[5]

Cognitive Learning Disabilities

Other learning disabilities are related to cognitive skills. Dyslexia, for example, is a common developmental reading disorder. Though a person can have problems with any of the tasks involved in reading, scientists have found that a significant number of people with dyslexia share an inability to distinguish or separate the sounds in spoken words. For instance, people with dyslexia sometimes have difficulty assigning the appropriate sounds to individual letters or to letters that have been combined to form words. Reading is more than recognizing words, however. If the brain is unable to form images or relate new ideas to those stored in memory, the reader can't understand or remember the new concepts. So other types of reading disabilities can appear when the focus of reading shifts from word identification to comprehension.[6]

Writing involves several brain areas and functions as well. The brain networks for vocabulary, grammar, hand movement, and memory must all be in good working order. A developmental writing disorder might result from problems in any of these areas. Someone who can't distinguish the sequence of sounds in a word will often have problems with spelling. People with writing disabilities, particularly expressive language disorders (the inability to express oneself using accurate language or sentence structure), are often unable to write complete, grammatical sentences.[7]

A student with a developmental arithmetic disorder will have difficulty recognizing numbers and symbols, memorizing facts such as multiplication tables, and understanding abstract concepts such as place value and fractions.[8]

---

[5]"Attention Deficit Hyperactivity Disorder." U.S. Department of Health and Human Services, National Institutes of Health, NIH Publication No. 12-3572, p. 17 (Revised 2012). www.nimh.nih.gov/health/publications/attention-deficit-hyperactivity-disorder/index.shtml, accessed September 3, 2014.

[6]Ibid.

[7]Ibid.

[8]Ibid.

The following questions may help you determine whether you or someone you know should be screened for a possible learning disability:

Do you perform poorly on tests, even when you feel that you have studied and are capable of performing better?

Do you have trouble spelling words?

Do you work harder than your classmates at basic reading and writing?

Do your instructors point out inconsistencies in your classroom performance, such as answering questions correctly in class but incorrectly on a written test?

Do you have a really short attention span, or do your family members or instructors say that you do things without thinking?

Although responding *yes* to any of these questions does not mean that you have a disability, your campus learning center or the office for student disability services can help you address any potential problems and devise ways for you to learn more effectively.

If you have a documented learning disability, make sure to notify the office of student disability services at your college or university to receive reasonable accommodations, as required by law. Reasonable accommodations might include use of a computer during some exams, readers for tests, in-class note-takers, extra time for assignments and tests, or the use of audio textbooks, depending on your needs and the type of disability you have.

Anyone who is diagnosed with a learning disability is in good company. According to national data, between 15 and 20 percent of Americans have a learning disability. Pop star Jewel, National Football League host and former player Terry Bradshaw, actor Patrick Dempsey, and CNN news anchor Anderson Cooper are just a few of the famous and successful people who have diagnosed learning disabilities. Here is a final important message: A learning disability is a learning *difference*, but is in no way related to intelligence. Having a learning disability is not a sign that you are stupid. In fact, some of the most intelligent individuals in human history have had a learning disability.

IN CLASS > Share information on where students should go for help on campus if they have a learning disability, or if they think they might have one and want to be evaluated.

your turn   Make Good Choices

Accept the Challenge to Do Your Best, No Matter What!

Although you generally won't be able to select courses and instructors based on your learning style, you can choose how to handle yourself in each class. Think about your courses this term and look at how you filled in Table 4.2. Which classes are challenging you because of the way the instructors teach? If you are using an instructor's teaching style as an excuse for your poor performance, you are making a choice that may affect your overall college success. Your college or university has plenty of resources available to help you. Seek them out and choose to get the assistance you need to do your best.

The concept of "critical thinking" might not be new to you; you have probably heard the term before. Here we define **critical thinking** as the thoughtful consideration of the information, ideas, observations, and arguments that you encounter. In essence, critical thinking is a search for truth. It is similar to slow thinking as described by Kahneman, but it also emphasizes the importance of analyzing and evaluating information to guide belief and action—this is the kind of thinking you will do in college, and it's what this chapter is all about. We will explain how developing and applying your critical-thinking skills can make the search for answers a worthwhile and stimulating adventure.

COLLEGE-LEVEL THINKING: HIGHER AND DEEPER

In college, the level of thinking that your instructors expect from you exceeds that which you did in high school, both in terms of the questions that are asked and the answers that are expected. For instance, if a high school teacher asked, "What are the three branches of the U.S. government?" he or she would ask you to give the one right answer: "legislative, executive, and judicial." A college instructor, on the other hand, might ask, "Under what circumstances might conflicts arise among the three branches of government, and what do the circumstances and the conflicts reveal about the democratic process?" There is no simple, quick, or single acceptable answer to the second question—that's the point of higher education. Questions that suggest complex answers engage you in the process of deep thinking. The shift to this higher or deeper level of thinking can be an adjustment—it might even catch you off guard and cause you some stress.

One step toward deep and critical thinking is becoming comfortable with uncertainty. In college, it's important to challenge assumptions and conclusions, even those presented by so-called experts. Rather than just

RETENTION STRATEGY > One thing that keeps students motivated to stay in college is engaging in learning that they think is relevant to improving their employment options. This chapter focuses on how to develop a skill that is highly sought by employers—critical thinking!

IN CLASS > Critical thinking is one of the most important concepts in this book. Point out the relationship between this concept and your institution's mission statement on its Web site or catalog. Discuss the college mission statement to help your students understand your institution's educational goals; tie in the meaning of a liberal education as appropriate. You might want to point out that most employers value the ability to think critically more than they value specific content knowledge.

taking in information, studying it, and then recalling it for a test, in college you'll go far beyond these skills and gain the ability and the confidence to arrive at your own conclusions—to think for yourself. Educational researchers describe this process as "constructing" knowledge for yourself rather than merely "receiving" knowledge from others. Courses in every discipline will encourage you to ask questions, sort through competing information and ideas, form well-reasoned opinions, and defend them.

It is natural to feel frustrated by answers that are neither entirely wrong nor right, yet the complicated questions are usually the ones that are the most interesting and worthy of study. Working out the answers can be both intellectually exciting and personally rewarding.

Problem Solving in and out of Class

College will give you experience in decision making and problem solving—processes that are linked to your abilities to use logical thinking processes, to weigh evidence, and to formulate conclusions. Your success both in college and in your future life will depend on how well you make decisions and solve problems. Here are some examples of situations commonly encountered in college that will call upon these skills:

- Deciding how to allocate your research and writing time when you have two papers due on the same day
- Finding a way to ask your roommate to compromise on a suitable lights-out time because you're not getting the sleep you need
- Mapping out how to incorporate time for exercising into your busy schedule in order to maintain a healthy fitness level and avoid weight gain
- Deciding whether to go home on the weekends or stay on campus to study and participate in campus events
- Understanding the advantages and disadvantages of the variety of readily available information sources, including Facebook, Twitter feeds, CNN, *USA Today*, *The New York Times*, the *Onion*, and your school newspaper.

In addition to these situations, which provide opportunities for you to flex your problem-solving muscles on a more personal level, the college years also represent a time in your life when you get to know yourself. You will begin to develop your own positions on societal and political issues, learn more about what is important to you, and develop into a contributing citizen of your country and also the world.

In college, you'll be exposed to ideas and often-conflicting opinions about contemporary issues such as same-sex marriage, U.S. military operations, global human rights, animal rights, comprehensive sex education, food safety, the state of public education in the U.S., student loan debt and loan forgiveness, and economic inequality. The list goes on and on. Before accepting any opinion on any issue as "the truth," look for evidence that supports different positions on these debates. In fact, look for opportunities to participate in such debates. In most colleges, these opportunities abound.

Making a Choice between Slow and Fast Thinking

At the start of the chapter, we introduced the concepts of slow and fast thinking. While fast thinking has its place, improving your slower and more logical thinking abilities will allow you to become a better learner. But you might notice that some people seem to do no real thinking at all, or at least no thinking of their own.

IN CLASS > Ask students why some people do not think for themselves, instead relying on others to think for them.

People who do not develop their thinking skills often make spur-of-the-moment decisions based on what seems easiest, results in the least conflict, or conforms to preconceived notions. You probably know a lot of people like that—who do not think critically, depend on others to think for them, and assume that what they believe is true simply because they wish, hope, or feel that it is true. You might also know people who like things just because they are popular, and still others whose beliefs may be based on what they heard growing up, without ever examining the underlying assumptions that support those beliefs. As you might have noticed, the followers, the wishful believers, and the rigid thinkers tend not to have much control over their lives or to have any real power in business or society.

The slow thinkers, those who use critical-thinking skills, are different. They examine problems, ask questions, suggest new answers that challenge the existing situation, discover new information, question authorities and traditional beliefs, make independent judgments, and develop creative solutions. Being a good critical thinker does not mean that you are "critical" or negative in your dealings with others. Rather, the term refers to thoughtful consideration of the information, ideas, and arguments that you encounter. When employers say they want workers who can find reliable information, analyze it, organize it, draw conclusions from it, and present it convincingly to others, that means they want employees who are good critical thinkers.

Whatever else you do in college, make it a point to develop and sharpen your critical-thinking skills. You won't become a great critical thinker overnight. With practice, however, you can learn how to tell if information is truthful and accurate. Thinking critically—mastering slow thinking—will help you make better decisions, come up with fresh solutions to difficult problems, and communicate your ideas effectively.

---

your turn   Make Good Choices

If You Had a "Do-Over"

Think about a past problem or difficult situation you were unsuccessful in solving. If you could go back in time, how would you choose to solve the problem to get the outcome you desire? What would you do differently? What different choices would you make? Could you more deliberately use slow thinking in approaching the situation?

Rate Your Critical-Thinking Skills

It will be interesting to see how your critical-thinking skills change over the next few weeks and months. Given where you are currently, rate yourself as a "critical" thinker. At the end of the term, return to this table, and see how much you've changed.

Circle the number that best fits you in each of the critical situations described below.

Critical Situations	Never				Sometimes					Always
In class, I ask lots of questions when I don't understand.	1	2	3	4	5	6	7	8	9	10
If I don't agree with what the group decides is the correct answer, I challenge the group opinion.	1	2	3	4	5	6	7	8	9	10
I believe there are many solutions to a problem.	1	2	3	4	5	6	7	8	9	10
I admire those people in history who challenged what was believed at the time, such as "the earth is flat."	1	2	3	4	5	6	7	8	9	10
I make an effort to listen to both sides of an argument before deciding which way I will go.	1	2	3	4	5	6	7	8	9	10
I ask lots of people's opinions about a political candidate before making up my mind.	1	2	3	4	5	6	7	8	9	10
I am not afraid to change my belief system if I learn something new.	1	2	3	4	5	6	7	8	9	10
Authority figures do not intimidate me.	1	2	3	4	5	6	7	8	9	10

The more 7–10 scores you have circled, the more likely it is that you use your critical-thinking skills often. The lower scores indicate that you may not use critical-thinking skills very often, or that you use them only during certain activities.

high-impact practice 3

IN CLASS > Discuss the value of collaborative thinking as it applies to critical thinking, especially in the area of creative brainstorming.

HIGH-IMPACT PRACTICE > The findings about the link between collaboration and critical thinking are an important reason that student collaboration is found to be a high-impact educational practice.

Collaboration

One way to become a better critical thinker is to practice with other people. By getting feedback from others, you can see the possible flaws in your own position or approach. Whether debating an issue in a political science class or making a dress in a fashion design class, appreciate how people bring their own life experiences, personal taste, knowledge, and expertise to the table. Most questions do not have clear-cut answers, and there are often several ways of approaching any task. Getting input from others can help make your finished product a masterpiece.

Researchers who study thinking of elementary school students, high school students, and college students find that critical thinking and collaboration go hand in hand. Students at all levels are more likely to exercise their critical-thinking abilities when they are confronted by the experiences and opinions of others. Having more than one student involved in the learning process generates a greater number of ideas than one person can generate alone. People think more clearly when they talk as well as listen, which is a very good reason to participate actively in your classes. Creative brainstorming and group discussion encourage original thought. These habits also teach participants to consider alternative points of view carefully and to express and defend their own ideas clearly. As a group negotiates ideas and learns to agree on the most reliable concepts, it moves closer to a conclusive solution.

As you leave college and enter the working world, you will find that collaboration—not only with people in your work setting but also with others around the globe—is essential to almost any career you may pursue. Whether in person or through electronic communication, teamwork improves your ability to think critically.

Creativity

Our society is full of creative individuals who think outside the box, challenge the status quo, or simply ask questions that others are not asking. Many have achieved fame by using their thinking skills and actions to change our world. Even a single thought can have a ripple effect that leads to major progress. As you move through your other first-year courses such as sociology, psychology, history, or technology, you will learn about people who have used their creative-thinking abilities to become world changers in their academic areas.

Below are some critical thinkers of our past and present. Some might surprise you. What contributions to our world did each of these individuals make, and how do these contributions continue to affect our lives?

- **Abraham Lincoln** When we think of great leaders, Lincoln often comes to mind. Lincoln was able to think about the relationship between national policy and human rights in new and different ways. By working slowly and deliberately, Lincoln changed American laws and began a long process toward guaranteeing equal rights for all U.S. citizens—a journey that culminated in the civil rights legislation of the 1960s.
- **Martin Luther King Jr.** King could be considered one of the greatest activists of all time. When segregation ruled in the South, he contributed to the civil rights movement by voicing his concerns and presenting his dream of a different world. He created opportunities for change in many unfair societal policies and practices.
- **Twitter creators Jack Dorsey, Evan Williams, Biz Stone, and Noah Glass** Twitter was created in 2006 as a social networking and microblogging site to enhance communication around the world through hashtag statements that are limited to 140 characters each. In spite of early public resistance, the site quickly gained popularity and changed our way of communicating in times of national and international crisis due to its ability to disseminate information to millions of people instantly.
- **Steve Jobs** As an innovative and dynamic thinker, Jobs shaped the way our society viewed technology and digital capabilities. He persevered with passion, even through tough times, such as when he was ousted from his position as the head of Apple.

- **Lady Gaga** Pushing her artistic expression through fashion and activism, Lady Gaga projects an androgynous identity that challenges gender expectations and voices her belief in equality for all individuals.
- **Your instructors** You may not know it yet, but many of your instructors have conducted and written about cutting-edge research in their respective fields. Some may have even written textbooks that you are currently using in class!

---

your turn | Stay Motivated

Follow the Examples of Others

People who make a difference in their communities, nation, or the world stay motivated. They don't quit, even when they experience tough times. What other people in our world today—religious leaders, politicians, scientists, athletes, or entrepreneurs—have maintained their motivation and achieved major successes within their spheres of influence? What can you learn from them about what it means to stay motivated?

BECOMING A CRITICAL THINKER

As you've read, a high-priority goal in college is to develop strong thinking and decision-making skills. Not only will you develop your own competence and confidence, you will contribute to the larger society by helping solve community and national problems.

Asking Questions

The first step of thinking at a deeper level, of true critical thinking, is to be curious. This involves asking questions. Instead of accepting statements and claims at face value, question them. Here are a few suggestions:

- When you come across an idea or a statement that you consider interesting, confusing, or suspicious, first ask yourself what it means.
- Do you fully understand what is being said, or do you need to pause and think to make sense of the idea?
- Do you agree with the statement? Why or why not?
- Can the statement or idea be interpreted in more than one way?

Don't stop there.

- Ask whether you can trust the person or group making a particular claim, and ask whether there is enough evidence to back up that claim (more on this later).
- Ask who might agree or disagree and why.
- Ask how a new concept relates to what you already know.
- Think about where you might find more information about the subject, and what you could do with what you learn.

- Ask yourself about the effects of accepting a new idea as truth.
  - Will you have to change or give up what you have believed in for a long time?
  - Will it require you to do something differently?
  - Will it be necessary to examine the issue further?
  - Should you try to bring other people around to a new way of thinking?

© Randy Glasbergen.
www.glasbergen.com

WATER 99¢

LO-CARB WATER $2.99

GLASBERGEN

Considering Multiple Points of View and Drawing Conclusions

Before you draw any conclusions about the validity of information or opinions, it's important to consider more than one point of view. College reading assignments might deliberately expose you to conflicting arguments and theories about a subject, or you might encounter differences of opinion as you do research for a project. Your own belief system will influence how you interpret information, just as others' belief systems and points of view might influence how they present information. For example, consider your own ideas about the issue of K–12 education in the United States. American citizens, politicians, and others often voice opinions on options such as charter, private, and public schools. What kind of pre-college education do *you* think is best, and *why* do you hold this viewpoint?

The more ideas you consider, the more sophisticated your thinking will become. Ultimately, you will discover not only that it is okay to change your mind but also that a willingness to do so is the mark of a reasonable, educated person. Considering multiple points of view means synthesizing material, evaluating information and resources that might contradict each other or offer multiple points of view on a topic, and then honoring those differences. After considering multiple viewpoints and drawing

IN CLASS ❯ Ask whether students have been told that once they make up their minds, they have to stick with their decisions. If so, who told them that? Under what circumstances? Why does it make more sense to be able to change your mind if you believe that you have a better solution? Suggest that they think about these questions with reference to how U.S. presidents make—or unmake—major policy decisions.

conclusions, the next step is to develop your own viewpoint based on credible evidence and facts, while staying true to your values and beliefs. Critical thinking is the process you go through in deciding how to align your experience and value system with your viewpoint.

This process isn't necessarily a matter of figuring out the right idea. Depending on the goals of the activity, the "right" idea might simply be the one that you think is the most fun or the most practical, or it might be a new idea of your own creation.

Drawing conclusions based on your consideration of many opinions and other types of evidence involves looking at the outcome of your inquiry in a more demanding, critical way. If you are looking for solutions to a problem, which ones seem most promising after you have conducted an exhaustive search for materials? If you have found new evidence, what does that new evidence show? Do your original beliefs hold up in the face of new evidence? Do they need to be modified? Which notions should be abandoned? Most important, consider what you would need to do or say to persuade someone else that your ideas are valid. Thoughtful conclusions are the most useful when you can share them with others.

high-impact practice 3

HIGH-IMPACT PRACTICE ❯ This "Work Together" exercise will help your students dig deeply for evidence that would support or reject this position. By working together, students can challenge each other to go beyond personal opinion and learn about the implications of the First Amendment.

> **your turn** Work Together
>
> **Moving from Opinion to Logical Conclusion**
>
> Imagine that your state has just approved a license plate design incorporating a cross and the slogan, "I Believe." Almost immediately, a number of organizations begin protesting that this license plate is a violation of the First Amendment of the U.S. Constitution. Work with a small group of other students in your class and decide whether you agree or disagree with the state's action. Ask all members of the group to set aside their personal opinions and try to reach the best conclusion using solid evidence.

Making Arguments

IN CLASS ❯ Select a topic on which there are differences of opinion. The topic could relate to your institution, your community, your state, or the nation. One possibility would be the legalization of marijuana. Divide the class into two teams and schedule a debate on this topic. Some of the group members could be assigned to do background research, and some could be assigned to debate the issue. After the debate, ask class members to critique the arguments presented and determine which group presented the strongest case in support of its position.

What does the word *argument* mean to you? If you're like most people, the first image it conjures up might be an ugly fight you had with a friend, a yelling match you witnessed on the street, or a heated disagreement between family members. True, such unpleasant confrontations are arguments, but the word also refers to a calm, reasoned effort to persuade someone of the value of an idea.

When you think of it this way, you'll quickly recognize that arguments are central to academic study, work, and life in general. Scholarly articles, business memos, and requests for spending money all have something in common: The effective ones make a general claim, provide reasons to support it, and back up those reasons with evidence. That's what argument is.

It's important to consider multiple points of view, or arguments, in tackling new ideas and complex questions, but arguments are not all equally valid. Good critical thinking involves analyzing assumptions that might have been omitted and scrutinizing the quality of the evidence used to support a claim. Whether examining an argument or making one, a good critical thinker is careful to ensure that ideas are presented in an understandable, logical way.

Challenging Assumptions and Beliefs

To some extent, it's unavoidable to have beliefs based on gut feelings or blind acceptance of something you've heard or read. However, some assumptions should be examined more thoughtfully, especially if they will influence an important decision or serve as the foundation for an argument.

We develop an understanding of information based on our value systems and how we view the world. Our family backgrounds influence these views, opinions, and assumptions. College is a time to challenge those assumptions and beliefs and to think critically about ideas we have always had.

FYI ❯ Sharing examples from personal experience should help students generate their own examples and feel comfortable sharing them.

Well-meaning people will often disagree. It's important to listen to both sides of an argument before making up your mind. If you follow the guidelines in this chapter, we can't promise that your classes will be easier or that you'll solve major problems, but you will be better equipped to handle them. You will have the skills to use critical thinking to figure things out instead of depending purely on how you feel or what you've heard. As you listen to a lecture, debate, or political argument about what is in the public's best interest, try to predict where it is heading and why. Ask yourself whether you have enough information to justify your own position.

Examining Evidence

Another important part of thinking critically is checking that the evidence supporting an argument—whether someone else's or your own—is of the highest possible quality. To do that, simply ask a few questions about the argument as you consider it:

- What general idea am I being asked to accept?
- Are good and sufficient reasons given to support the overall claim?
- Are those reasons backed up with evidence in the form of facts, statistics, and quotations?
- Does the evidence support the conclusions?
- Is the argument based on logical reasoning, or does it appeal mainly to emotions?
- Do I recognize any questionable assumptions?

is**this**you?

When New Knowledge and Old Beliefs Collide

Are you having conversations in class or with your friends about topics or ideas that go against what you have been taught? Do you feel anxious that these new ideas don't align with what your family has taught you? Ideas presented by college instructors are almost always supported by evidence and research, much of which is derived from data and cutting-edge technology. It is important to keep an open mind, even if it makes you uncomfortable. Develop a relationship with a mentor or colleague who can help you process some of the more sensitive information you hear.

- Can I think of any counterarguments, and if so, what facts can I muster as proof?
- What do I know about the person or organization making the argument?
- What credible sources can I find to support the information?

If you have evaluated the evidence used in support of a claim and are still not certain of its quality, it's best to keep looking for more evidence. Drawing on questionable evidence for an argument has a tendency to backfire. In most cases, a little persistence will help you find better sources.

Recognizing and Avoiding Faulty Reasoning

Although logical reasoning is essential to solving any problem, whether simple or complex, you need to go one step further to make sure that an argument hasn't been compromised by faulty reasoning. Here are some of the most common missteps—referred to as logical fallacies or flaws in reasoning—that people make in their use of logic:

- **Attacking the person.** Arguing against other people's positions or attacking their arguments is perfectly acceptable. Going after their

Logic That Just Doesn't Fly

This cartoon presents an obvious example of faulty reasoning. Some conversations or arguments tend to include reasoning like this. Can you think of a similarly illogical leap that someone used in an argument with you? Did you use critical thinking to counter it, or did your emotions get the best of you?

© Randy Glasbergen

PENGUINS ARE BLACK AND WHITE.
SOME OLD TV SHOWS ARE BLACK AND WHITE.
THEREFORE, SOME PENGUINS ARE OLD TV SHOWS.

GLASBERGEN

Logic: another thing that penguins aren't very good at.

personalities, however, is not OK. Any argument that resorts to personal attack ("Why should we believe a cheater?") is unworthy of consideration.

- **Begging.** "Please, officer, don't give me a ticket! If you do, I'll lose my license, and I have five little children to feed, and I won't be able to feed them if I can't drive my truck." None of the driver's statements offer any evidence, in any legal sense, as to why she shouldn't be given a ticket. Pleading *might* work if the officer is feeling generous, but an appeal to facts and reason would be more effective: "I fed the meter, but it didn't register the coins. Since the machine is broken, I'm sure you'll agree that I don't deserve a ticket."

- **Appealing to false authority.** Citing authorities, such as experts in a field or the opinions of qualified researchers, can offer valuable support for an argument. However, a claim based on the authority of someone whose expertise is questionable relies on the appearance of authority rather than on real evidence. We see examples of false authority all the time in advertising: Sports stars who are not doctors, dieticians, or nutritionists urge us to eat a certain brand of food; famous actors and singers who are not dermatologists extol the medical benefits of a costly remedy for acne.

- **Jumping on a bandwagon.** Sometimes we are more likely to believe something that many others also believe. Even the most widely accepted truths can turn out to be wrong, however. At one time, nearly everyone believed that the world was flat, until someone came up with evidence to the contrary.

- **Assuming that something is true because it hasn't been proven false.** If you go to a bookstore or look online, you'll find dozens of books detailing close encounters with flying saucers and extraterrestrial beings. These books describe the people who had such encounters as beyond reproach in their integrity and sanity. Because critics could not disprove the claims of the witnesses, the events are said to have actually occurred. Even in science, few things are ever proved completely false, but evidence can be discredited.

- **Falling victim to false cause.** Frequently, we make the assumption that just because one event followed another, the first event must have caused the second. This reasoning is the basis for many superstitions. The ancient Chinese once believed that they could make the sun reappear after an eclipse by striking a large gong, because they knew that on a previous occasion the sun had reappeared after a large gong had been struck. Most effects, however, are usually the result of a complex web of causes. Don't be satisfied with easy before-and-after claims; they are rarely correct.

- **Making hasty generalizations.** If someone selected a green marble from a barrel containing a hundred marbles, you wouldn't assume that the next marble drawn from the barrel would also be green. After all, you know nothing about the colors of the ninety-nine marbles still in the barrel. However, if you were given fifty draws from the barrel, and each draw produced a green marble after the barrel had been shaken thoroughly, you would be more willing to conclude that the next marble drawn would be green, too. Reaching a conclusion based on the opinion of one source is like assuming that all the marbles in the barrel are green after pulling out only one marble.

- **Slippery slope.** "If we allow tuition to increase, the next thing we know, it will be $20,000 per term." Such an argument is an example of "slippery slope" thinking. Fallacies like these can slip into even the most careful reasoning. One false claim can derail an entire argument, so be on the lookout for weak logic in what you read and write. Never forget that accurate reasoning is a key factor in succeeding in college and in life.

your turn Write and Reflect

Tempted to Use a Logical Fallacy?

Have you ever used a logical fallacy to justify decisions you have made? In looking back, did your flawed argument convince anyone that you were right? Why or why not? Describe your experiences in a journal entry.

APPLYING BLOOM'S TAXONOMY

Benjamin Bloom, a professor of education at the University of Chicago during the second half of the twentieth century, worked with a group of other researchers to design a system of classifying goals for the learning process. This system is known as Bloom's taxonomy, and it is now used at all levels of education to define and describe the process that students use to understand and think critically about what they are learning.

Bloom's Six Levels of Learning

Bloom identified six levels of learning, as represented in Figure 5.1. The higher the level, the more critical thinking it requires. Bloom's taxonomy is used in developing curricula, textbooks, learning management systems, and other academic work. You have been using the levels of Bloom's taxonomy throughout your education, perhaps without being aware of it.

Bloom's Taxonomy and the First Year of College

As you progress through your first year of college, you will notice that your level of comprehension and reflection begin to deepen as you engage with material and apply it to your experience in order to retain and synthesize it. If you pay close attention, you will discover that Bloom's taxonomy is often the framework that college instructors use to design classroom activities and out-of-class assignments. No matter what the topic is, this framework will help move you to deeper understanding and an ability to apply what you learn to other situations and concepts. Now we'll take a closer look at Bloom's taxonomy and then we'll take a concept you're likely to encounter in your first year of college—diversity—and match your cognitive development of the concept to Bloom's taxonomy.

chapter will also explore different strategies you can use when reading textbooks across the academic disciplines. These strategies include building your overall vocabulary and increasing your familiarity with terms that are unique to your particular field of study. Choose to make your textbook reading something you do every day. Reading in small chunks will help you concentrate and will increase your comprehension.

Depending on how much reading you did before coming to college—reading for pleasure, for your classes, or for work—you might find that reading is your favorite or least favorite way to learn. When you completed the VARK learning styles inventory in the chapter "How You Learn," you determined your preferences about reading and writing as a learning strategy. Even if reading *isn't* your favorite thing to do, it is absolutely essential to doing well in college and at work—no matter your major or profession.

IN CLASS ❯ Have students share what they are reading in college, including textbooks or other sources. The results will illustrate the different demands of college reading and why students need to pay attention to this chapter.

RETENTION STRATEGY ❯ To increase retention, we have to increase student motivation. Most college students are highly motivated to secure a job, or to secure a better job than the one they currently have. Therefore, point out that to accomplish their employment goals, students must understand and remember what they read because employers will require them to constantly read new information.

A PLAN FOR ACTIVE READING

Active reading involves using strategies, such as highlighting and taking notes, that help you stay focused. Active reading is different from reading for pleasure, which doesn't require you to do anything while you are reading. By choosing active rather than passive reading, you will increase your focus and concentration, understand more of what you read, and prepare more effectively for tests and exams.

These are the four active reading steps designed to help you read college textbooks:

1. Previewing
2. Marking
3. Reading with concentration
4. Reviewing

IN CLASS ❯ In response to the inevitable argument that a systematic reading method takes too much time, emphasize that students will understand more of the chapter using this method, and will therefore spend less time rereading.

yourturn Work Together

Comparing Textbook Reading Strategies

With a group of your classmates, share which of these four steps you always, sometimes, or never do. Have one member of the group keep a tally and report results to the class. Are there steps that almost everyone avoids? If so, discuss the reasons why.

Previewing

Previewing involves taking a first look at your assigned reading before you really tackle the content. Think of previewing as browsing in a newly remodeled store. You locate the pharmacy and grocery areas. You get a feel for the locations of the men's, women's, and children's clothing departments; housewares; and electronics. You pinpoint the restrooms and checkout areas. You get a sense for where things are in relation to each other and compared to where they used to be. You identify where to find the items that you buy most often, whether they are diapers, milk, school supplies, or prescriptions. You get oriented.

Previewing a chapter in your textbook or other assigned reading is similar. The purpose is to get the big picture, to understand the main ideas covered in what you are about to read and how those ideas connect both with what you already know and with the material the instructor covers in class. Here's how you do it:

- Begin by reading the title of the chapter. Ask yourself: What do I already know about this subject?
- Next, quickly read through the learning objectives, if the chapter has them, or the introductory paragraphs. **Learning objectives** are the main ideas or skills that students are expected to learn from reading the chapter.
- Then turn to the end of the chapter and read the summary, if there is one. A **summary** highlights the most important ideas in the chapter.
- Finally, take a few minutes to skim the chapter, looking at the headings, subheadings, key terms, tables, and figures. You should also look at the end-of-chapter exercises.

As you preview, note how many pages the chapter contains. It's a good idea to decide in advance how many pages you can reasonably expect to cover in your first study session. This can help build your concentration as you work toward your goal of reading a specific number of pages. Before long, you'll know how many pages are practical for you to read in one sitting.

Previewing might require some time up front, but it will save you time later. As you preview the text material, look for connections between the text and the related lecture material. Remember the related terms and concepts in your notes from the lecture. Use these strategies to warm up. Ask yourself: Why am I reading this? What do I want to know?

Keep in mind that different types of textbooks can require more or less time to read. For example, depending on your interests and previous knowledge, you might be able to read a psychology text more quickly than a biology text that includes many scientific words that might be unfamiliar to you. Ask for help from your instructor, another student, or a tutor at your institution's learning assistance center.

Mapping. **Mapping** is a preview strategy in which you draw a wheel or branching structure to show relationships between main ideas and secondary ideas and how different concepts and terms fit together; it also helps you make connections to what you already know about the subject (see Figure 6.1). Mapping the chapter during the previewing process provides a visual guide for how different chapter ideas work together. Because many students identify themselves as visual learners, visual mapping is an excellent learning tool, not only for reading, but also for test preparation.

In the wheel structure, place the central idea of the chapter in the circle. The central idea should be in the chapter introduction; it might even be in the chapter title. Place secondary ideas on the lines connected to the circle, and place offshoots of those ideas on the lines attached to the main lines. In the branching map, the main idea goes at the top, followed by supporting ideas on the second tier, and so forth. Fill in the title first. Then, as you skim the chapter, use the headings and subheadings to fill in the key ideas.

FIGURE 6.1 **>** Wheel and Branching Maps

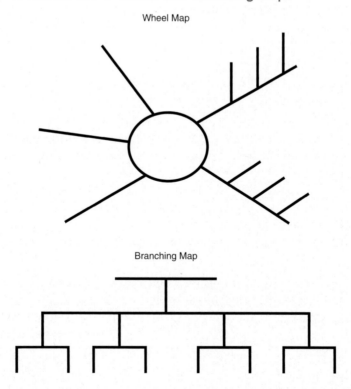

Wheel Map

Branching Map

Outlining or Listing. Perhaps you are more of a read/write learner than a visual learner and prefer a more step-by-step visual image. If so, consider making an outline of the headings and subheadings in the chapter. You can usually identify the text's main topics, subtopics, and specific terms within each subtopic by the size of the print. Notice, also, that the different levels

RETENTION STRATEGY **>** This is another occasion to remind your students of the positive correlation between seeking assistance and academic success in college. Also, point out that, disproportionately, it is the students who are already performing well who make the most use of such learning centers. The key idea here is to stress that these centers are not for dummies! They are for all students, and the best students use them.

OUTSIDE CLASS **>** After discussing how to map a chapter, have students map a chapter from a textbook they're using in another course.

IN CLASS **>** Have students bring the maps to class for sharing.

PEER LEADERS **>** As a peer leader, you can teach by example. Students will be interested in seeing whatever methods you use to identify important topics in the readings. If you create maps, bring them to class. If you prefer outlines, lists, or other methods, share these with your students.

of headings in a textbook look different. In a textbook, headings are designed to show relationships among topics and subtopics covered within a section. Flip through this textbook to see how the headings are designed. See a sample outline of this chapter in Figure 6.2 below. (Review the chapter "Getting the Most from Class" for more on outlining.)

To save time when you are outlining, don't write full sentences. Rather, include clear explanations of new technical terms and symbols. Pay special attention to topics that the instructor covered in class. If you aren't sure whether your outlines contain too much or too little detail, compare them with the outlines your classmates or members of your study group have made. You can also ask your instructor to check your outlines

FIGURE 6.2 ❯ Sample Outline
Here is how an outline of the first section of this chapter might look.

I. Active Reading

    A. Previewing
        1. Mapping
        2. Alternatives to Mapping
           a. Outlines
           b. Lists
           c. Chunking
           d. Flash cards
    B. Marking textbooks—Read and think BEFORE
        1. Underlining
        2. Highlighting
        3. Annotating (Margin notes)
    C. Reviewing—Each week, review
        1. Notes
        2. Study questions
        3. Annotations
        4. Flash cards
        5. Visual maps
        6. Outlines
    D. Reading with concentration—Use suggestions like
        1. Find proper location
        2. Turn off electronic devices
        3. Set aside blocks of time with breaks
        4. Set study goals

during office hours. In preparing for a test, review your chapter outlines so you can see how everything fits together.

Another previewing technique is listing. A list can be effective when you are dealing with a text that introduces many new terms and their definitions. Set up the list with the terms in the left column, and fill in definitions, descriptions, and examples on the right as you read or reread. Divide the terms on your list into groups of five, seven, or nine, and leave white space between the clusters so that you can visualize each group in your mind. This practice is known as **chunking**. Research has shown that we learn material best when it is presented in chunks of five, seven, or nine.

Creating Flash Cards. **Flash cards** are like portable test questions—you write a question or term on the front of a small card and the answer or definition on the back. In a course that requires you to memorize dates, like American history, you might write a key date on one side of the card and the event that correlates to that date on the other. To study chemistry, you would write a chemical formula on one side and the ionic compound on the other. You might use flash cards to learn vocabulary words or practice simple sentences for a language course. (See Figure 6.3.) Creating the cards from your readings and using them to prepare for exams are great ways to retain information, and they are especially helpful for visual and kinesthetic learners. Some apps, such as Flashcardlet and Chegg Flashcards, enable you to create flash cards on your electronic devices.

FIGURE 6.3 ❯ Examples of Flash Cards

Soy un estudiante del colegio.

Soy un estudiante universitario.

I am a college student.

iglesia

church

Strategies for Marking Your Textbook

After completing your preview, you are ready to read the text actively. With your map, outline, list, or flash cards to guide you, mark the sections that are most important. To avoid marking too much or marking the wrong information, first read without using your pencil or highlighter. This means you should read the text *at least* twice.

Marking is an active reading strategy that helps you focus and concentrate as you read. When you mark your textbook, you underline, highlight, or make margin notes or annotations. **Annotations** are notes or remarks about a piece of writing. Figure 6.4 provides an example of each method:

FIGURE 6.4 › Examples of Marking

Using a combination of highlighting, underlining, and margin notes, the reader has made the content of this page easy to review. Without reading the text, review the highlighted words and phrases and the margin notes to see how much information you can gather from them. Then read the text itself. Does the markup serve as a study aid? Does it cover the essential points? Would you have marked this page any differently? Why or why not? Source: Adapted from *Discovering Psychology*, 6th ed., p. 534, by D. H. Hockenbury and S. E. Hockenbury. Copyright © 2013 by Worth Publishers. Used with permission.

CULTURE AND HUMAN BEHAVIOR

The Stress of Adapting to a New Culture

differences affecting cultural stress

Refugees, immigrants, and even international students are often unprepared for the dramatically different values, language, food, customs, and climate that await them in their new land. The process of changing one's values and customs as a result of contact with another culture is referred to as *acculturation*. **Acculturative stress** is the stress that results from the pressure of adapting to a new culture (Sam & Berry, 2010).

acceptance of new culture reduces stress

also speaking new language, education, & social support

Many factors can influence the degree of acculturative stress that a person experiences. For example, when the new society accepts ethnic and cultural diversity, acculturative stress is reduced (Mana & others, 2009). The transition is also eased when the person has some familiarity with the new language and customs, advanced education, and social support from friends, family members, and cultural associations (Schwartz & others, 2010). Acculturative stress is also lower if the new culture is similar to the culture of origin.

how attitudes affect stress

Cross-cultural psychologist John Berry (2003, 2006) has found that a person's attitudes are important in determining how much acculturative stress is experienced (Sam & Berry, 2010). When people encounter a new cultural environment, they are faced with two questions: (1) Should I seek positive relations with the dominant society? (2) Is my original cultural identity of value to me, and should I try to maintain it?

4 patterns of acculturation

The answers produce one of four possible patterns of acculturation: integration, assimilation, separation, or marginalization (see the diagram). Each pattern represents a different way of coping with the stress of adapting to a new culture (Berry, 1994, 2003).

1 *Integrated* individuals continue to value their original cultural customs but also seek to become part of the dominant society. They embrace a *bicultural* identity (Hunyh & others, 2011). Biculturalism is associated with higher self-esteem and lower levels of depression, anxiety, and stress, suggesting that the bicultural identity may be the most adaptive acculturation pattern (Schwartz & others, 2010). The successfully integrated individual's level of acculturative stress will be low (Lee, 2010).

2 *Assimilated* individuals give up their old cultural identity and try to become part of the new society. They adopt the customs and social values of the new environment, and abandon their original cultural traditions.

possible rejection by both cultures

Assimilation usually involves a moderate level of stress, partly because it involves a psychological loss—one's previous cultural identity. People who follow this pattern also face the possibility of being rejected either by members of the majority culture or by members of their original culture (Schwartz & others, 2010). The

Acculturative Stress Acculturative stress can be reduced when immigrants learn the language and customs of their newly adopted home. Here, two friends, one from China, one from Cuba, help each other in an English class in Miami, Florida.

process of learning new behaviors and suppressing old behaviors can also be moderately stressful.

3 *Individuals who follow the pattern of *separation* maintain their cultural identity and avoid contact with the new culture. They may refuse to learn the new language, live in a neighborhood that is primarily populated by others of the same ethnic background, and socialize only with members of their own ethnic group.

In some cases, separation is not voluntary, but is due to the dominant society's unwillingness to accept the new immigrants. Thus, it can be the result of discrimination. Whether voluntary or involuntary, the level of acculturative stress associated with separation tends to be high.

4 *Finally, the *marginalized* person lacks cultural and psychological contact with *both* his traditional cultural group and the culture of his new society. By taking the path of marginalization, he lost the important features of his traditional culture but has not replaced them with a new cultural identity.

Although rare, the path of marginalization is associated with the greatest degree of acculturative stress. Marginalized individuals are stuck in an unresolved conflict between their traditional culture and the new society, and may feel as if they don't really belong anywhere. Fortunately, only a small percentage of immigrants fall into this category (Schwartz & others, 2010).

*separation may be self-imposed or discriminating

higher stress with separation

*marginalized = higher level of stress

	Question 1: Should I seek positive relations with the dominant society?	
	Yes	**No**
Question 2: Is my original cultural identity of value to me, and should I try to maintain it? **Yes**	Integration	Separation
No	Assimilation	Marginalization

Patterns of Adapting to a New Culture
According to cross-cultural psychologist John Berry, there are four basic patterns of adapting to a new culture (Sam & Berry, 2010). Which pattern is followed depends on how the person responds to the two key questions shown.

No matter what method you prefer, remember these important guidelines:

1. **Read before you mark.** Finish reading a section before you decide which are the most important ideas and concepts.

2. **Think before you mark.** When you read a text for the first time, everything can seem important. After you complete a section, reflect on it to identify the key ideas. Ask yourself: What are the most important ideas? What terms has the instructor emphasized in class? What will I see on the test? Knowing the likely answers to these questions can help you avoid marking too much material. On a practical note, if you find that you have made mistakes in how you have highlighted or that your textbooks were already highlighted by another student, use a different color highlighter.

3. **Take notes along with marking.** If you only make notes or underline in your textbook, you will have to read all the pages again. Rather than relying on marking alone, consider taking notes as you read. You can add your notes to the map, outline, list, or flash cards that you created while previewing the text. These methods are also more practical if you intend to review with a friend or study group. One more step in the note-taking process—putting your notes in your own words—will help you learn the material. When you rewrite your notes in your own words, you are not only predicting exam questions but also evaluating whether you can answer them.

A few words of caution about marking: For some students, highlighting or underlining is actually a form of procrastination and can lead to a false sense of security—just noting what's most important doesn't mean you've learned the material. Some students highlight or underline nearly everything they read, which does more harm than good. Remember, highlights and underlines are intended to pull your eye to key words and important facts. You won't be able to identify important concepts quickly if they're lost in a sea of color or lines. Ask yourself whether highlighting or underlining helps you take a more active role in your learning process. If not, you might want to try a different technique, such as making margin notes or annotations.

Reading with Concentration

Students often have trouble concentrating or understanding the content when they read textbooks. This is normal, and many factors contribute to this problem: the time of day, your energy level, your interest in the material, and your study location.

IN CLASS ❯ Students might complain that a marked book won't get a high buyback price when the course is over. As an exercise in values, ask them to consider which they value more: a few bucks or a better grade. Ask them to check buyback policies at local bookstores to find out how much of the book's value they will lose by marking their books.

IN CLASS ❯ Divide the class into groups of four students. In each group, ask students to choose two or more of the tips for building concentration and understanding. Ask them to practice these tactics over the next few days and report on what worked, what did not work, and why.

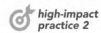
*high-impact
practice 2*

HIGH-IMPACT PRACTICE > As part of their ongoing journal, this writing exercise will help students monitor their own reading behavior and reflect more deeply on it.

your turn Write and Reflect

Improving Your Powers of Concentration

The next time you are reading a textbook, monitor your ability to concentrate. Check your watch when you begin and check it again when your mind begins to wander. How many minutes did you concentrate on your reading? Write a journal entry listing some strategies to keep your mind from wandering.

Consider these suggestions and decide which would help you improve your reading ability:

- **Find a quiet place to study.** Choose a room or location away from traffic and distracting noises, such as the campus information commons. Avoid studying in your bed because your body is conditioned to go to sleep there.
- **Mute or turn off your electronic devices.** Store your cell phone in your book bag or some other place where you aren't tempted to check it. If you are reading on a device like a laptop or tablet, download what you need and disconnect from Wi-Fi so that you aren't tempted to e-mail, chat, or check social media sites.
- **Read in blocks of time, with short breaks in between.** Some students can read for 50 minutes, while others may find that a 50-minute reading period is too long. By reading in small blocks of time throughout the day instead of cramming in all your reading at the end of the day, you should be able to process material more easily.
- **Set goals for your study period.** A realistic goal might be "I will read twenty pages of my psychology text in the next 50 minutes." Reward yourself with a 10-minute break after each 50-minute study period.
- **Engage in physical activity during breaks.** If you have trouble concentrating or staying awake, take a quick walk around the library or down the hall. Stretch or take some deep breaths, and think positively about your study goals. Then go back to studying.
- **Actively engage with the material.** Write study questions in the margins, take notes, or recite key ideas. Reread confusing parts of the text, and make a note to ask your instructor for clarification on any material that remains unclear.
- **Focus on the important portions of the text.** Pay attention to the first and last sentences of paragraphs and to words in italics or bold type.
- **Understand the words.** Use the text's glossary or a dictionary to define unfamiliar terms.
- **Use organizers as you read.** Have the maps, outlines, lists, or flash cards you created during your preview available as you read, and add to them as you go. The next page shows an example of an organizer to use when you are reading; you can use it to organize a chapter you are currently reading in this or any other class.

IN CLASS > Explain that maps, outlines, lists, and flash cards might also include students' reactions to the material or questions they need to ask in class.

Date:	Title:
Textbook:	Chapter:

What is the overall idea of the reading?	
What is the main idea of each major section of the reading?	Section 1: Section 2: Section 3:
What are the **supporting ideas** presented in the reading? Examples? Statistics? Any reference to research?	1. 4. 2. 5. 3.
What are the key terms and what do they mean?	
What are the conclusions from the reading?	
What are two or three things that I remember after reading?	1. 2. 3.

Reviewing

The final step in active textbook reading is reviewing. **Reviewing** involves looking through your assigned reading again. Many students expect to be able to read through their text material once and remember the ideas four, six, or even twelve weeks later when it's time for their exam. More realistically, you will need to include regular reviews in your study process. Your notes, study questions, margin notes and annotations, flash cards, visual maps, or outlines will prove very useful during the reviewing process. Your study goal should be to review the material from each chapter every week. Here are some strategies:

- Consider ways to use your senses to review.
- Recite aloud.
- Tick off each item on a list on your fingers.
- Post diagrams, maps, or outlines around your living space so that you will see them often and will likely be able to visualize them while taking the test.

Mark and Review

Marking the text and reviewing carefully are among the best approaches to getting more from your reading. These strategies seem to be good enough for George Clooney. Are they good enough for you?

Michael Buckner/Getty Images for American Foundation for Equal Rights

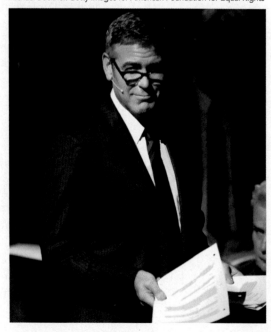

STRATEGIES FOR READING TEXTBOOKS

As you begin to read, be sure to learn more about the textbook and its author by reading the sections at the beginning of the book, such as the preface, foreword, introduction, and the author's biographical sketch. The **preface**, which is a brief overview near the beginning of a book, is usually written by the author(s) and will tell you why they wrote the book and what material the book covers. It will also explain the book's organizational structure and give insight into the author's viewpoint—all of which can help you see the relationships among the facts presented and comprehend the ideas discussed throughout the book. Reading the preface can come in handy if you are feeling a little lost at different points in the term. The preface often lays out the tools available in each chapter to guide you through the content, so if you find yourself struggling with the reading, be sure you go back and read this section.

The **foreword** is often an endorsement of the book written by someone other than the author. Some books have an additional **introduction** that describes the book's overall organization and its contents, often chapter by chapter. Some textbooks include study questions at the end of each chapter. Take time to read and respond to these questions, whether or not your instructor requires you to do so.

---

yourturn Stay Motivated

Do ALL the Required Reading

Some first-year students, especially those who have trouble managing their time, believe that they can skip some of the required reading and still get good grades on tests and exams. The best students, however, will tell you that this isn't a smart strategy. Instructors assign readings because they believe they're important to your understanding, and concepts and details in the readings will be on the tests. Maintain your motivation to do well by reading all the materials assigned by your instructors.

All Textbooks Are Not Created Equal

Textbooks in different **disciplines**—areas of academic study—can differ in their organization and style of writing. Some may be easier to understand than others, but don't give up if the reading level is challenging.

Math and science texts are filled with graphs and figures that you will need to understand in order to grasp the content and the classroom lectures. They are also likely to have less text and more practice exercises than other textbooks. If you have trouble reading and understanding any of your textbooks, get help from your instructor or your college's learning center.

Textbooks cover a lot of material in a limited space, and they won't necessarily provide all the information you want to know about a topic. If you find yourself interested in a particular topic, go to the **primary sources**—the original research or documents on that subject. You'll find those sources referenced in almost all textbooks, either at the end of each chapter or at the back of the book.

You can also refer to other related sources that make the text more interesting and easier to understand. Your instructors might use the textbook only to supplement their lectures. Some instructors expect you to read the textbook carefully, while others are much more concerned that you understand broad concepts that come primarily from their lectures. Ask your instructors what the tests will cover and what types of questions will be used.

Finally, not all textbooks are written in the same way. Some are better designed and written than others. If your textbook seems disorganized or hard to understand, let your instructor know your opinion. Other students likely feel the same way. Your instructor might spend some class time explaining the text, and he or she can meet with you during office hours to help you with the material.

Math Texts

While the previous suggestions about textbook reading apply across the board, mathematics textbooks present some special challenges because they usually have lots of symbols and few words. Each statement and every line in the solution of a problem needs to be considered and processed slowly. Typically, the author presents the material through definitions, theorems, and sample problems. As you read, pay special attention to definitions. Learning all the terms that relate to a new topic is the first step toward understanding.

Math texts usually include derivations of formulas and proofs of theorems. You must understand and be able to apply the formulas and theorems, but unless your course has a particularly theoretical emphasis, you are less likely to be responsible for all the proofs. So if you get lost in the proof of a theorem, go to the next item in the section. When you come to a sample problem, it's time to get busy. Pick up a pencil and paper, and work through the problem in the book. Then cover the solution and think through the problem on your own.

Of course, the exercises in each section are the most important part of any math textbook. A large portion of the time you devote to a math course will be spent completing these assigned exercises. It is absolutely necessary to work out these exercises before the next class, whether or not your instructor collects the work. Success in mathematics requires regular practice, and students who keep up with their math homework, either by working alone or in groups, perform better than students who don't, particularly when they include in their study groups other students who have more advanced math skills.

After you complete the assignment, skim through the other exercises in the problem set. Reading the unassigned problems will increase your comprehension. Finally, talk through the material to yourself, and be sure your focus is on understanding the problem and its solution, not on memorization. Memorizing something might help you remember how to work through one problem, but it does not help you learn the steps involved so that you can use them to solve other, similar problems.

high-impact practice 3

HIGH-IMPACT PRACTICE ❯ This group exercise can be the beginning of a math study group that meets frequently. Group study, especially in math, correlates with better grades and a greater understanding of math concepts.

> **your turn** Work Together
>
> **Tackle Math as a Team**
>
> In a small group, discuss with classmates two or three of your challenges in learning from your math textbooks. Find students who are taking the same math course, share some strategies that you use to study the material for this course, and consider forming a study group.

IN CLASS ❯ Ask a reading specialist from your campus developmental skills center or learning assistance center to come to class to provide tips on how to approach a science textbook.

Science Texts

Your approach to your science textbook will depend somewhat on whether you are studying a math-based science, such as physics, or a text-based science, such as biology. In either case, you need to become familiar with the overall format of the book. Review the table of contents and the **glossary** (a list of key words and their definitions), and check the material in the **appendixes** (supplemental materials at the end of the book). There you will find lists of physical constants, unit conversions, and various charts and tables. Many physics and chemistry books also include a mini-review of the math you will need in those science courses. (See Figure 6.5.)

Notice the organization of each chapter, and pay special attention to graphs, charts, and boxes. The amount of technical detail might seem overwhelming. Remember that textbook authors take great care to present material in a logical format, and they include tools to guide you through the material. Chapter-opening learning objectives and end-of-chapter summaries can be useful to study both before and after reading the chapter. You will usually find answers to selected problems in the back of the book. Use the answer key or the student solutions manual to make sure that you're solving problems and answering questions accurately.

FIGURE 6.5 › Reading Science Textbooks

This page from an allied-health-themed chemistry textbook includes abbreviations you'd need to know for dosages, practice exercises, and a formula for calculating medicine dosages. If you need help with any of your textbooks, ask your instructor or classmates. Source: Excerpt from page 23 of *Essentials of General, Organic, and Biochemistry*, 2nd ed., by Denise Guinn. Copyright © 2012 by W. H. Freeman. Used by permission.

PRACTICE EXERCISES

23 Using the conversions on page 12, convert the following units into calories:
   a. 5.79 kcal   **b.** 48.8 J
24 How many joules are there in 2.45 cal?
25 How many joules are there in 2,720 Calories, the amount of energy the average person consumes in a day?

Dosage Calculations

For some medicines prescribed for patients, the dosage must be adjusted according to the patient's weight. This is especially true when administering medicine to children. For example, a dosage of "8.0 mg of tetracycline per kilogram body weight daily" is a dosage based on the weight of the patient. A patient's weight is often given in pounds, yet many drug handbooks give the dosage per kilogram body weight of the patient. Therefore, to calculate the correct amount of medicine to give the patient, you must first convert the patient's weight from pounds into kilograms with an English-metric conversion, using Table 1-3.

It is important to recognize that the dosage is itself a conversion factor between the mass or volume of the medicine and the weight of the patient. Whenever you see the word *per*, it means *in every* and can be expressed as a ratio or fraction where *per* represents a division operation (divided by). For example, 60 miles *per* hour can be written as the ratio 60 mi/1 hr. Similarly, a dosage of 8.0 mg *per* kg body weight can be expressed as the fraction 8.0 mg/1 kg. Hence, dosage *is* a conversion factor:

$$\frac{8 \text{ mg}}{1 \text{ kg}} \quad \text{or} \quad \frac{1 \text{ kg}}{8 \text{ mg}}$$

Dimensional analysis is used to solve dosage calculations by multiplying the patient's weight by the appropriate English-metric conversion factor and then multiplying by the dosage conversion factor, as shown in the following worked exercise.

> Some common abbreviations indicating the frequency with which a medication should be administered include *q.d.* and *b.i.d.*, derived from the Latin meaning administered "daily" and "twice daily," respectively. If the medicine is prescribed for two times daily or four times daily, divide your final answer by two or four to determine how much to give the patient at each administration.

WORKED EXERCISE | Dosage Calculations

1-19 Tetracycline elixir, an antibiotic, is ordered at a dosage of 8.0 mg per kilogram of body weight q.d. for a child weighing 52 lb. How many milligrams of tetracycline elixir should be given to this child daily?

Solution

Step 1: Identify the conversions. Since the dosage is given based on a patient's weight in kilograms, an English-to-metric conversion must be performed. From Table 1-3 this is 1.000 kg = 2.205 lb. The dosage itself is already a conversion factor.

Step 2: Express each conversion as two possible conversion factors. The English-to-metric conversion factors for the patient's weight are

$$\frac{1 \text{ kg}}{2.205 \text{ lb}} \quad \text{or} \quad \frac{2.205 \text{ lb}}{1 \text{ kg}}$$

The dosage *is* a conversion factor between the mass of medicine in milligrams and the weight of the patient in kilograms:

$$\frac{8.0 \text{ mg}}{1 \text{ kg}} \quad \text{or} \quad \frac{1 \text{ kg}}{8.0 \text{ mg}}$$

IN CLASS ❯ Explain that a large percentage of students have difficulty with introductory science and mathematics courses such as calculus, physics, and organic chemistry. Discuss why doing well in introductory courses is especially critical for some majors.

As you begin an assigned section in a science text, skim the material quickly to gain a general idea of the topic and to familiarize yourself with any new vocabulary and technical symbols. Then look over the end-of-chapter problems so that you'll know what to look for in your detailed reading of the chapter. State a specific goal: "I'm going to learn about recent developments in plate tectonics," or "I'm going to distinguish between mitosis and meiosis," or "Tonight I'm going to focus on the topics in this chapter that were stressed in class."

Should you underline and highlight, or should you outline the material in your science textbooks? You might decide to underline or highlight for a subject such as anatomy, which involves a lot of memorization. In most sciences, however, it is best to outline the text chapters.

Social Sciences and Humanities Texts

Many of the suggestions that apply to science textbooks also apply to reading in the **social sciences** (academic disciplines that examine human aspects of the world, such as sociology, psychology, anthropology, economics, political science, and history). Social science textbooks are filled with special terms that are specific to a particular field of study. (See Figure 6.6.) These texts also describe research and theory building and contain references to many primary sources. Your social science texts might also describe differences in opinions or perspectives. Social scientists do not all agree on any one issue, and you might be introduced to a number of ongoing debates about particular topics. In fact, your reading can become more interesting if you seek out differing opinions on an issue. You might have to go beyond your course textbook, but your library is a good source of various viewpoints about ongoing controversies.

Textbooks in the **humanities** (branches of knowledge that investigate human beings, their culture, and their self-expression, such as philosophy, religion, literature, music, and art) provide facts, examples, opinions, and original material such as stories or essays. You will often be asked to react to your reading by identifying central themes or characters.

> **your turn**   Make Good Choices
>
> **Buy Your Course Materials**
>
> Textbooks are expensive, and it may be tempting to think that you can borrow one from another student, find the text in the library, or even do well in the course without having access to the textbook. No one will force you to purchase your textbooks—it's really up to you. To succeed in college, however, it's critically important that you choose to buy them and do all the assigned reading. Read the Tech Tip in this chapter for information on the benefits of e-books and for help in evaluating whether these are a good option for you.

your turn — Write and Reflect

Building Your Vocabulary

Choose a chapter in this or another textbook. As you read it, list the words that are new to you or that you don't understand. Using a dictionary, write out the definition of each word, and then write a short paragraph using the word in an appropriate context. Set a goal to add at least one new word a week to your personal vocabulary.

high-impact practice 2

HIGH-IMPACT PRACTICE ❯ This writing exercise gives your students an opportunity to practice and improve their writing and build vocabulary at the same time. Remember that writing is a high-impact key to learning.

What to Do When You Fall Behind on Your Reading

From time to time, life might get in the way of doing your assigned readings on time. You may get sick or have to take care of a sick family member, you may have to work extra hours, or you may have a personal problem that prevents you from concentrating on your courses for a short time. Unfortunately, some students procrastinate and think they can catch up. That is a myth. The less you read and do your assignments, the harder you will have to work to make up for lost time.

A Marathon, Not a Sprint

If you fall behind in your reading, you're not alone—many students do. Remember that your studies are more like a marathon than a sprint; you should take time to catch up, but do so at a steady pace. Do your assigned readings, study with others, get help, and do not give up!

© Jerome Prevost/TempSport/Corbis

If you try to stay on schedule with your assigned readings but fall behind, do not panic. Here are some suggestions for getting back on track:

- **Add one or two hours a day to your study time to go back and read the material that you missed.** In particular, take advantage of every spare moment to read; for example, read during your lunch hour at work, while you are waiting for public transportation, or in the waiting room at the doctor's office.
- **Join a study group.** If everyone in the group reads a section of the assigned chapter and shares and discusses his or her notes, summaries, or outlines with the group, you can cover the content more quickly.
- **Ask for help.** Visit your college learning center to work with a tutor who can help you with difficult concepts in the textbook.
- **Talk to your instructor.** Ask for extra time to make up your assignments if you have fallen behind for a valid reason such as sickness or dealing with a personal problem. Most instructors are willing to make a one-time exception to help students catch up.
- **Do not give up.** You may have to work harder for a short period of time, but you will soon get caught up.

If English Is Not Your First Language

RETENTION STRATEGY ❯ Non-native English speakers are at risk for poor academic performance and loss of self-confidence. Although many such students are highly intelligent and motivated to persist and may have been academically successful in another country, they will likely experience barriers to their academic progress. Make sure that these students and their families understand the policies and procedures of higher education, and that ESL students are given the help they need to improve their English-language skills.

The English language is one of the most difficult languages to learn. Words are often spelled differently from the way they sound, and the language is full of **idioms**—phrases that cannot be understood from the individual meanings of the words. For example, if your instructor tells you to "hit the books," she does not mean for you to physically pound your texts with your fist, but rather to study hard.

If you are learning English and are having trouble reading your texts, don't give up. Reading slowly and reading the material more than once can help you improve your comprehension. Make sure that you have two good dictionaries—one in English and one that links English with your primary language—and look up every key word you don't know. Be sure to practice thinking, writing, and speaking in English, and take advantage of your college's services. Your campus might have English as a second language (ESL) tutoring and workshops. Ask your adviser or your first-year seminar instructor to help you find out where those services are offered on your campus.

assess your strengths

Students who are engaged in college life, both in and out of class, practice many of the behaviors that are reviewed in this chapter. What about you? Were you engaged in classes and activities in high school? Which were your favorites and why? Most students find that engagement makes them more enthusiastic and actually increases their learning. As you begin to read this chapter, consider your strengths in the area of engagement.

set goals

What are your most important objectives in learning the material in this chapter? Do you have a good method of note taking? Do you devote time and energy to academic work by attending class and studying out of class? Use this chapter to help you develop strategies and goals that relate to engagement in learning. Do all the assigned reading and warm up for each class session so you can see how being prepared for class makes a difference. Consider scheduling visits with your instructors during their office hours to show them your notes from recent classes and ensure that you are writing down the most important points.

says is probably not possible and because you might need some help to determine which are the most important ideas presented, ask questions in class and become comfortable reviewing your notes with your instructor, either after class or during office hours. You might consider making an audio recording of the lecture and discussion, if you have the instructor's permission. Reviewing your notes with a tutor, someone from your campus learning center, a friend from class, or in a study group can also help you clarify your understanding of a lecture's most important points.

RETENTION STRATEGY ❯ Share with students that one of their textbook's authors was failing all his courses in his first year of college until he learned how to take notes. For him, note taking was the single most important study technique he learned in college.

BECOME ENGAGED IN LEARNING

Engaged students are those who are fully involved with the college experience and spend the time and energy necessary to learn, both in and out of class. Engaged learners who have good listening and note-taking skills get the most out of college.

You can learn by listening to a lecture, and you can better understand that lecture by considering what the information presented means to you. Practice the techniques of **active learning** by talking with others, asking questions in class, studying in groups, and seeking out information beyond the lecture material and required reading. Explore other information sources in the library or on the Internet. Think about how the material relates to your own life or experience. For instance, what you learn in a psychology class might help you recognize patterns of behavior in your own family, or the material presented in a sociology class may shed light on the group dynamics in a team or group to which you belong. When you are actively engaged in learning, you will not

RETENTION STRATEGY ❯ Engaged students are more likely to be retained! That's why it's worth your effort in class to encourage and monitor student engagement.

Stay Engaged

Students of all kinds benefit from active learning strategies, whether in arts and sciences courses or professional training situations, like the one in which these military cadets are engaged.

Yana Paskova/For *The Washington Post* via Getty Images

only learn the material in your notes and textbooks, but you will also build valuable skills that you can apply to college, work, and your personal life, such as:

- **Working with others.** Learning to work with others is one of the most important skills you can develop for success in college and your career.
- **Improving your thinking, listening, writing, and speaking skills.** These are the primary skills that define a college-educated person.
- **Functioning independently and teaching yourself.** Your first year of college will help you become an **independent learner.** Independent learners are self-motivated and do not always wait for an instructor to point them in the right direction.
- **Managing your time.** Time management sounds easy, but it is a challenge for almost all students, regardless of their academic abilities.
- **Gaining sensitivity to cultural differences.** The world we live in requires all of us to develop our own knowledge about, and respect for, cultures that are different from our own.

Engagement in learning requires your full and active participation in the learning process. Your instructors will set the stage and provide valuable information, but it's up to you to do the rest. For instance, if you disagree with what your instructor says, politely share your opinion. Most instructors will listen. They might still disagree with you, but they might also appreciate your efforts to think independently.

Not all instructors teach in a way that includes active learning. Ask your friends to recommend instructors who encourage students to participate in class, work in groups, explore materials independently, and otherwise engage fully in learning.

FIGURE 7.2 ❯ Note Taking in the Outline Format

Psychology 101, 1/27/16: Theories of Personality

I. Personality trait = "durable disposition to behave in a particular way in a variety of situations"
II. Big 5-McCrae + Costa
    A. Extroversion (or positive emotionality)=outgoing, sociable, friendly, upbeat, assertive
    B. Neuroticism=anxious, hostile, self-conscious, insecure, vulnerable
    C. Openness to experience=curiosity, flexibility, imaginative
    D. Agreeableness=sympathetic, trusting, cooperative, modest
    E. Conscientiousness=diligent, disciplined, well organized, punctual, dependable
III. Psychodynamic Theories-focus on unconscious forces-- Freud—psychoanalysis
    A. 3 components of personality
        1. Id=primitive, instinctive, operates according to pleasure principle (immediate gratification)
        2. Ego=decision-making component, operates according to reality principle (delay gratification until appropriate)
        3. Superego=moral component, social standards, right + wrong
    B. 3 levels of awareness
        1. Conscious=what one is aware of at a particular moment
        2. Preconscious=material just below surface, easily retrieved
        3. Unconscious=thoughts, memories, + desires well below surface, but have great influence on behavior

Outline Format. Some students find that an **outline** is the best way for them to organize their notes. In a formal outline, Roman numerals (I, II, III, etc.) mark the main ideas. Other ideas relating to each main idea are marked by uppercase letters (A, B, C, etc.). Arabic numerals (1, 2, 3, etc.) and lowercase letters (a, b, c, etc.) mark related ideas in descending order of importance or detail. Using the outline format allows you to add details, definitions, examples, applications, and explanations (see Figure 7.2).

IN CLASS ❯ Discuss the kinds of courses and topics that might be difficult to outline. Ask students how they might supplement regular note taking in these situations.

FIGURE 7.3 > Note Taking in the Paragraph Format

Psychology 101, 1/27/16: Theories of Personality

A personality trait is a "durable disposition to behave in a particular way in a variety of situations"

Big 5: According to McCrae + Costa most personality traits derive from just 5 higher-order traits: extroversion (or positive emotionality), which is outgoing, sociable, friendly, upbeat, assertive; neuroticism, which means anxious, hostile, self-conscious, insecure, vulnerable; openness to experience characterized by curiosity, flexibility, imaginative; agreeableness, which is sympathetic, trusting, cooperative, modest; and conscientiousness means diligent, disciplined, well organized, punctual, dependable

Psychodynamic Theories: Focus on unconscious forces

Freud, father of psychoanalysis, believed in 3 components of personality: id, the primitive, instinctive, operates according to pleasure principle (immediate gratification); ego, the decision-making component, operates according to reality principle (delay gratification until appropriate); and superego, the moral component, social standards, right + wrong

Freud also thought there are 3 levels of awareness: conscious, what one is aware of at a particular moment; preconscious, the material just below surface, easily retrieved; and unconscious, the thoughts, memories, + desires well below surface, but have great influence on behavior

IN CLASS > Lecture to the class and ask students to take notes. Give them an additional five minutes to revise and complete their notes. Collect and review their notes, or prepare a handout for taking notes and using a recall column.

Paragraph Format. When you take notes while you read, you might decide to write **summary paragraphs**—two or three sentences that sum up a larger section of material (see Figure 7.3). This method might not work well for class notes because it's difficult to summarize a topic until your instructor has covered it completely. By the end of the lecture, you might have forgotten critical information.

FIGURE 7.4 > Note Taking in the List Format

Psychology 101, 1/27/16: Theories of Personality

- A personality trait is a "durable disposition to behave in a particular way in a variety of situations"
- Big 5: According to McCrae + Costa most personality traits derive from just 5 higher-order traits
  - extroversion, (or positive emotionality)=outgoing, sociable, friendly, upbeat, assertive
  - neuroticism=anxious, hostile, self-conscious, insecure, vulnerable
  - openness to experience=curiosity, flexibility, imaginative
  - agreeableness=sympathetic, trusting, cooperative, modest
  - conscientiousness=diligent, disciplined, well organized, punctual, dependable
- Psychodynamic Theories: Focus on unconscious forces
- Freud, father of psychoanalysis, believed in 3 components of personality
  - id=primitive, instinctive, operates according to pleasure principle (immediate gratification)
  - ego=decision-making component, operates according to reality principle (delay gratification until appropriate)
  - superego=moral component, social standards, right + wrong
- Freud also thought there are 3 levels of awareness
  - conscious=what one is aware of at a particular moment
  - preconscious=material just below surface, easily retrieved
  - unconscious=thoughts, memories, + desires well below surface, but have great influence on behavior

List Format. The list format can be effective in taking notes on terms and definitions, facts, or sequences, such as the body's digestive system (see Figure 7.4). It is easy to use lists in combination with the Cornell format, with key terms on the left and their definitions and explanations on the right.

Note-Taking Techniques

Whatever note-taking format you choose, follow these important steps:

1. **Identify the main ideas.** The first principle of effective note taking is to identify and write down the most important ideas around which the lecture is built. Although supporting details are important as well, focus your note taking on the main ideas. These ideas can be buried in details, statistics, examples, or problems, but you will need to identify and record them for further study. Some instructors announce the purpose of a lecture or offer an outline of main ideas, followed by details. Other instructors develop PowerPoint presentations. If your instructor makes such materials available on a

Web site prior to class, you can print them out and take notes on the outline or next to the PowerPoint slides during the lecture. Some instructors change their tone of voice or repeat themselves for each key idea. Some ask questions or provide an opportunity for discussion. If an instructor says something more than once, chances are it is important. Ask yourself, "What does my instructor want me to know at the end of today's class?"

2. **Don't try to write down everything.** Some first-year students try to do just that. They stop being thinkers and become just note-takers. As you take notes, leave spaces so that you can fill in additional details that you might have missed during class but remember or read about later. Take the time to review and complete your notes as soon as you can after class. Once you have decided on a format for taking notes, you might also want to develop your own system of abbreviations. For example, you might write "inst" instead of "institution" or "eval" instead of "evaluation." Just make sure you will be able to understand your abbreviations when it's time to review.

3. **Don't be thrown by a disorganized lecturer.** When a lecture is disorganized, it's your job to try to organize the material presented into general and specific points. When information is missing, you will need to indicate in your notes where the gaps are. After the lecture, review the reading material, ask your classmates to fill in these gaps, or ask your instructor for help. Some instructors have regular office hours for student appointments, while others are willing to spend time after class answering students' questions. However, it is amazing how few students use these opportunities for one-on-one instruction. The questions you ask might help your instructor realize which parts of the lecture need more attention or repetition.

FYI ❯ New college students do not yet understand how courses are sequential and build on each other. Explain to them how saving their notes and textbooks can help them in later courses.

4. **Keep your notes and supplementary materials for each course separate.** Whether you use folders, binders, or some combination, label your materials with the course number and name. Before class, label and date the paper you will use to take notes; after class, organize your notes chronologically. In your folder or binder, create separate tabbed sections for homework, lab assignments, graded and returned tests, and other materials. If you take notes electronically, you should create separate files and folders for each class, with specific names and dates. You can create a folder for each course and add subfolders for notes, assignments, and projects within each folder.

5. **Download notes, outlines, diagrams, charts, and graphs from the CMS site and bring them to class.** You might be able to save yourself a lot of time during class if you do not have to copy graphs and diagrams while the instructor is talking. Instead, you can focus on the ideas being presented while adding labels and notes to the printouts.

6. **If handouts are distributed in class, label them and place them near your notes.** Buy a portable three-hole punch, and use it to add handouts to your binder or folder as you review your notes each day.

What Note-Taking Method Works Best for You?

Over the next week, try a variety of note-taking methods, such as the Cornell format, the outline format, and a random format where you write down what you think is important in no particular order. Then compare your notes and decide which format you like best—which is easiest for you and which helps you the most when you study and prepare for tests. Write a short essay describing your experience using these methods.

Taking Notes in Nonlecture Courses.
Always be ready to change your note-taking methods based on the situation. Group discussion is a popular way to teach in college because it engages students in active participation. On your campus, you might also have courses with **Supplemental Instruction (SI)** opportunities, which allow students to discuss the information covered in class lectures and discussions outside of class.

How do you keep a record of what's happening in such classes? Let's assume that you are taking notes on a problem-solving group assignment. You would begin your notes by writing down the problem that the group is being asked to solve. As the group discussion continues, you would list the solutions that are offered. These would be your main ideas. The important details might include the pros and cons of each viewpoint or suggested solution. The important thing to remember when taking notes in non-lecture courses is that you need to record the information presented by your classmates as well as the information presented by your instructor, and you need to consider all reasonable ideas, even those that differ from your own.

When a course has separate lecture and discussion sessions, you will need to understand how the discussion sessions relate to and supplement the lectures. If the material covered in the discussion session differs from what was covered in the lecture, you might need to ask for help in organizing your notes. When similar topics are covered, you can combine your lecture and discussion notes so that you have full coverage of each topic.

How you organize the notes you take in a class discussion session depends on the purpose or form of the discussion. It usually makes sense to begin with a list of the issues or topics under discussion. Another approach is to list the questions raised for discussion. If the discussion explores reasons for and against a particular argument, divide your notes into columns or sections for each set of reasons. When different views are presented in discussion, record all the ideas. Your instructor might ask you to compare your own opinions to those of other students and explain why and how you formed those opinions.

Taking Notes in Science and Mathematics Courses.
Many mathematics and science courses build on one another from term to term and from year to year. When you take notes in these courses, you will likely need to go back to them in the future. For example, when taking organic

TAKE BETTER NOTES IN BETTER WAYS

Studies have shown that people remember only half of what they hear, which is a major reason to take notes during lectures. Solid note taking will help you distill key concepts and make it easier to study for tests. Note taking also engages the brain in a process known as rehearsal. Writing things down is important for you to start the process of creating your own way of understanding the materials.

The Problem

You don't take good notes because you aren't sure what is important. You have access to technology, but aren't sure how to use it to take notes.

The Fix

Along with making use of the note-taking formats presented in this chapter, use your smart phone, tablet, or laptop to save information and create tools that will help you study.

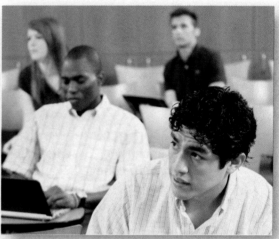

© Erik Isakson/Tetra Images

How to Do It

1. Microsoft Word is great for most classes. To highlight main ideas, you can bold or underline text, change the size and color, highlight whole sections, and insert text boxes or charts. You can make bullet points or outlines and insert comments. As you review your notes, you can cut and paste to make things more coherent. You can also create a folder for each class so you can find everything you need easily.
2. Microsoft Excel is especially good for any class that involves calculations or financial statements. You can embed messages in the cells of a spreadsheet to explain calculations. (The notes will appear whenever you hover your cursor over that cell.)
3. Microsoft PowerPoint can be invaluable for visual learners. Instead of creating one giant, potentially confusing Word file, you can make a slideshow with a new slide for each key point. Some instructors also post the slides that they plan to use in class before class begins. You can write notes on printouts of the slides, or download them and add your notes in PowerPoint.

Some Cool Apps for Note Taking and Reviewing:

- Pocket (iOS and Android) allows you to store and review written content from your phone.
- Evernote (iOS and Android) lets you take a picture of handwritten or printed notes—or anything else you want to recall later—then you can file content and search it by keyword later.

- CamScanner (iOS and Android) allows you to photograph, scan, and store notes.
- Scan Edit (iOS) lets you scan any document and convert it into a PDF, saving time and money.
- Tiny Tap (iOS) lets you create multiple-choice quizzes that you can take as practice and share with other students.
- StudyBlue (iOS, Android, and Web Apps) allows you to make amazing-looking flash cards.

EXTRA STYLE POINTS: No matter what program or app you use, some rules always apply:

- Write down main points using phrases or key terms instead of long sentences.
- Date your notes; keep them in order and in one place; save files using filenames with the course number, name, and date of the class; and back up everything.
- Keep a pen and paper handy for sketching graphs and diagrams.
- If you find it hard to keep up, keep practicing your listening and typing skills. Consider a typing class, program, or app to learn how to type properly.
- If you prefer a spiral notebook and a ballpoint pen, that's OK; these formats are tried and true.
- Practice teaching others what you learned in class. You can also learn note-taking strategies from your peers.

chemistry, you might need to review the notes you took in earlier chemistry courses. This can be particularly important if some time has passed since you completed your last related course, such as after a summer or winter break.

Taking notes in math and science courses can be different from taking notes in other classes. The following tips can help:

- Write down any equations, formulas, diagrams, charts, graphs, and definitions that the instructor puts on the board or screen.
- Write the instructor's words as precisely as possible. Technical terms often have exact meanings that cannot be changed.
- Use standard symbols, abbreviations, and scientific notation.
- Write down all worked problems and examples step by step. The steps are often necessary in answering exam questions. Actively engage in solving the problem yourself as it is being solved during class. Be sure that you can follow the logic and understand the sequence of steps. If you have questions you cannot ask during the lecture, write them down in your notes so that you can ask them in a discussion session, in the lab, or during the instructor's office hours.
- Consider taking your notes in pencil or erasable pen. You might need to make changes if you are copying long equations while trying to pay attention to the instructor. You want to keep your notes as neat as possible. Later, you can use colored ink to add other details.
- Listen carefully to other students' questions and the instructor's answers. Take notes on the discussion and during question-and-answer periods.
- Use asterisks, exclamation points, question marks, or symbols of your own to highlight both important points in your notes and questions that you need to come back to when you review.
- Refer to the textbook after class; the text might contain better diagrams and other visual representations than you can draw while taking notes in class. If they are not provided in handouts or on the instructor's Web site, you might even want to scan or photocopy diagrams from the text and include them with your notes in your binder.
- Keep your binders for math and science courses until you graduate (or even longer if you are planning to go to graduate or professional school). They will serve as good review materials for later classes in math and science. In some cases, these notes can also be helpful in the workplace.

Using Technology to Take Notes.

While some students use laptops, tablets, or other mobile devices for note taking, others prefer taking notes by hand so that they can easily circle important items or copy equations or diagrams while they are being presented. If you handwrite your notes, entering them on a computer after class for review purposes might be helpful, especially if you are a kinesthetic learner who prefers to learn through experience and practice. After class, you can also cut and paste diagrams and other visuals into your notes and print a copy, since a printout might be neater and easier to read than notes you wrote by hand.

IN CLASS > In the Hawaiian language, the words for *teaching* and *learning* are the same. Ask students: How can someone teach and learn at the same time?

IN CLASS ❯ Ask how many students use laptops to take notes during class. Have these students discuss the advantages and drawbacks of taking notes this way. Ask how they use their notes to study for exams. Encourage students to ask advanced students these questions, or invite guest speakers to share their experiences with note taking in class.

IN CLASS ❯ To demonstrate how easy it is to forget information, ask students to think back to a lecture from the previous day and then write down as many main ideas and supporting details as they can remember.

Some students—especially aural learners, who prefer to hear information—find it is advantageous to record lectures. But if you record, don't become passive; listen actively. Students with specific types of learning disabilities might be urged to record lectures or use the services of note-takers, who type on a laptop while the student views the notes on a separate screen.

Review Your Notes

Unless we take steps to remember it, we forget much of the information we receive within the first twenty-four hours; in fact, the decline of memory over time is known as the **forgetting curve**. So if you do not review your notes almost immediately after class, it can be difficult to remember the material later. In two weeks, you will have forgotten up to 70 percent of it! Forgetting can be a serious problem when you are expected to learn and remember many different facts, figures, concepts, and relationships for a number of classes.

Immediate reviewing will help your overall understanding as well as your ability to remember important details during exams. Use the following three strategies:

1. **Write down the main ideas.** For five or ten minutes, quickly review your notes and select key words or phrases. Fill in the details you still remember but missed writing down during class. You might also want to ask your instructor or a classmate to quickly look at your notes to see if you have covered the major ideas.

2. **Repeat your ideas out loud.** Repeat a brief version of what you learned from the class either to yourself or to someone else. For many, the best way to learn something is to teach it to others. You will understand something better and remember it longer if you try to explain it in your own words. This helps you discover your own reactions and find the gaps in your understanding of the material. Asking and answering questions in class can also provide you with the feedback you need to make sure that your understanding is accurate.

3. **Review your notes from the previous class just before the next class session.** As you sit in class the next time it meets, waiting for the instructor to begin, use the time to quickly review your notes from the previous class session. This will prepare you for the lecture that is about to begin and help you to ask questions about material from the earlier lecture that was not clear to you.

What if you have three classes in a row and no time to study between them? Repeat the information as soon as possible after class. Review the most recent class first. Never delay doing this; if you do, it will take you longer to review, select main ideas, and repeat the ideas. With practice, you can complete the review of your main ideas from your notes quickly, perhaps between classes, during lunch, or while waiting for or riding the bus.

high-impact practice 3

Compare Notes

Comparing notes with other students in a study group, SI session, or learning community has a number of benefits: You will probably take better notes when you know that someone else will see them, you can tell whether

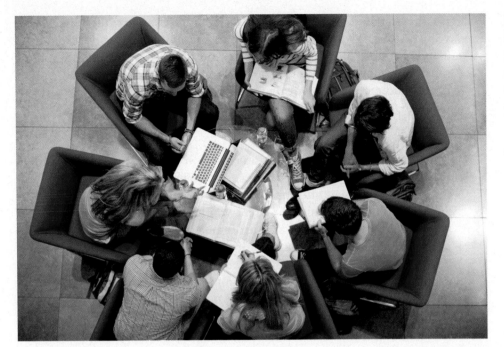

Many Heads Are Better Than One

Educational researchers have discovered that learning is enhanced by group study. Give it a try.

Clerkenwell/Getty Images

your notes are as clear and organized as those of other students, and you can use your comparisons to see whether you agree on what the most important points are.

Take turns testing each other on what you have learned. This will help you predict exam questions and find out if you can answer them. In addition to sharing specific information from the class, you can also share tips on how you take and organize your notes. You might get new ideas that will help your overall learning.

Be aware, however, that merely copying another student's notes, no matter how good those notes are, does not benefit you as much as comparing notes. If you had to be absent from a class because of illness or a family emergency, it's fine to look at another student's notes to see what you missed, but just rewriting those notes might not help you learn the material. Instead, summarize the other student's notes in your own words to enhance your understanding of the important points.

Class Notes and Homework

Once you have reviewed your notes, you can use them to complete homework assignments. Follow these steps:

1. **Do a warm-up for your homework.** Before doing the assignment, look through your notes again. Use a separate sheet of paper to rework examples, problems, or exercises. If there is related assigned material in the textbook, review it. Go back to the examples. Try to respond to the questions or complete the problems without looking at the answers or solutions. Keep in mind that it can help to go back through your course notes, reorganize them, highlight the important items, and create new notes that let you connect with the material.

IN CLASS ❯ Talk about comparing notes for the purpose of learning versus plagiarism and cheating. Emphasize that sharing notes can be good practice for retaining information, but it can be counterproductive when students rely on someone else's notes because they missed class or failed to take good notes themselves.

RETENTION STRATEGY ❯ Suggest that students compare their notes with those of successful students from previous first-year seminars. Remember: The greatest impact on students is the experience of other students. Advanced students can help retain beginning students.

OUTSIDE CLASS ❯ Ask students to practice these steps and report the results to the rest of the class, or have them write about the results in a journal or a blog.

2. **Do any assigned problems, and answer any assigned questions.** When you start doing your homework, read each question or problem and ask: What am I supposed to find or find out? What is most important? What is not that important? Read each problem several times, and state it in your own words. Solve the problem without referring to your notes or the text, as though you were taking a test. In this way, you will test your knowledge and know whether you are prepared for exams.

3. **Don't give up too soon.** Start your homework with the hardest subject first while you are most energetic. When you face a problem or question that you cannot easily solve or answer, move on only after you have tried long enough. After you have completed the whole assignment, come back to any problems or questions that you could not solve or answer. Try once more, and then take a break. You might need to think about a particularly difficult problem for several hours or even days. Inspiration might come when you are waiting at a stoplight or just before you fall asleep.

4. **Complete your work.** When you finish an assignment, talk to yourself about what you learned from it. Think about how the problems and questions were different from one another, which strategies were successful, and what form the answers took. Be sure to review any material you have not mastered. Ask for help from the instructor, a classmate, a study group, the campus learning center, or a tutor to learn how to answer questions that stumped you.

FYI ❯ After reviewing this chapter's suggestions on getting the most out of class, remind students where they can go on campus or at their college's Web site to get help with these strategies. Tell them that it is the most successful students who are most likely to seek such assistance, and that such actions correlate with higher probabilities for retention and graduation.

your turn Stay Motivated

Use What You Have Learned

Now that you've read these suggestions about taking notes and studying for class, which ideas are you motivated to implement in your own note taking? Come to class ready to explain which ideas appeal to you most and why.

FIGURE 8.1 > Sample Mind Map

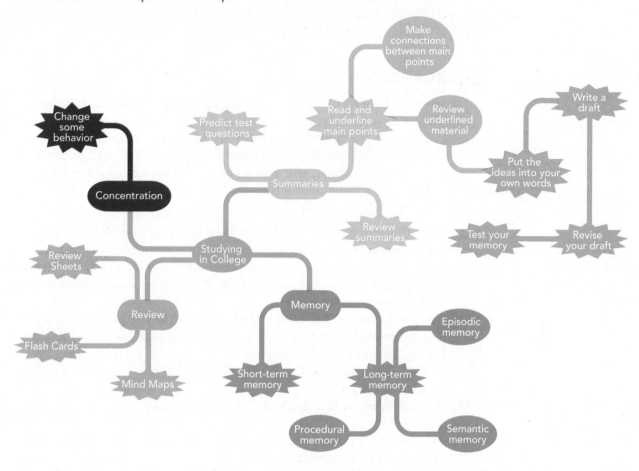

To create a mind map, start with a main idea and place it in the center. Then add major categories that branch out from the center. To these branches, add pieces of related information to form clusters. You can use different shapes and/or colors to show the relationships among the various pieces of information. You can find many apps for creating mind maps on your computer or mobile device. Figure 8.1 shows a mind map of this chapter, created by using an app called Total Recall. Other mind-map apps include MindMeister and SimpleMind.

Flash Cards

Just as you can create flash cards during the process of active reading, you can also use them as a tool for improving your memory. Flash cards—with a question, term, or piece of information on one side and the answer, definition, or explanation on the other—can serve as memory aids. One of the advantages of flash cards is that you can keep them in your backpack or jacket, or on your mobile device. Then you can look at them anywhere, even when you don't have enough time to take out your notebook to study.

Flash cards can help you make good use of time that might otherwise be wasted, such as time spent on the bus or waiting for a friend. Flash cards are excellent tools for improving your vocabulary, especially if you are learning English as a second language. See the "Reading to Learn" chapter for more information about creating and using flash cards.

Summaries

An immediate benefit of writing summaries of class topics is that they can help you answer short-answer and essay questions successfully. They also allow you to see connections between ideas and help you identify major and minor details. By summarizing the main ideas and putting them into your own words, you will be able to remember information better. Here's how you can create a good summary in preparation for taking a test:

1. **Read the assigned material, your class notes, or your instructor's presentation slides.** Underline or mark the main ideas as you go, make explanatory notes or comments about the material, or make an outline on a separate sheet of paper. Predict test questions based on your active reading.

2. **Make connections between main points and key supporting details.** Reread to identify each main point and its supporting evidence. Create an outline in the process.

3. **Review underlined material.** Put those ideas into your own words in a logical order.

4. **Write your ideas in a draft.** In the first sentence, state the purpose of your summary. Follow this statement with each main point and its supporting ideas. See how much of the draft you can develop from memory without relying on your notes.

5. **Review your draft.** Read it over, adding missing details or other information.

6. **Test your memory.** Put your draft away, and try to repeat the contents of the summary out loud to yourself or to a study partner who can let you know whether you have forgotten anything.

7. **Schedule time to review your summary and double-check your memory shortly before the test.** You might want to do this with a partner, but some students prefer to review alone. Some instructors might be willing to help you with this process and give you feedback on your summaries.

OUTSIDE CLASS ▸ Have students write a summary of this chapter by following the outlined steps on this page. Ask students to discuss the differences between the mind map and the summary. Which tool is more helpful to them? Why?

PEER LEADERS ▸ How good is your memory? Be candid with the students in your class about any challenges you have had remembering course information. Tell them about your particular memory strategies, such as your note-taking method, visual methods such as mind maps, and mnemonics.

high-impact practice 3

HIGH-IMPACT PRACTICE ▸ When students who share the same learning style work together on memory strategies, they will inevitably come up with new ideas they can share with each other.

your turn   Work Together

Using Learning Styles to Study and Remember

With your instructor's help, identify other students in your class who share your learning style. Get together to brainstorm strategies for remembering material for exams using your learning style, and keep track of the most helpful ideas.

and apply what you have learned. Knowing your preferred learning style, managing your time and energy, and using the study and memory strategies discussed in previous chapters will help you prepare for any kind of test or exam you face. This chapter provides you with several strategies to prepare for and take tests and exams successfully, describes types of tests and test questions you may encounter, and includes tips for managing test anxiety and maintaining academic honesty.

GETTING READY . . .

Believe it or not, you actually began preparing for tests on the first day of the term. Your lecture notes, assigned readings, and homework are all part of that preparation. As you get closer to the test day, you should know how much additional time you will need for review, what material the test will cover, and what format the test will take. It is very important to double-check the exam dates on the syllabus for each of your classes, as in Figure 9.1 on the next page, and to incorporate these dates into your overall plans for time management—for example, in your daily and weekly to-do lists.

Prepare for Test Taking

Tests are usually a major portion of your grade in college, so proper preparation for them is essential. Of course you need to understand the material, but there are many ways you can prepare for exams in addition to your regular study routines.

Find Out about the Test. Ask your instructor about the test format, how long the test will last, and how it will be graded. Find out the types of questions and the content that will be covered. Talk with your instructor to clarify any misunderstandings you might have about your reading or lecture notes. If you have a part-time instructor who does not have office hours, try to talk to him or her before or after class. Some instructors might let you view copies of old exams so that you can see the types of questions they use. Never miss the last class before an exam; your instructor might take part or all of that class session to summarize and review valuable information.

RETENTION STRATEGY › Many of us tell our students that learning is more important than grades. We should acknowledge, however, that grades do matter. First-year students who have earned A's and B's in high school may be shocked to see their first C, D, or worse. The material in this chapter will help students do their best to earn good grades, but make sure that you also encourage them not to give up on college if they receive a disappointing grade on a particular test or exam.

IN CLASS › Ask students what they know about midterm and final exam periods. Why do colleges set these times aside for examinations?

IN CLASS › Have your students check their schedules, and make sure that they have written down all their exam dates for each of their classes.

IN CLASS › Most college instructors would agree that essay exams measure learning far better than objective tests do. Explain why so many objective tests are given (e.g., large classes, easier to grade). Why do students need to alter their study methods according to the type of exam?

FIGURE 9.1 > Exam Schedule from Sample Course Syllabus

History 111, US History to 1865
Fall 2016

Examinations
Note: In this course, most of your exams will be on Fridays, except for the Wednesday before Thanksgiving and the final. This is to give you a full week to study for the exam and permit me to grade them over the weekend and return the exams to you on Monday. I believe in using a variety of types of measurements. In addition to those scheduled below, I reserve the right to give you unannounced quizzes on daily reading assignments. Also, current events are fair game on any exam! Midterm and final exams will be cumulative (on all material since beginning of the course). Other exams cover all classroom material and all readings covered since the prior exam. The schedule is as follows:

Friday, 9/9: Objective type

Friday, 9/23: Essay type

Friday, 10/14: Midterm: essay and objective

Friday, 11/4: Objective

Wednesday, 11/16: Essay

Tuesday, 12/20: Final exam: essay and objective

RETENTION STRATEGY > Your efforts to get students to learn more about different types of tests and what they might cover provides another chance for you to urge students to take advantage of your institution's academic support opportunities. Supplemental Instruction (SI) is a highly validated strategy for doing this. If your institution doesn't offer SI, then an alternative is for your learning center personnel to advise students about testing procedures in any given course.

Design an Exam Plan. Use information about the test as you design an exam-preparation plan. Create a schedule that will give you time to review for the exam without waiting until the night before. Develop a to-do list of the major steps you need to take to be ready, and schedule review dates. Be sure that your schedule is flexible enough to allow for unexpected distractions or emergencies. If you are able to schedule your study sessions over several days, your mind will continue to process the information between study sessions, which will help you during the test. Be sure you have read and learned all the material one week before the exam. That way, you can use the week before the exam to review. In that final week, set aside several one-hour blocks for review, and make specific notes on what you plan to do during each hour. Also, let your friends and family know when you have important exams coming up and how that will affect your time with them.

Use Online Quizzing. Many textbooks have related Web sites that offer a number of study tools such as flash cards, videos, or online quizzing. Ask your instructors about these sites, and also check the preface of your textbooks for information on accessing these sites. You might also use Google to find them.

Join a Study Group. As mentioned in previous chapters, joining a study group is one of the best ways to prepare for exams. Group members can share different views of the most important topics to review, quiz one another on facts and concepts, and gain support from other serious students. Some instructors will provide time in class for the formation of study groups, or you might choose to approach classmates on your own. You can always ask your instructor, academic adviser, or the college's tutoring or learning center professionals to help you find other interested students and decide on guidelines for the group. Study groups can meet throughout the term, or they can just review for midterms or final exams. Group members should prepare questions or discussion points before the group meets. If your study group decides to meet just before exams, allow enough time to share notes and ideas.

⊙ **high-impact practice 3**

HIGH-IMPACT PRACTICE > Study groups are among the most powerful and well-researched collaborative strategies to improve student learning, especially in math and science.

Talk to Other Students. Other students, especially those who have previously taken a course you are currently taking from the same instructor, may be able to give you a good idea of what to expect on tests and exams. If your college is small, you shouldn't have any trouble finding students who have taken the same courses you are taking now. If you're at a large college, your instructor may be able to suggest a former student who could serve as a tutor. But keep in mind that your instructor might decide to take a different approach in your class than he or she did in past classes.

RETENTION STRATEGY > You can enhance student retention by facilitating meetings between your current students and your successful former students.

Get a Tutor. Most colleges and universities offer free tutoring services. Ask your academic adviser, counselor, or college learning center staff members about arranging for tutoring. Keep in mind that some of the best

Strength in Numbers
Study groups can meet anytime, but studying and reviewing with others in your class can be most helpful just before and just after a test or exam.

students seek out tutoring, not just students who are struggling. Most students who receive tutoring are successful in their courses. Many learning centers employ student tutors who have done well in the same courses you are taking. These students might have some good advice on how to prepare for tests given by particular instructors. If you earn good grades in a specific course, you could eventually become a tutor and be paid for your services. Serving as a tutor also deepens your own learning and helps you become more successful in your major.

Prepare for Math and Science Exams

Math and science exams often require additional—and sometimes different—preparation techniques. Here are some suggestions for doing well on these exams:

- Do your homework regularly even if it is not graded, and do all the assigned problems. As you do your homework, write out your work as carefully and clearly as you will be expected to on your tests. This practice will allow you to use your homework as a review for the test. Figure 9.2 shows a page from a textbook with practice problems.
- Attend each class, always be on time, and stay for the entire class. Many instructors use the first few minutes of class to review homework, and others may end the class by telling you what will be on the test.
- Build a review guide throughout the term. As you begin your homework each day, write out a problem from each homework section in a notebook that you use solely to review material for that course. Then when you need to review for your exam, you can come back to this notebook to make sure you have a representative problem from each section you've studied.
- Throughout the term, keep a list of definitions or important formulas and put them on flash cards. Review several of them as part of every study session. Another technique is to post the formulas and definitions in your living space—on the bathroom wall, around your computer work area, or on the door of the microwave. Seeing this information frequently will help you keep it in your mind.

If these strategies don't seem to help you, ask a tutor to give you a few practice exams so you can review your responses together.

Prepare Physically

Keeping your body healthy is another key part of preparing yourself for quizzes, tests, and exams. The following strategies will help you prepare physically:

- **Maintain your regular sleep routine.** To do well on exams, you will need to be alert so that you can think clearly, and you are more likely to be alert when you are well rested. Last-minute, late-night cramming does not allow you to get sufficient sleep, so it isn't an effective study strategy. Most students need seven to eight hours of sleep the night before the exam.

IN CLASS > Have your students fill out an anonymous survey that asks how many hours of sleep they get each night, how much exercise they get each week, what kinds of foods they are most likely to eat, and what their overall levels of energy and concentration are. Compile and discuss the results. A staff member from the health and wellness center can be invited to class for this discussion.

IN CLASS > Ask the class how often they have crammed in a last-minute review of their notes just before a test is to begin. Tell the class that last-minute cramming usually will not improve a test score. It is better to prepare early and try to relax before the test starts.

FIGURE 9.2 ❯ Solving Practice Problems

Completing plenty of practice problems, like the ones shown here, is a great way to study for math and science classes. So try your hand at all the problems provided in your textbook—even those that your instructor hasn't assigned—and check out Web sites offering such problems. Source: Excerpt from page 315, COMAP, *For All Practical Purposes: Mathematical Literacy in Today's World*, 9th ed. Copyright © 2013 by W. H. Freeman. Used by permission.

(c) What is the probability that 5 cards drawn at random from a 52-card deck will yield a royal flush?

■ **30.** Biblical permutations: The King James Version of the Old Testament has its 39 books canonized in a different order than the Hebrew Bible does. What mathematical expression would yield the number of possible orders of these 39 books? Is this number larger than you expected?

8.4 Continuous Probability Models

31. Generate two random real numbers between 0 and 1 and take their sum. The sum can take any value between 0 and 2. The density curve is the shaded triangle shown in Figure 8.13.

Figure 8.13 The density curve for the sum of two random numbers, for Exercise 31.

(a) Verify by geometry that the area under this curve is 1.
(b) What is the probability that the sum is less than 1? (Sketch the density curve, shade the area that represents the probability, and then find that area. Do this for part (c) as well.)
(c) What is the probability that the sum is less than 0.5?

32. Suppose two data values are each rounded to the nearest whole number. Make a density curve for the sum of the two roundoff errors (assuming each error has a continuous uniform distribution).

33. On the TV show *The Price Is Right*, the "Range Game" involves a contestant being told that the suggested retail price of a prize lies between two numbers that are $600 apart. The contestant has one chance to position a red window with a span of $150 that will contain the price. On one episode, the price of a piano is between $8900 and $9500. If we assume a uniform continuous distribution (i.e., that all prices within the $600 interval are equally likely), what is the probability that the contestant will be successful?

8.5 The Mean and Standard Deviation of a Probability Model

34. You have a campus errand that will take only 15 minutes. The only parking space anywhere nearby is a faculty-only space, which is checked by campus police about once every hour. If you're caught, the fine is $25.

(a) Give the probability model for the money that you may or may not have to pay.
(b) What's the expected value of the money that you will pay for your unauthorized parking?

35. Exercise 15 gives a probability model for the grade of a randomly chosen student in Statistics 101 at North Carolina State University, using the 4-point scale. What is the mean grade in this course? What is the standard deviation of the grades?

36. In Exercise 14, you gave a probability model for the intelligence of a character in a role-playing game. What is the mean intelligence for these characters?

37. Exercise 16 gives probability models for the number of rooms in owner-occupied and rented housing units. Find the mean number of rooms for each type of housing. Make probability histograms for the two models and mark the mean on each histogram. You see that the means describe an important difference between the two models: Owner-occupied units tend to have more rooms.

38. Typographical and spelling errors can be either "nonword errors" or "word errors." A nonword error is not a real word, as when "the" is typed as "teh." A word error is a real word, but not the right word, as when "lose" is typed as "loose." When undergraduates write a 250-word essay (without spell-checking), the number of nonword errors has this probability model:

Errors	0	1	2	3	4
Probability	0.1	0.2	0.3	0.3	0.1

The number of word errors has this model:

Errors	0	1	2	3
Probability	0.4	0.3	0.2	0.1

(a) What is the mean number of nonword errors in an essay?
(b) What is the mean number of word errors in an essay?
(c) How does the difference between the means describe the difference between the two models?

39. Find (and explain how you found) the mean for:
(a) the continuous probability model in Exercise 31.
(b) the probability model in Exercise 32.

■ **40.** The idea of insurance is that we all face risks that are unlikely but carry a high cost. Think of a fire destroying your home. Insurance spreads the risk: We all pay a small amount, and the insurance policy pays a large amount to those few of us whose homes burn down. An insurance

- **Follow your regular exercise program.** Exercise is a positive way to relieve stress and to give yourself a much-needed break from long hours of studying.
- **Eat right.** Eat a light breakfast before a morning exam, and avoid greasy or acidic foods that might upset your stomach. Limit the amount of caffeinated beverages you drink on exam day because caffeine can make you jittery. Choose fruits, vegetables, and other foods that are high in energy-rich complex carbohydrates. Avoid eating sweets before an exam; the immediate energy boost they create can be quickly followed by a loss of energy and alertness. Ask the instructor whether you may bring a bottle of water with you to the exam.

Prepare Emotionally

Just as physical preparation is important, so is preparing your attitude and your emotions. You'll benefit by paying attention to the following ideas:

- **Know the material.** If you have given yourself enough time to review, you will enter the classroom confident that you are in control. Study by testing yourself or quizzing others in a study group so that you will be sure you really know the information.
- **Practice relaxing.** Some students experience test anxiety, which can lead to upset stomachs, sweaty palms, racing hearts, and other unpleasant physical symptoms. The section on test anxiety later in this chapter includes an anxiety quiz; if that quiz reveals that test anxiety is a problem for you, consult your counseling center about relaxation techniques. Some campus learning centers also provide workshops on reducing test anxiety.
- **Use positive self-talk.** Instead of telling yourself, "I never do well on math tests" or "I'll never be able to learn all the information for my history essay exam," make positive statements, such as "I have always attended class, done my homework, and passed the quizzes. Now I'm ready to do well on the test!"

---

your turn | Stay Motivated

Avoid Becoming Discouraged

Are you sometimes down on yourself when you've performed poorly on a test or exam? Does your disappointment negatively affect your motivation to do well in a particular course or in college? Remember that a positive attitude, plus a clear plan for improvement, will both help you stay motivated to do your best and make you more resilient. Believe in your ability to overcome the temporary stumbling blocks that are part of everyone's college experience.

TIPS FOR TEST TAKING

Throughout your college career, you will take tests in many different formats, in many subject areas, and with many different types of questions. It may surprise you to find that your first-year tests are likely to be more challenging than those in later years because, as a new student, you are still developing your college test-taking skills. The following test-taking tips apply to any test situation.

IN CLASS ▶ Remind students that many errors on tests, especially those that require problem solving, occur when a student does not read or follow directions. Ask students whether failing to follow directions has ever resulted in a poor test score for them. How does test anxiety relate to reading and following directions?

1. **Write your name on the test.** Usually you will have to write your name on a test booklet or answer sheet. Some instructors, however, may require you to fill in your student ID number.
2. **Look over the whole test and stay calm.** Carefully read all the directions before beginning the test so that you understand what to do.

Ask the instructor or exam monitor for clarification if you don't understand something. Be confident. Don't panic. Answer one question at a time.

3. **Make the best use of your time.** Quickly review the entire test and decide how much time you will spend on each section. Be aware of the point values of different sections of the test. If some questions are worth more points than others, you need to spend more of your time answering them.

4. **Jot down idea starters before the test.** Check with your instructor ahead of time to be sure that it is OK to write some last-minute notes on the test or on scrap paper. If so, then before you even look at the test questions, turn the test paper over and take a moment to write down the formulas, definitions, or major ideas you have been studying. This will help you go into the test with confidence and knowledge, and your notes will provide quick access to the information you may need throughout the test.

5. **Answer the easy questions first.** Expect that you won't completely understand some questions. Make a note to come back to them later. If different sections have different types of questions (such as multiple-choice, short-answer, and essay questions), first finish the types of questions that are easiest for you to answer. Be sure to leave enough time for any essays.

6. **If you feel yourself starting to panic or go blank, stop whatever you are doing.** Take a deep breath, and remind yourself that you will be OK and you do know the material and can do well on this test. If necessary, go to another section of the test and come back later to the item that triggered your anxiety.

7. **Try to answer each question, even if you can only provide a partial answer.** You may not be able to answer all the questions fully; provide as much information as you can remember. Particularly for math and science test questions, you may get some credit for writing down equations and descriptions of how to solve the problems even if you cannot fully work them out or if you run out of time before you finish them.

8. **If you finish early, don't leave immediately.** Stay and check your work for errors. Reread the directions one last time.

TYPES OF TESTS

While you are in college, you will take many different types of tests. Some may be used in specific subjects such as English or math; others can be used in any class you might take. This section discusses the different test types and presents helpful tips for succeeding on each one.

Problem-Solving Tests

In science, mathematics, engineering, and statistics courses, some tests will require you to solve problems and show all the steps that led to the solution. Even if you know a shortcut, it is important to document how you got from step A to step B. For these tests, you must also be careful to avoid errors in your scientific notation. A misplaced sign, parenthesis, or bracket can make all the difference.

If you are allowed to use a calculator during the exam, it is important to check that your input is accurate. The calculator does what you tell it to, and if you miss a zero or a negative sign, the calculator will not give you the correct answer to the problem.

Read all directions carefully. Whenever possible, after you complete the problem, work it in reverse to check your solution. Also check to make sure that your solution makes sense. You can't have negative bushels of apples, for example, or a fraction of a person, or a correlation less than negative 1 or greater than 1.

Machine-Scored Tests

For some tests, you may have to enter your answers on a Scantron form. The instructor will feed those forms into a machine that scans the answers and prints out your score. When taking any test, especially a machine-scored test, carefully follow the directions. In addition to your name, be sure to provide all other necessary information on the answer sheet. Each time you fill in an answer, make sure that the number on the answer sheet corresponds to the number of the item on the test.

Although scoring machines have become more sophisticated over time, they might still misread stray marks or incomplete bubbles on your answer sheet. When a machine-scored test is returned to you, check your answer sheet against the scoring key, if one is provided, to make sure that you receive credit for all the questions you answered correctly.

Example of a Scantron Answer Sheet

Each time you fill in a Scantron answer sheet, make sure that the number on the answer sheet corresponds to the number of the item on the test, and make sure that all bubbles are filled in completely.

Vixit/Shutterstock

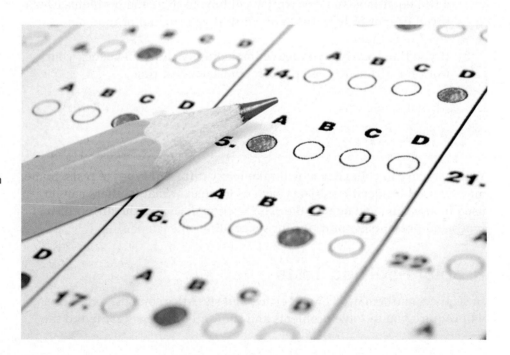

checklist for success

Test Taking

■ **Learn as much as you can about the type of test you will be taking.** You will study differently for an essay exam than you will for a multiple-choice test.

■ **Realize that you started preparing for test taking the very first day of the course.** Make the most of the first class sessions of the term—they are the most important ones *not* to miss. If you skip class, you are behind on your test preparation from day one.

■ **Prepare yourself physically through proper sleep, diet, and exercise.** These behaviors are as important as studying the actual material. You may not control what is on the exams, but you can control your physical readiness to do your best.

■ **Prepare yourself emotionally by being relaxed and confident.** Confidence comes from the knowledge that you have prepared well and know the material.

■ **If you experience moderate to severe test anxiety, seek help from your counseling center.** Professionals can help you deal with this problem.

■ **Develop a systematic plan of preparation for every test.** Be specific about when you are going to study, for how long, and what material you will cover.

■ **Join a study group and participate conscientiously and regularly.** Students who join study groups perform better on tests. It's a habit you should practice.

■ **Never cheat or plagiarize.** Experience the satisfaction that comes from learning and doing your own work and from knowing that you don't have to worry about getting caught or using material that may be incorrect.

■ **Make sure that you understand what constitutes cheating and plagiarism on your campus so that you don't inadvertently do either.** If you are not clear about policies, ask your instructors or the professionals in your campus learning center or writing center.

9 build your experience

REFLECT ON CHOICES

high-impact practice 2 Test taking is an inevitable part of college life. But you can choose how you are going to prepare for tests, deal with any test anxiety you might feel, and pay attention to your grades and instructor feedback. Reflect on your biggest problem in taking tests. Is it with certain types of tests or all of them? Is it related to certain subjects or any subject? Write a brief summary of strategies you have learned in this chapter to deal with this problem.

APPLY WHAT YOU HAVE LEARNED

Now that you have read and discussed this chapter, consider how you can apply what you have learned to your academic and personal life. The following prompts will help you reflect on the chapter material and its relevance to you both now and in the future.

1. Identify your next upcoming test or exam. What time of day is it scheduled, and what type of test will it be? What strategies have you read about in this chapter that will help you prepare for and take this test?

2. Is there one course you are taking this term that you find especially difficult? If you are anxious about taking tests in that class, adopt a positive self-message to help you stay focused. It could be a favorite quote or even something as simple as "I know I can do it!"

USE YOUR RESOURCES

> **Learning Center**
Before you take your first tests, locate your campus's learning center. Almost every campus has one, and helping students study for tests is one of its specialties. The best students, good students who want to be the best students, and students with academic difficulties use learning centers and tutoring services.

These services are offered by both full-time professionals and highly skilled student tutors, and they are usually free. If you are an online student, there may be a special learning center that focuses on helping you do your best in online courses.

> **Counseling Services**
College and university counseling centers offer a wide array of services, including workshops and individual or group counseling for test anxiety. Sometimes these services are also offered by the campus health center. Ask your first-year seminar instructor where you can find counseling services on your campus. If you are an adult student, you may be very anxious about your first tests. Seek out services designed specifically for adults.

> **Fellow College Students and Peer Leaders**
Often the best help we can get is the closest to us. Keep an eye out in your classes, residence hall, and extracurricular activities for the best students, those who appear to be the most serious, purposeful, and directed. Find a tutor. Join a study group. Talk with your peer leader. Students who do these things are much more likely to be successful than those who do not.

> **College and University Exam Preparation Resources**
A wealth of helpful resources is available from many institutions. For instance, Florida Atlantic University's Center for Learning and Student Success (CLASS) offers a list of tips to help you prepare for exams: **fau.edu/CLASS /success/keys_to_success.php.** The State University of New York offers some excellent strategies for exam preparation: **blog.suny.edu/2013 /12/scientifically-the-best-ways-to-prepare-for -final-exams.** And here is some exam preparation advice from the University of Leicester in England: **le.ac.uk/offices/ssds/healthy-living -for-students/preparation-for-exams.**

LaunchPad

LaunchPad is a great resource! For *Your College Experience*, go to macmillanhighered.com/gardner12e. For the Concise edition, go to macmillanhighered.com/collegesuccessmedia.

10
INFORMATION LITERACY AND COMMUNICATION

YOU WILL EXPLORE

What it means to be information literate

How to choose a topic, narrow it down, and research it

How to use your college or university library and get help from librarians

Strategies for evaluating sources

How to move from research to writing and effectively use all steps in the writing process

Guidelines for effective public speaking

♂ High-impact practices 2 (writing) and 3 (collaboration)

Analee Bracero, 26

Criminal Justice major
Montclair State University

" **Start researching the topic you will be writing about as soon as possible.** "

When Analee was looking into going to college, she found that Montclair State University in New Jersey had everything she wanted: affordability, online courses, and a variety of student clubs. The college also has a good library that allows her to conduct research and write papers while on campus.

Analee grew up in a small town in Puerto Rico where she attended high school, completed a certificate program in medical office billing and coding, and then worked for a few years. When she decided that she wanted to change careers, she realized a degree in criminal justice was just what she needed. "I intend to join a law enforcement agency," she says. "My goal is to join the FBI as a behavior analyst."

Now that she is in college, Analee has had to develop a number of strategies to help her write well-researched papers that are very different from those she wrote in high school. "In high school, they didn't emphasize how important it was to include your opinions," she says. "In college, they

want you to research your work, cite as many sources as you can, think about your topic, and form opinions. It is very different for me." She tells us that her best strategy is to start early and prepare to write, rewrite, and edit the same material a few times before handing it in for a grade. "Start researching the topic you will be writing about as soon as possible," she advises. "Every day, look for more data and take additional notes. That way you can prevent procrastination and reduce your stress when it's time to put the research together on the paper."

Analee does most of her research online, where information is at her fingertips. She is careful about checking the validity of material she finds on the Web, especially on sites like Wikipedia. "I use Wikipedia and other online encyclopedias to start learning about a topic," she explains, "but I rely on other sources for writing my paper and carefully check any information I pull from the Web to ensure accuracy." She can access the databases she needs from her laptop or at the library.

A s Analee's story illustrates, developing the skills to locate and use information will increase your ability to keep up with what is going on in the world, participate in activities that interest you, and succeed in college, career, and community. The research skills you learn and use as a student will serve you well as a successful professional in whatever career you choose. Whether you're a student of nursing, political science, or business, one of your main tasks in college is to manage information. In a few years, as a nurse, lawyer, or accountant, one of your main tasks will be the same: to manage and present information for your employers and clients. All colleges and many companies provide libraries for this purpose.

Finding information and using it involves more than operating a computer or browsing the bookshelves. To make sense of the enormous amount of information at your fingertips in a reasonable amount of time, you'll need to develop a few key research and information-literacy skills.

INFORMATION LITERACY

Information literacy is the ability to find, interpret, and use information to meet your needs. It includes computer literacy, media literacy, and cultural literacy:

- **Computer literacy** is the ability to use electronic tools to conduct searches and to communicate and present to others the information you have found and analyzed. This ability involves using different computer programs, digital video and audio tools, and social media.
- **Media literacy** is the ability to think deeply about what you see and read through both the content and context of television, film, advertising, radio, magazines, books, and the Internet.
- **Cultural literacy** is knowing what has gone on and is going on around you. You have to understand the difference between the American Civil War and the Revolutionary War, U2 and YouTube, and Eminem and M&Ms so that you can keep up with everyday conversation and with your college reading material.

Information matters. It helps people make good choices. The choices people make often determine their success in careers, their happiness as friends and family members, and their well-being as citizens of our planet.

RETENTION STRATEGY > Retention is related to student motivation, and the greatest motivator for students these days is the belief that attaining a college degree will improve employment opportunities. Information literacy is an essential skill for employment. Being able to find and use information will help students discover both a career path and the majors that prepare them for that path. Students who are committed to a career goal are more likely to be retained.

IN CLASS > Ask students what it means to be information literate. Can we believe everything we read? If not, why not?

PEER LEADERS > Ask your students to search the Internet for articles defining youth culture and describing its components. Engage your students in an introductory discussion of "youth culture." Then divide the class into groups and ask each group to do a presentation on some component of youth culture, using PowerPoint, Prezi, photographs, music, drama, or other kinds of presentation techniques.

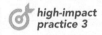

high-impact practice 3

HIGH-IMPACT PRACTICE > By collaborating in small groups, your students will learn more about the specifics of information literacy and have a chance to consider how information literacy is a contemporary "survival skill."

your turn Work Together

Information Literacy—A Survival Skill?

Brainstorm with a group of classmates and make a list of the components of "information literacy." How many separate components did your group identify? This chapter asserts that information literacy is the premier survival skill for the modern world. Does your group agree? Why or why not? Share your group's ideas with others in the class.

Learning to Be Information Literate

People are amazed at the amount of information available to them everywhere, especially online. Many think that because they checked out some links they found on a search engine, they are informed or can easily become informed. Most of us, though, are unprepared for the number of available sources and the amount of information that we can find at the press of a button. What can we do about information overload? To become an informed and successful user of information, keep three basic goals in mind.

1. **Know how to find the information you need.** Once you have figured out where to look for information, you'll need to ask good questions and learn how to search information systems, such as the Internet, libraries, and databases. You'll also want to get to know your college librarians, who can help you ask questions, decide what sources you need to investigate, and find the information you need.

2. **Learn how to interpret the information you find.** It is important to find information, but it is even more important to make sense of that information. What does the information mean? Have you selected a source you can understand? Is the information correct? Can the source be trusted?

3. **Have a purpose for collecting information and then do something with it once you have it.** Even the best information won't do much good if you don't know what to do with it. True, sometimes you'll hunt down a fact simply to satisfy your own curiosity, but more often, you'll communicate what you've learned to someone else. First you should decide how to put your findings into an appropriate format, such as a research paper for a class or a presentation at a meeting. Then you need to decide what you want to accomplish. Will you use the information to make a decision, solve a problem, share an idea, prove a point, or something else?

In this chapter, we'll explore ways to work toward each of these goals.

What's Research—and What's Not?

In the past, you might have completed assignments that required you to find a book, journal article, or Web page related to a particular topic. While finding information is an essential part of research, it's just one step, not the end of the road. Research is not just copying a paragraph from a book or putting together bits and pieces of information without adding any of your own comments. In fact, such behavior could easily be considered plagiarism, a form of cheating that could result in a failing grade or worse. (Plagiarism is discussed later in this chapter.) At the very least, repeating information or ideas without thinking about or interpreting them puts you at risk of careless use of old, incorrect, or biased resources.

Research is a process of steps used to collect and analyze information to increase understanding of a topic or issue. Those steps include asking questions, collecting and analyzing data related to those questions, and presenting one or more answers. Good research is information literacy in action. If your instructor asks you to select and report on a topic, you might search for information about it, find a dozen sources, evaluate them, interpret them, discard a few, organize the ones you wish to keep, select related portions, write a paper or presentation that cites your sources, write an introduction that explains what you have done, draw some conclusions of your own, and submit the results. That's research. The conclusion that you make based on your research is new information!

IN CLASS ❯ These days, many students confuse retrieval for research. Be sure to push them further. Emphasize the importance of evaluating, analyzing, and using information effectively, and consider giving assignments designed to have them truly benefit from working with a librarian.

RETENTION STRATEGY ❯ Ask your students to research the topics of "college student success" or "college student retention." Encourage them to explore videos on college student success. Students are more likely to take their college success course seriously if they know there is credibility in what your institution is doing.

CHOOSING, NARROWING, AND RESEARCHING A TOPIC

Assignments that require the use of library materials can take many forms and will be a part of most of your classes. We'll consider several ways to search for information later in the chapter. Before you start searching, however, you need to have an idea of what you're looking for.

Choosing a topic is often the most difficult part of a research project. Even if an instructor assigns a general topic, you'll need to narrow it down to a particular aspect that interests you enough to research it. Imagine, for example, that you have been assigned to write a research paper on the topic of global warming. What steps should you take? Your first job is to get an overview of your topic. You can begin by conducting a Google search. Once you've found some basic information to guide you toward an understanding of your topic, you have a decision to make: What aspects of the subject will you research? Soon after you start researching your topic, you may realize that it is really large (for example, simply typing "global warming" into Google will return millions of hits) and that it includes many related subtopics.

You can use this new information to create keywords. A **keyword** is a word or phrase that tells an online search tool what you're looking for. You can create a list of keywords by brainstorming different terms and subtopics within your general topic. For example, for the topic "global warming," keywords may include "climate change," "greenhouse effect," "ozone layer," "smog," or "carbon emissions." Even those terms will generate a large number of hits, and you will probably need to narrow your search several times.

What you want are twelve or so focused and highly relevant hits that you can use to write a well-organized essay. Begin by figuring out what you already know and what you would like to learn more about. Perhaps you know a little about global warming's causes and effects, and you're curious about its impacts on animals and plants. In that case, you might decide on a two-part topic: impacts on animals, impacts on plants. By consulting a few general sources, you'll find that you can narrow a broad topic to something that interests you and is a manageable size. You may end up focusing on the impact of global warming on one particular animal or plant in one specific geographical area.

If you are having trouble coming up with keywords, you can begin your research in an encyclopedia. Encyclopedias provide general overviews of topics. They can help you understand the basics of a concept or event, but you will need to use other resources for most college-level research projects. An encyclopedia is a great place to start your research, but not a good place to end it.

You have probably used an encyclopedia recently—you may use one all the time without thinking about it: Wikipedia. A *wiki* is a type of Web site that allows many different people to edit its content. This means that information on wikis can be constantly changing. Wikipedia is controversial in college work. Many instructors feel that the information on Wikipedia cannot be guaranteed to be reliable because anyone can change it; they instead want students to use sources that have gone through a formal editing and reviewing process. Your instructors might even forbid Wikipedia; if so, avoid it altogether. Even if an instructor permits the use of Wikipedia, it's best to use it only as a *starting point* for your research. Do not plan on citing Wikipedia in your final paper. Rather, check the references at the bottom of Wikipedia pages, or otherwise verify claims made at Wikipedia in another trustworthy source.

Even with an understanding of various types of sources, it can be difficult to determine exactly what you need for your assignment. Figure 10.1 provides an overview of when to use different common research sources and gives examples of what you'll find in each source.

OUTSIDE CLASS > Create an assignment that shows students how important it is to narrow their research topics. They can also ask a librarian for help and practice keyword searches, as described later in the chapter.

USING THE LIBRARY

Whenever you have research to do for a class, your job, or your personal life, visit a library. We can't stress this enough. Although the Internet is loaded with billions of pages of information, don't be fooled into thinking

FIGURE 10.1 ❯ Using Common Research Sources

This information time line helps identify when and how to use each type of source, whether for classwork or for your personal life.

INFORMATION TIME LINE		
Source	**When to access information**	**What it offers**
Newspapers (print and online)	Daily/hourly after an event	Primary-source, firsthand discussions of a current event, and of what happened at the time of the event; short articles
Magazines	Weekly/monthly after an event	Analysis by a journalist or reporter of an event days or weeks after it occurred; longer articles than in newspapers; informally credits sources; might include more interviews or research as well as historical context
Scholarly articles	Months after an event	In-depth analyses of issues; research-based scientific studies with formally credited sources, written and reviewed by experts; contains graphs, tables, and charts
Books	Months/years after an event	A comprehensive overview of a topic with broad and in-depth analyses

it will serve all of your needs. For one thing, you'll have to sort through a lot of junk to find your way to good-quality online sources. More important, if you limit yourself to the Web, you'll miss out on some of the best materials. Although we often think that everything is electronic and can be found through a computer, a great deal of valuable information is still stored in traditional print formats and in your college library database.

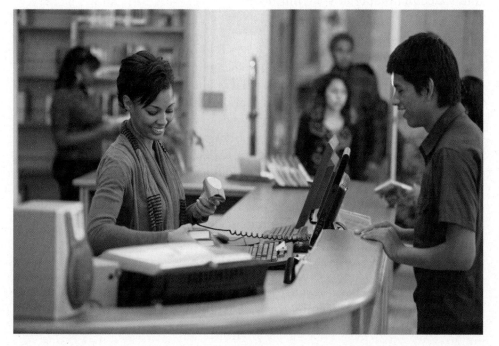

Get to the Library

How often do you go to your campus library? Beyond having a library tour, have you explored this important academic resource? Although information is available from many sources, the most reliable resource will be a professional librarian, who can guide you to relevant books, articles, and online information.

Blend Images-Hill Street Studios/ Getty Images

IN CLASS > Share information with your students on the rich research resources available in your campus library. Have your students select a method—phone, e-mail, or in person—to contact a librarian and ask a question. Follow up with a short discussion about their experiences in contacting a librarian.

OUTSIDE CLASS > Many librarians will be glad to host a visit from you and your class. Provide the librarian with a copy of your assignment, and he or she will talk your students through the research process. Have a conversation with the librarian beforehand to ensure that he or she covers the topics you consider necessary for the assignment.

Every library has books, journals, and a great number of items in electronic databases that aren't available on public Web sites. Librarians at your college work with your instructors to determine the kinds of materials that support their teaching. Librarians carefully select well-respected and credible resources with you and your research in mind. Most libraries also have several other types of collections, such as government documents, microfilm, rare books, manuscripts, dissertations, fine art, photographs, historical documents, maps, music, and films, including archival and documentary productions. A key component of being information literate is determining the kinds of sources you need to satisfy your research questions.

A college library is far more than a document warehouse, however. For starters, most campus libraries have Web sites and apps that offer lots of help to students. Some provide guidelines on writing research papers, conducting online searches, or navigating the **stacks**—the area of a library where most of the books are shelved.

Of course, no one library can possibly own everything you might need or have enough copies of each item to satisfy demand, so groups of libraries share their materials with each other. If your college library does not have a journal or book that looks promising for your project, or if the item you need is checked out, you can use **interlibrary loan**, a service that allows you to request an item at no charge from another library at a different college or university. The request process is simple, and the librarians can help you get started.

If it is difficult for you to go to your college library because of commuting, family, work challenges, time constraints, or because you are an online student who lives far from campus, you will still have off-campus, online access to library materials through a school-provided ID and password. You can also have online chats with librarians who can help you in real time. To learn more, check your library's Web site, or e-mail or phone the reference desk. Be sure to use the handouts and guides that are available at the reference desk or online. You will also find tutorials and virtual tours that will help you become familiar with the collections, services, and spaces available at your library.

The 20-Minute Rule

If you have been working hard trying to locate information for a research project for 20 minutes and haven't found what you need, stop and ask a librarian for help. Let the librarian know what searches you've tried, and he or she will be able to help you figure out new strategies to get to the books, articles, and other sources you need. In addition, the librarian can help you develop strategies to improve your research and writing skills. Doing research without a librarian is like driving cross-country without a map or GPS—technically, you can do it, but you will get lost along the way and you may not get to your destination on time. Get to know at least one librarian as your go-to expert. College librarians are dedicated to helping students like you.

Scholarly Articles and Journals

Many college-level research projects will require you to use articles from **scholarly journals**, collections of original, peer-reviewed research articles written by experts or researchers in a particular academic

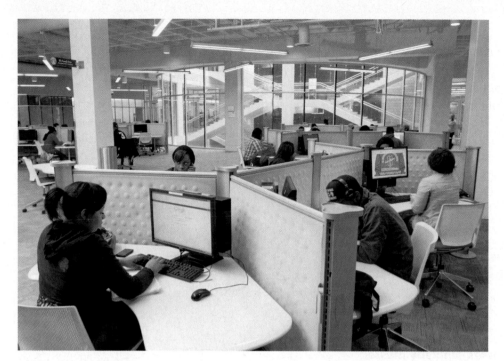

discipline. Examples are the *Journal of Educational Research* and the *Social Psychology Quarterly*. The term **peer-reviewed** means that other experts in the field read and evaluate the articles in the journal before they are published. You might find that some of your instructors use the terms *peer-reviewed* or *academic* to refer to scholarly articles or journals. Be sure to clarify what your instructor expects of your sources before you begin your research.

Scholarly articles focus on a specific idea or question and do not usually provide a general overview of a topic. For example, for the topic of climate change, you might find scholarly articles that compare temperature data over a certain period, analyze the effects of pollution, or explore public and political conversations on the topic. Scholarly articles always include a reference list that contains other sources related to the topic; you may find those sources useful in finding other relevant articles.

The most popular way to find scholarly articles is to use an online **database**, an organized and searchable set of information often categorized by subject areas. Some databases are specific to one subject, like chemistry, while others include articles from many different disciplines. Many libraries have dozens, if not hundreds, of databases. It can be difficult to figure out which ones you should use, but your librarian can help you determine which databases are best for your research.

When you use a database, you can easily add filters to ensure that your results include scholarly articles only, and you can clearly see who the authors are. Your database search should result in article and journal titles, descriptions, and sometimes full articles.

While some databases are available to anyone, whether that person is a student or instructor at a college, most of the databases you'll use for research in college are offered through subscription and are available only

IN CLASS > Use an analogy to illustrate that there are different databases for different resources: You wouldn't go to the grocery store to buy lumber. Not everything is available in the same location. This is why it's important that students ask their professor or a librarian where to look.

techtip

CONDUCT EFFECTIVE SEARCHES

Most of us frequently do casual research. But while Google, Wikipedia, and IMDb.com can provide some helpful answers, you will have to ramp it up a notch for a college-level research project.

When academic research is done properly, the question being researched is clear and the answers that are found become part of the body of research that other professionals in that field would recognize and respect. To do that, researchers use "peer-reviewed" publications, which means that other professionals in that field read their research to verify information before it is published.

The Problem

You understand the basics of online research but don't know how to apply it to an academic setting.

The Fix

Learn what research passes scholarly muster: peer-reviewed academic journals (e.g., Harvard Business Review), government Web sites (U.S. ones usually end in .gov), or newspaper Web sites (e.g., New York Times, Washington Post).

"It's a new syndrome we're seeing more of... "Google-itis"."

www.CartoonStock.com

How to Do It

Unlike the examples above, much of the information that you find online isn't objective or factual; the Internet is a digital free-for-all. When doing academic research, you need to be picky and filter out what is not helpful by using your critical-thinking skills.

Your college library offers free online access to a wealth of academic databases, LexisNexis, e-journals, and so on. If you have questions about how to use them, or about what kinds of materials qualify as academic research in general, make an appointment with a reference librarian. It's also worth visiting the Web site of the library at Bowling Green State University at libguides.bgsu.edu/library_basics for helpful "getting started" guides. Here are some quick tips:

- *Hone your online research skills.* Make sure that you understand common Boolean operators such as the words AND, OR, and NOT. How you use them affects your search results.
- *If you are looking for an exact phrase, use quotation marks or asterisks.* For instance, if you search for "rock and roll 1957" or *rock and roll 1957* your results will include that exact phrase. If you get too few hits, omit a search term.

Good to Know: Get familiar with the databases that your college subscribes to; many colleges subscribe to over one hundred. In advance of assignments, make yourself aware of the kinds of information you are likely to find in the various databases. Come up with your own list of questions and see which database yields the best results in answering them. Databases often offer tools to help you save, store, and cite that information for your research.

EXTRA STYLE POINTS: Avoid Internet plagiarism and intentional or unintentional cheating. Check with your professor about his or her policies if you are unclear, and always seek research help from reference librarians. You cannot cut and paste whole sentences from the Internet into your essays. Instructors can easily catch you, and the penalties are stiff. When in doubt, footnote. Paraphrasing anything off the Internet or from any other source without attribution is cheating. Most colleges have a zero-tolerance policy on this issue.

Whenever you copy online research into your notes, be sure to add a URL in brackets at the end. While you're at it, place quotation marks around all cited materials, or highlight them in a bright color.

students consider cheating or plagiarizing because they think that doing so will help them get a better grade, but you can avoid the temptation if you keep in mind the high likelihood of getting caught, as well as the serious consequences that will follow if you do get caught.

Because there is no universal rule about plagiarism, ask your instructors about the guidelines they set in their classes. Once you know the rules, plagiarism is easy to avoid. Keep careful notes as you do your research, so that later on you don't mistake someone else's words or ideas for your own. Finally, be sure to check out your college's official definition of what constitutes plagiarism, which you will find in the student handbook, college catalog, college Web site, course syllabi, or first-year course materials. If you have any questions about what is and isn't acceptable, be sure to ask someone in charge.

It should go without saying (but we'll say it anyway) that intentional plagiarism is a bad idea on many levels. Aside from the possibility of being caught and the potential for punishment—a failing grade, suspension, or even expulsion—submitting a paper purchased from an Internet source, copying and pasting passages from someone else's paper, or lifting material from a published source will cause you to miss out on the discovery and skill development that research assignments are meant to teach.

USING YOUR RESEARCH IN PRESENTATIONS

IN CLASS > Ask students to discuss how writing and speaking are both processes and products. Brainstorm a list of ways that writing and speaking are processes, and then create a second list of how they are products. Discuss the topic further with your students.

What you have learned in this chapter about writing also applies to public speaking: Both are processes that you can learn and master, and each results in a product. Because the fear of public speaking is a common one—it is more common, in fact, than the fear of death—you might think: What if I plan, organize, prepare, and rehearse my speech, but my mind goes completely blank, I drop my note cards, or I say something totally embarrassing? Remember that people in your audience have been in your position and will understand your anxiety. Your audience wants you to succeed. Be positive, rely on your wit, and keep speaking. Your recovery is what they are most likely to recognize; your success is what they are most likely to remember. The following guidelines can help you improve your speaking skills significantly, including losing your fear of speaking publicly.

IN CLASS > Review your college's core requirements (found in the institution's print or online catalog) to determine whether a communications or speech course is mandated. If it is, show students the course description and discuss why speech and communication skills are important to students who want to become successful professionals.

Guidelines for Successful Speaking

Just as there is a process for writing a paper, there is a process for developing a good speech. The following guidelines can help you both improve your speaking skills and lose your fear of public speaking.

Step 1: Clarify Your Objective.
Begin by identifying the goals of your presentation. Do you want to persuade your listeners that your campus needs additional student parking, or inform your listeners about the student government? What do you want your listeners to know, believe, or do when you are finished?

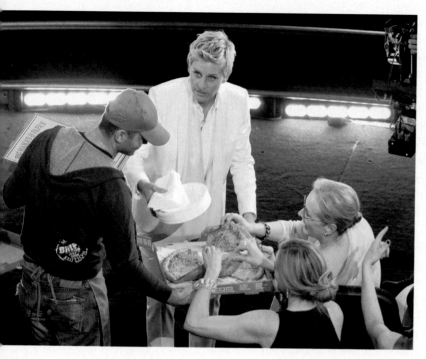

They Make It Look So Easy

When television icon Ellen DeGeneres hosted the Academy Awards for the second time, she surprised everybody by having pizza delivered to the hungry celebrity audience. While this comedian's use of humor and creativity to engage with the audience seems effortless, she wasn't always so comfortable onstage. "I got so nervous I would choke," she has said when talking about her early days doing stand-up comedy. When you feel nervous about speaking in front of others, consider taking a cue from Ellen: How can you work some audience interaction into your presentation?

Kevin Winter/Getty Images

Step 2: Understand Your Audience. To understand the people you'll be talking to, ask yourself the following questions:

- What do they already know about my topic?
- What do they want or need to know?
- Who are my listeners?
- What are their attitudes toward me, my ideas, and my topic?

Step 3: Organize Your Presentation. Now comes the most critical part of the process: building your presentation by selecting and arranging blocks of information to guide your listeners through the ideas they already have to the new knowledge, attitudes, and beliefs that you would like them to have. You can use the suggestions from earlier in the chapter for creating a writing outline to create an outline for your speech.

Step 4: Choose Appropriate Visual Aids. You might use presentation software, such as Prezi or PowerPoint, to prepare your presentations. When creating PowerPoint slides or Prezi templates, you can insert images and videos to support your ideas while making your presentations animated, engaging, and interactive. You might also prepare a chart, write on the board, or distribute handouts. As you select and use your visual aids, consider these guidelines:

- Make visuals easy to follow.
- Make sure that words are large enough to be read, and don't overload your audience by including a lot of information on one slide.
- Use font colors to make your slides visually attractive. Use light colors for text on a dark background or dark colors on a light background.
- Explain each visual clearly.

- Allow your listeners enough time to process visuals.
- Proofread carefully. Misspelled words hurt your credibility as a speaker.
- Maintain eye contact with your listeners while you discuss the visuals. Don't turn around and address the screen.

A fancy slideshow can't make up for a lack of careful research or sound ideas, but using clear, attractive visual aids can help you organize your material and help your listeners understand what they're hearing. The quality of your visual aids and your skill in using them can help make your presentation effective.

Step 5: Prepare Your Notes.
If you are like most speakers, having an entire written copy of your speech in front of you may tempt you to read much of your presentation, but a speech that is read word for word will often sound artificial. A better strategy is to memorize the introduction and conclusion, and then use a carefully prepared outline to guide you in between. You should practice in advance. Because you are speaking mainly from an outline, your choice of words will be slightly different each time you give your presentation, with the result that you will sound prepared but natural. Since you're not reading, you will be able to maintain eye contact with your listeners. Try using note cards; number them in case you accidentally drop the stack on your way to the front of the room. After you become more experienced, your visuals can serve as notes. A handout or a slide listing key points can provide you with a basic outline.

Step 6: Practice Your Delivery.
Practice delivering your speech before an audience: a friend, your dog, even the mirror. As you rehearse, form a mental image of success rather than failure. Practice your presentation aloud several times to control your anxiety. Begin a few days before your

speech date, and make sure you rehearse out loud, as thinking through your speech and talking through your speech have very different results. Consider making an audio or video recording of yourself to hear or see your mistakes and reinforce your strengths. If you ask a practice audience to give you feedback, you'll have some idea of what changes you might make.

Step 7: Pay Attention to Word Choice and Pronunciation.
As you reread your presentation, make sure that you have used the right words to express your ideas. Get help ahead of time with words that you aren't certain how to pronounce. Try your best to avoid *like, um, uh, you know*, and other fillers.

Step 8: Dress Appropriately and Give Your Presentation.
Now you're almost ready to give your presentation, but don't forget one last step: Dress appropriately. Leave the baseball cap, the T-shirt, and the tennis shoes at home. Don't overdress, but do look professional. Experts suggest that your clothes should be a "little nicer" than what your audience is wearing. Some speakers find that when they dress professionally, they deliver a better presentation!

Step 9: Request Feedback from Someone in Your Audience.
After you have completed your speech, ask a friend or your instructor to give you some honest feedback. If you receive written evaluations from your audience, read them and pay attention to suggestions for ways you can improve.

Your first public presentation in college might be a scary experience for you, and you might even try to select courses that allow you to avoid public speaking. You're really not doing yourself any favors, though. Nearly all employers will expect you to make an occasional speech or presentation, and the only way to improve as a speaker is through practice. If you receive negative feedback on a presentation, don't let it get you down. Show your instructors and your fellow students that you are resilient—you can bounce back from a less-than-perfect presentation and can use feedback to improve.

---

your turn | **Stay Motivated**

Learning from Motivational Speakers

Think about public speakers you have heard either in person or on TV. Which ones were the most effective? Which ones motivated you to accept their ideas? Why? What are some of the specific ways that the best public speakers communicate with and motivate an audience? What can you learn from them about what motivates you?

common with other students than you think. Now your individual efforts, dreams, courage, determination, and ability to stay focused can be the determinants of your success.

Learning and Physical Challenges. Although the majority of college students have reasonably average learning and physical abilities, the numbers of students with physical or learning challenges are rising on most college campuses, as are the services that are available to these students. Physical challenges can include hearing impairment, visual impairment, paralysis, or specific disorders such as cerebral palsy or multiple sclerosis. As discussed earlier in this book, many students have a learning disability that makes college work a challenge.

A person with a physical or learning challenge wants to be treated just as you would treat anyone else—with respect. If a student with such a challenge is in your class, treat him or her as you would any student; too much eagerness to help might be seen as an expression of pity.

If you have, or think you might have, a learning disability, visit your campus learning center for testing, diagnosis, and advice on getting extra help for learning problems. Unlike in high school, college students with disabilities need to inform the appropriate office if they require accommodations.

Sexuality. The word *sexuality* refers to the people to whom you are romantically attracted. You are probably familiar with the terms *gay, straight, homosexual, heterosexual,* and *bisexual.* In college you will likely meet students, staff members, and instructors whose sexual orientation differs from yours. While some people are lucky enough to come from welcoming environments, for many students, college is the first time they have been able to express their sexual identity openly. Sexual orientation can be

IN CLASS > Ask students whether they have been around people with learning or physical disabilities. If so, how did they act and feel in their company? Did the disability make them feel uncomfortable? If so, why? Would they do things differently now? Why or why not?

difficult to talk about, and it is important that you respect all individuals that you meet. Check to see if your campus has a center for the lesbian, gay, bisexual, transgendered, and questioning (LGBTQ) community. If there are educational events about sexual identity on your campus, consider going to hear some speakers and expanding your worldview.

IN CLASS > Ask students to define and discuss the words *bias, stereotyping,* and *prejudice.* What are the sources of these attitudes and beliefs? You might want to introduce students to the lyrics of "You've Got to Be Carefully Taught," a song about prejudice from the Rodgers and Hammerstein musical *South Pacific.*

Stereotyping: Why We Believe What We Believe

Many of our beliefs are the result of our personal experiences. Others are a result of a **stereotype**, which is a generalization—usually exaggerated or oversimplified, and often offensive—that is used to describe or distinguish a group. A negative experience with members of a particular group may result in the stereotyping of people in that group. We may acquire stereotypes about people we have never met before, or we may have bought into a stereotype without even thinking about it. Children who grow up in an environment in which dislike and distrust of certain types of people are openly expressed might adopt those judgments, even if they have had no direct interaction with those being judged.

In college, you might encounter personal values and belief systems that run counter to yours. When your friendships with others are affected by differing values, tolerance is generally a good goal. Talking about diversity with someone else whose beliefs seem to conflict with your own can be very rewarding. Your goal in this kind of discussion is not to reach agreement, but to enhance your understanding of why people have different

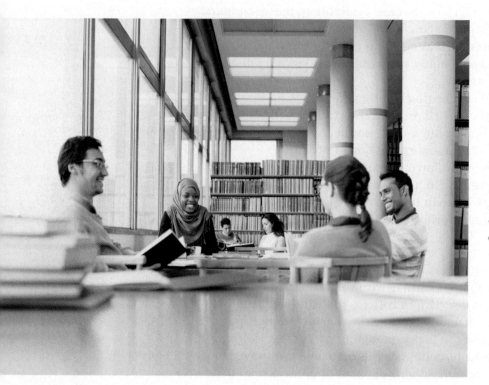

Expand Your Worldview

How has coming to college changed your experience with diversity? Are you getting to know people of different races or ethnic groups? Do your classes have both traditional-aged and older students? Are you seeking out people who are different from you and sharing personal stories and worldviews?

© Ocean/Corbis

values and beliefs, and how this understanding can enrich your college experience and your life beyond college.

Before coming to college, you might never have coexisted with most of the groups you now see on campus. In college, you have the opportunity to learn from many kinds of people, possibly many more than in your home community. Your lab partner in biology may be a veteran, and your sociology study group may include international students. Even your roommate or suitemate in a residence hall may be someone of a different racial or ethnic group. If you are taking one or more online courses, explore the diversity among other online students. You may get to know students from other states, adult students, students with disabilities, and others who could be taking classes on campus but prefer to learn in an online format. Your college experience will be enriched if you are open to the possibility of learning from all members of the college or university community.

While in college, your openness to diversity will add to your understanding of the many ways in which people are different from one another. Learn not to make assumptions, rely on stereotypes, or rush to judgment. Give yourself time to get to know someone before forming an opinion about him or her.

IN CLASS ❯ Discuss with students why understanding perspectives on diversity is an important element of a college education. Why is it important for personal growth and development? Why will learning about others help us better understand ourselves?

SEEKING DIVERSITY IN COLLEGE

🎯 *high-impact practice 4*

Because research in higher education[1] confirms the importance of diversity to learning, colleges and universities have committed to assuring diversity in college admissions and in learning opportunities. Your campus will provide you with opportunities to interact with and learn alongside a kaleidoscope of individuals who represent diversity in religious affiliation, sexual orientation, gender, ethnicity, age, culture, economic status, and ability.

The Curriculum

Many institutions offer an **inclusive curriculum**, one that offers courses that introduce students to diverse people, worldviews, and approaches. Today you can find many courses with a diversity focus, and many of them meet graduation requirements. The college setting is ideal for promoting education about diversity because it allows students and faculty of varying backgrounds to come together for the common purpose of learning and critical thinking.

College students have led the movement that resulted in a curriculum that reflects disenfranchised groups such as women, people of color, the

IN CLASS ❯ *Eyes on the Prize* is an excellent video series on the civil rights movement. After watching parts of the series, have students share their reactions. How could racism like this exist in the United States? What was the role of youth in the civil rights movement?

IN CLASS ❯ At your college, how is multiculturalism reflected in the curriculum? Are there multicultural organizations? Ask students to discuss their feelings about multiculturalism. Are there any negative points of view? If so, what are they, and why do you think that they exist?

[1]*Does Diversity Make a Difference: Three Research Studies on Diversity in College Classrooms* (Washington, DC: American Council on Education and American Association of University Professors, 2000) and Gloria M. Ameny-Dixon, "Why Multicultural Education Is More Important in Higher Education Now Than Ever: A Global Perspective." *National Forum.* Accessed January 9, 2015.

Commit to Coexist

In a college or university environment, students often learn that they have a lot in common with others who have been on the opposite side of the fence for centuries. By learning to coexist respectfully and peacefully, students can take the first step toward building a better world.

Jamie Smith-Skinny Genes Photography

elderly, the disabled, gays, lesbians, bisexuals, and the transgendered. In public protests, students have demanded the hiring of more instructors from different ethnic groups, the creation of ethnic studies departments, and a variety of initiatives designed to support diverse students academically and socially, including multicultural centers, women's resource centers, enabling services, and numerous academic-support programs.

In almost all colleges and universities, you will be required to take some general education courses that will expose you to a wide range of topics and issues. We hope that you will take a course or two with a multicultural focus. Such courses can provide you with new perspectives and an understanding of issues that affect your fellow students and community members. They can also affect you, possibly in ways you had not considered. Just as your college or university campus is diverse, so too is the workforce you will enter. Therefore, a multicultural education can improve the quality of your entire life.

---

your turn   Make Good Choices

Go for Diversity

Whether or not your college or university requires you to include a diversity or multicultural course in your curriculum, you should choose to take at least one. These courses will introduce you to different views on common issues and will help prepare you for the contemporary and multicultural world in which you live and work.

Study Abroad

If your college or university offers study-abroad opportunities, take advantage of them. Visiting or living in another country for a period of time (a few weeks to an entire year) is a great way to expand your horizons, learn about another culture, and become competent speaking another language. Many colleges and universities offer scholarships or grants for study abroad, and some even have student residential accommodations in the host country.

Student-Run Organizations

Student-run organizations can provide multiple avenues to express ideas, pursue interests, and cultivate relationships. According to our definition of culture, all student-run organizations provide an outlet for the promotion and celebration of a culture. Let's take, for instance, a gospel choir and an animation club and apply the components of culture to both of them. Both groups promote a belief system that is common among their members: The first is based on a love of music in the gospel tradition, and the second is based on the appreciation of animation as an art form. Both have aspects that can be taught: the musical tradition of gospel singing and the rules and techniques used in drawing. Both groups use a specific language related to the group's belief system. Most campus organizations bring like-minded students together and are open to anyone who wants to be involved.

To promote learning and discovery both inside and outside the classroom, colleges and universities provide programming that highlights ethnic and cultural celebrations, such as Chinese New Year and Kwanzaa; gender-related activities, such as initiatives sponsored by the group Sexual Assault and Relationship Violence Activists; and a broad range of entertainment, including concerts and art exhibits. These events expose you to new and exciting ideas and viewpoints, enhancing your education and challenging your current views.

Career/Major Groups. You can also explore diversity through your major and your career interests. Groups that focus on a specific field of study can be great assets as you explore your interests. Are you interested in helping minority and majority groups interact more effectively? Consider majoring in sociology or social work. Do you want to learn more about human behavior? Study psychology. If you join a club that is affiliated with the major that interests you, not only will you find out more about the major, but you can also make contacts in the field that could lead to career opportunities.

Political/Activist Organizations. Organizations devoted to specific political affiliations and causes—such as Campus Republicans, Young Democrats, Students for Human Rights, and Native Students in Social Action—add to the diversity mix on campus. These organizations provide debating events and forums and contribute diverse ideas on current issues and events.

Special-Interest Groups. Perhaps the largest subgroup of student organizations is the special-interest category, which encompasses everything from recreational interests to hobbies. On your campus, you might find special-interest clubs such as the Brazilian jujitsu club, a belly dance club, the flamenco club, Ultimate Frisbee, and the video gamers' society. Students can cultivate an interest in bird watching or indulge their curiosity about ballroom dance without ever leaving campus. If a club for your special interest is not available, create one yourself.

Intramural Sports. Believe it or not, you can often experience multiculturalism through intramural sports, especially soccer, tennis, and basketball. These sports and others may be a way for you to develop close friendships with teammates whom you might never have met in any other way.

high-impact practice 4

IN CLASS ❯ Confusion can arise when students use the words *prejudice* and *racism* interchangeably. Racism is prejudice directed at a racial group that often stems from one group's fear of losing power and privilege to another. Ask students whether they understand the difference between prejudice and racism, and how and why power can often be misdirected. The bottom line is that neither racism nor prejudice is tolerable; the latter is merely a prelude to the former.

OVERCOMING DISCRIMINATION, PREJUDICE, AND INSENSITIVITY ON COLLEGE CAMPUSES

You might feel uncomfortable when asked about your views on diversity. We all have **biases,** tendencies against or in favor of certain groups or value systems, but it is what we do with our individual beliefs that separates an unbiased and open-minded person from the racist, the bigot, and the extremist. Colleges strive to provide a welcoming and inclusive campus environment for all students. Because of acts of violence, intimidation, and stupidity occurring on campuses, college administrations have established policies against any and all forms of discriminatory actions, racism, and insensitivity. Many campuses have adopted zero-tolerance policies that prohibit verbal and nonverbal harassment and hate crimes such as physical assault, vandalism, and intimidation.

Some students instigate hate crimes because of deeply held negative views or fears about people who represent a different race, ethnic group, or sexual orientation. Other students might "follow the crowd" or feel pressured by peers to participate in organized harassment of a certain group. Commit to becoming involved in making your campus a safe place for all students. If you have been a victim of a racist, insensitive, or discriminatory act, report it to the proper authorities.

Raising Awareness

HIGH-IMPACT PRACTICE ❯ Most college campuses have policies against discrimination and intolerance. Ask students to research your campus policy and write a short paper on the subject. Have there been any recent incidents involving discrimination, racism, or insensitivity? If so, how did students react? What would students do if they observed this kind of activity?

While hate crimes on college and university campuses are, thankfully, infrequent, they do happen. In 2013, three first-year students at San Jose State University in California were suspended as a result of taunting their black roommate with racial slurs and references to slavery and trying to clamp a bicycle lock on his neck. In 2015, Sigma Alpha Epsilon fraternity at the University of Oklahoma was shut down because members engaged in racial chants; two members were expelled from the university. In 2014, students at both the University of Massachusetts and Colgate University protested acts of racism.

Although such actions are deliberate and hateful, others occur out of a lack of common sense. Consider a campus party to celebrate Cinco de Mayo. Party organizers asked everyone to wear sombreros. On arrival, guests encountered a mock-up of a border patrol station on the front lawn and were required to crawl under or climb over a section of chain-link fencing. Student groups voiced their disapproval over such insensitivity, which resulted in campus probationary measures for the organization that had thrown the party. At a Halloween party at a large university, members of a campus organization decided to dress in Ku Klux Klan outfits while other members dressed as slaves and wore black shoe polish on their faces. The group then simulated slave hangings during the party. When photos of the events surfaced, the university suspended the group from campus, and the community demanded that the group be banned indefinitely.

For a number of years, stereotypes that are used to identify school sports teams and their supporters have disturbed ethnic and cultural groups such as Native Americans. Mascots that incorporate a bow and arrow, a tomahawk, feathers, and war paint have raised awareness about the promotion and acceptance of stereotypes associated with the concept of the "savage Indian." Some schools have responded by altering the images while retaining the mascot. Other schools, such as Southeastern Oklahoma State University and the University of Illinois Urbana-Champaign, have changed their mascots to move away from references to Native Americans.

---

your turn Stay Motivated

Don't Let Harassment Ruin Your College Experience

Think back on your life. Can you recall an occasion in school or college when you were harassed for any reason, or when you witnessed harassment? Did that experience reduce your motivation to work toward a college degree? Discuss the event with a classmate, how it made you feel, and how you reacted. Don't let someone rob you of an important milestone like your college degree through harassment based on your race, ethnic group, gender, sexual orientation, or other characteristics.

What You Can Do to Fight Hate on Campus

Hate crimes, regardless of where they occur, should be taken very seriously. A hate crime is any prejudicial activity and can include physical assault, vandalism, and intimidation. One of the most common forms of hate crime on campus is graffiti that expresses racial, ethnic, and cultural slurs.

IN CLASS > Does your campus have a program that promotes diversity and understanding within the student body? If so, invite a speaker from this program to your class to describe the program's goals and activities.

Whatever form these crimes might take on your campus, it is important to examine your thoughts and feelings about their occurrence. The most important question to ask yourself is: Will you do something about it, or do you think that it is someone else's problem? If you or a group to which you belong is the target of the hate crime, you might be compelled to take a stand and speak out against the incident, but will you feel strongly enough to express your discontent if you are not a member of the target group?

Just because you or your particular group has not been targeted in a hate crime doesn't mean that you should do nothing. Commit to becoming involved in making your campus a safe place where students with diverse views, lifestyles, languages, politics, religions, and interests can come together and learn. If nothing happens to make it clear that hate crimes on campus will not be tolerated, it's anyone's guess as to who will be the next target.

Many students, whether or not they were directly targeted in a hate crime, find strength in unity, forming action committees and making it clear that hate crimes will not be ignored or tolerated. In most cases, instead of dividing students, hate crimes bring students together to work toward denouncing hate. It is important not to respond to prejudice and hate crimes with violence. It is more effective to unite with fellow students, faculty, staff, campus police, and administrators to address the issue, educate the greater campus community, and work to promote an environment of respect and tolerance. Recent news reports have also described the use of Twitter to identify and arrest perpetrators of hate crimes, whether the crime is hate speech or more serious instances of physical assault. The use of social media can make identifying harassers and responding to hate crimes quick and effective.

IN CLASS > Talk with your students about the career world of the future, when diversity will be the norm as demographics change. Preparing for future professional success will require a multicultural perspective.

Encouraging College Students to Vote

One of the simplest and most important ways to participate in your community is to vote. College students can have a significant impact on the outcome of an election, and the more regularly you vote, the more the politicians who represent you will pay attention to you. Be sure to exercise your right and privilege to "rock the vote."

Ann Hermes/*The Christian Science Monitor* via Getty Images

How can you get involved? Work with existing campus services such as the campus police, the multicultural center, faculty members, and the administration to plan and host educational opportunities, including training sessions, workshops, and symposiums centered on diversity, sensitivity, and multiculturalism. Organize an on-campus antidiscrimination event at which campus and community leaders address the issues and provide solutions. Join prevention programs to come up with ideas to battle hate crimes on campus or in the community. Finally, look into the antidiscrimination measures your college has in place. Do you think that they need to be updated or revised?

Challenge Yourself to Experience Diversity

Diversity enriches us all, and understanding the value of working with others and the importance of having an open mind will enhance your educational and career goals. Your college campus is diverse, and so is the workforce you will enter.

Challenge yourself to learn about various groups in and around your community, both at school and at home. These two settings might differ ethnically and culturally, giving you an opportunity to develop the skills you need to function in and adjust to a variety of settings. Attend events and celebrations outside of your regular groups. Whether they are in the general community or on campus, it is a good way to see and hear traditions that are specific to the groups being represented. Exposing yourself to new experiences through events and celebrations can be gratifying. Understanding viewpoints different from yours and learning from such differences will help you see similarities where you didn't think they existed.

You can also become active in your own learning by making time for travel. Seeing the world and its people can be an uplifting experience. Finally, if you want to learn more about a culture or group, ask a member of that group for information. If you do so in a tactful, genuine way, most people will be happy to share information about their viewpoints, traditions, and history. It is only through allowing ourselves to grow that we really learn.

techtip

GO BEYOND THE FILTER

When people learn new things, they increase their capacity to learn even more.

Technology can help us explore new ideas, products, and opportunities. However, when we are on the Internet, our preferences are tracked. The more we use Internet technology, the more information we make available about our opinions. Our online experience is continually shaped by our past searches, likes, and preferences. Author Eli Pariser defines this effect as our "filter bubble," which he describes as an unintended consequence of Web companies tailoring their services, including news and search results, to our personal tastes.[1] This effect causes us to miss all kinds of information that we might like or learn from—we never see it because it is being filtered away from us.

[1]Eli Pariser, *The Filter Bubble: What the Internet Is Hiding from You* (New York: Penguin Press, 2011).

The Problem

You want to be exposed to new things, but past preferences are shaping your current online experience.

The Fix

Push back on the "filter bubble." Be aware that it exists, and make a concerted effort to get exposure to information that could challenge or broaden your worldview. Shape your online research and reading so that you automatically receive a variety of sources of online information. And don't restrict yourself to the online world. Get out and experience the diverse world in which you live, in person!

How to Do It

1. *Join clubs or student groups to expand your interests.* Check with your campus center for student services. Most colleges have student activities, clubs, and events. College can be a time for you to meet new people and learn about new things, and not all of this will happen in the classroom. You can develop new interests by talking to new people about new things.

2. *Find ways to be of use.* Volunteering or interning can help you meet new people, explore new interests, understand others, and learn new skills. It can be tempting to avoid these kinds of activities because of the existing demands of your schoolwork or job. But the people you meet, the interests you explore, and the skills you learn can be important to your future career and long-term goals.

3. *When you are online, search in places other than Google or YouTube for new things to see, hear, or experience.* As you saw in the chapter on "Information Literacy and Communication," your college maintains access to a number of databases containing all kinds of cool information. These are not searchable by external search engines like Google or Bing, and your preferences and interests are not automatically tracked and

videos and music as well as text, you will become a better researcher and find new things to guide your professional interests.

4. *Expand your world.* Travel can be a great way for you to experience new people, music, food, history, and culture. No one will electronically track your interests if you explore the Camden Market in London or the Divisoria, a major market district in Manila. Travel will expose you to diverse ways of thinking that will challenge your ideas about who you are and what you have been taught—things you cannot learn in books or by watching television.

Money is often symbolically and realistically the key ingredient to independence and even, some people have concluded, to a sense of freedom. Money can also stir up problems. You probably know of instances when money divided a family or a relationship, or seemed to drive someone's life in a direction that person would not have taken otherwise.

The purpose of this chapter is to provide some basics of financial literacy—a specialized form of information literacy—and suggestions so that money issues will not be barriers to your success in college. Sources of financial assistance are available through loans, grants, and work-study programs, and this chapter will help you develop a strategy for investigating your options. Think of this chapter as a summary of needed financial skills; if you want more information, consider taking a personal finance class at your college or in your community.

LIVING ON A BUDGET

Face it: College is expensive, and most students have limited financial resources. Not only is tuition a major cost, but day-to-day expenses can also add up quickly. No matter what your financial situation, a budget for college is a must. A **budget** is a spending plan that tracks all sources of income (student loan disbursements, money from parents, etc.) and expenses (rent, tuition, etc.) during a set period of time (weekly, monthly, etc.). Creating and following a budget will allow you to pay your bills on time, cut costs, put some money away for emergencies, and finish college with as little debt as possible. A budget can help you become realistic about your finances so that you have a basis for future life planning.

Creating a Budget

A budget will condition you to live within your means, put money into savings, and possibly invest down the road. Here are a few tips to help you get started.

Gather Income Information. To create an effective budget, you need to learn more about your income and your spending behaviors. First, determine how much money is coming in and when. Sources of income

HIGH-IMPACT PRACTICE > In class, ask students to write about their financial situations, either anonymously or with attribution. Without using names, summarize their responses during the next class and ask students what they might do to solve any financial problems. Provide students with information on where they can go on campus or in the community for help with financial problems.

IN CLASS > Share the methods you use to keep your finances in order (e.g., balancing your checkbook, saving credit card and debit slips, reviewing your credit report). Ask the class whether these methods seem appropriate and manageable. Why or why not?

Too Much Month, Too Little Money

Are you having serious problems managing your money? Were you counting on a source of income that isn't going to be available after all? Do you need a budget, even though you aren't sure how to create one that will work for you? Are you using credit cards to buy things that you don't really need? To stay in college and do your best academically, you have to learn to manage your money. That might mean seeking out loans or scholarships, destroying or hiding your credit cards until they are paid off, or seeking financial counseling at your institution or through a community resource. This chapter will help you figure out what you need to do to be resilient—to stay on top of your financial situation so that money problems don't derail your college plans.

might include a job, your savings, gifts from relatives, student loans, scholarship dollars, or grants. List all your income sources, making note of how often you receive each type of income (weekly or monthly paychecks, quarterly loan disbursements, one-time gifts, etc.) and how much money you can expect. Knowing when your money is coming in will help you decide how to structure your budget. For example, if most of your income comes in on a monthly basis, you'll want to create a monthly budget. If you are paid every other week, a biweekly budget might work better.

Gather Expense Information for Your College or University. Your expenses will include tuition, residence hall fees if you live on campus, books and course materials, lab fees, and membership fees for any organizations you join. Some institutions offer a separate January or May term. Although your tuition for these one-month terms is generally covered in your overall tuition payment, you would have extra expenses if you wanted to travel to another location in the United States or abroad.

Gather Information about Living Expenses. First, do a "reality check." How do you *think* that you are spending your money? To find out for sure where your money is going and when, track your spending for a few weeks—ideally for at least a full month—in a notebook, a table, or a spreadsheet. The kinds of expense categories you should consider will vary depending on your situation. If you are a full-time student who lives with your parents or family members, your living expenses won't be the same as students living in a campus residence hall or in an off-campus apartment. If you are a returning student who holds down a job and has a family of your own to support, you will calculate your expenses differently. Whatever your situation, keeping track of your expenses and learning about your spending behaviors are important habits to develop. Consider which of the following expense categories are relevant to you:

- rent/utilities (electricity, gas, water)
- cell phone/cable/Internet/wi-fi
- transportation (car payment, car insurance, car repairs, gas, public transportation)
- child care
- groceries
- medical expenses (prescriptions, doctor visits, hospital bills)
- clothing/laundry

- entertainment (dining out, hobbies, movies)
- personal grooming (haircuts, toiletries)
- miscellaneous (travel, organization dues)

Be sure to recognize which expenses are fixed and which are variable. A *fixed expense* is one that will cost you the same amount every time you pay it. For example, your rent is a fixed expense because you owe your landlord the same amount each month. A *variable expense* is one that may change. Your textbooks are a variable expense because the number and cost of them will be different each term.

Find Out How You Are Doing. Once you have a sense of how your total income compares to your total weekly or monthly expenses, you can get a clearer picture of your current financial situation.

Make Adjustments. Although your budget might never be perfect, you can strive to improve it. In what areas did you spend much more or much less than expected? Do you need to reallocate funds to better meet the needs of your current situation? Be realistic and thoughtful in how you spend your money, and use your budget to help meet your goals, such as planning for a trip or getting a new pair of jeans.

Whatever you do, don't give up if your bottom line doesn't end up the way that you expected it would. Budgeting is a lot like dieting; you might slip up and eat a pizza (or spend too much buying one), but all is not lost. If you stay focused and flexible, your budget can lead you to financial stability and independence.

---

yourturn   Make Good Choices

Miscellaneous Expenses

Trying to get a handle on your "miscellaneous" expenses can be a challenge. Choose to write down everything you purchase over a two-week period, and see how many of those expenses don't fit into any of the categories listed above. Which of your miscellaneous expenses are necessary, and which aren't? The unnecessary expenses are places to reduce your spending. Make some tough choices to cut back, and start immediately. Track your spending for another two weeks. Can you tell the difference?

Cutting Costs

Once you have put together a working budget, have tried it out, and have adjusted it, you're likely to discover that your expenses still exceed your income. Don't panic. Simply begin to look for ways to reduce those expenses. Here are some tips for saving money in college:

- **Recognize the difference between your *needs* and your *wants*.** A *need* is something that you must have. For example, tuition and textbooks are considered *needs*. On the other hand, your *wants* are goods, services, or experiences that you wish to purchase but could reasonably live without. For example, concert tickets and mochas are *wants*. Your budget should always provide for your *needs* first.

- **Share expenses.** Having a roommate (or several) can be one of the easiest ways to cut costs on a regular basis. In exchange for giving up a little bit of privacy, you'll save hundreds of dollars on rent, utilities, and food. Make sure, however, that you work out a plan for sharing expenses equally and that everyone accepts his or her responsibilities. For instance, remember that if only your name is on the cable account, you (and only you) are legally responsible for that bill. You'll need to collect money from your roommates so that you can pay the bill in full and on time.

- **Consider the pros and cons of living on campus.** Depending on your school's location, off-campus housing might be less expensive than paying for a room and a meal plan on campus. Be aware, however, that although you might save some cash, you will give up a great deal of convenience by moving out of your campus residence. You almost certainly won't be able to roll out of bed 10 minutes before class, and you will have to prepare your own meals. Living on campus also makes it easier to make friends and develop a sense of connection to your college or university. Before you make the decision about where to live, weigh the advantages and disadvantages of each option.

- **Use low-cost transportation.** If you live close to campus, consider whether you need a car. Take advantage of lower-cost options such as public transportation or biking to class to save money on gasoline and parking. If you live farther away, check to see whether your institution hosts a ride-sharing program for commuter students, or carpool with someone in your area.

Go Vintage

Saving money doesn't mean you have to deprive yourself. Shopping at thrift stores for your clothes or apartment furnishings is a fun, affordable way to get one-of-a-kind pieces that won't break the bank.

© ANDREW WINNING/Corbis

- **Seek out discount entertainment options.** Take advantage of discounted or free programming through your college. Most institutions use a portion of their student fees to provide affordable entertainment options such as discounted or free tickets to concerts, movie theaters, sporting events, or other special events.
- **Embrace secondhand goods.** Use online resources such as Craigslist and thrift stores such as Goodwill to expand your wardrobe, purchase extras such as games and sports equipment, or furnish and decorate your room or apartment. You'll save money, and you won't mind as much when someone spills a drink on your "new" couch.
- **Avoid unnecessary fees.** Making late payments on credit cards and other bills can lead to expensive fees and can lower your credit score, which in turn will raise your interest rates. You might want to set up online, automatic payments to avoid making this costly mistake.

---

your turn | Stay Motivated

Using Money-Saving Strategies

Are you a bargain shopper or a coupon-clipper? Do you get a good feeling when you know you've saved money on a purchase or a service? Be on the lookout for ways to trim your budget, and let your successes motivate you to cut your expenses even more. Share your strategies with other students in your college success class.

UNDERSTANDING FINANCIAL AID

Few students can pay the costs of college tuition, fees, books, room and board, bills, and random expenses without some kind of help. Luckily, financial aid—student loans, grants, scholarships, work-study programs, and other sources of money to support your education—is available to help cover your expenses.

Types of Aid

While grants and scholarships are unquestionably the best forms of aid because they do not have to be repaid, the federal government, states, and colleges offer many other forms of assistance, such as loans, work-study opportunities, and cooperative education. A student loan is a form of financial aid that must be paid back with interest. We will discuss student loans in more detail later in this chapter.

Grants are funds provided by the government to help students pay for college. They are given to students based on their financial needs, and they do not need to be repaid. Some grants are specific to a particular academic major. Grants are awarded by the federal government, state

PEER LEADERS ❯ Some students might be embarrassed to share money-saving strategies in class because they don't want to be identified as someone who needs to keep a careful eye on expenses. You can play a major role in helping students understand that most of them have to live on a budget. Facilitate a class discussion in which you describe ways you save money, and invite students to share their ideas as well.

IN CLASS ❯ Consider sharing a time when you didn't handle your finances very well, perhaps when you were in college. Explain what went wrong and how long it took you to resolve your financial problem. Students can certainly learn from another person's mistakes.

IN CLASS ❯ Ask students to share their thoughts about financial aid and any experiences they have had in applying for financial aid. What advice would they give to other students about financial aid?

RETENTION STRATEGY ❯ Even though the term has already begun, many of your students may have registered without fully understanding or taking advantage of all the options available to them for financial aid. Financial aid could make the difference between leaving and persisting in college.

governments, and educational institutions. Students meet academic qualifications for grants by being admitted to a college and maintaining grades that are acceptable to the grant provider.

IN CLASS > Invite a financial aid adviser to visit class, or have the class meet in the financial aid office. Your students might not be aware of scholarship opportunities offered by your college or university. A financial aid adviser can give them up-to-date information and encourage them to apply for available scholarships.

A **scholarship** is money from your college or another institution that supports your education; it does not have to be repaid. Some scholarships are need-based—that is, they are awarded on the basis of both talent and financial need. "Talent" can refer to your past accomplishments in the arts or athletics, your potential for future accomplishments, or even where you are from. Some colleges and universities place importance on admitting students from other states or countries. "Need" in this context means the cost of college minus a federal determination of what you and your family can afford to contribute toward that cost. Your institution might provide scholarships from its own resources or from individual donors. Donors themselves sometimes stipulate the characteristics of scholarship recipients, such as age or academic major.

Other scholarships are known as **merit scholarships**. These are based on talent as defined above, but they do not require you to demonstrate financial need. It can be challenging to match your talent with merit scholarships. Most of them come through colleges and are part of the admissions and financial aid processes, which are usually described on the college's Web site.

Web-based scholarship search services are another good source for information on merit scholarships. Be certain that the Web site you use is free, will keep your information confidential unless you release your name, and will send you a notice—usually through e-mail—when a new merit scholarship that matches your qualifications is posted. Also be sure to ask your employer, your family's employers, and social, community, or religious organizations about any available merit scholarships.

Work-study programs provide part-time employment opportunities for students who receive financial aid if their aid amount is not enough to cover all their education costs. Students receive work-study notices as part of the overall financial aid notice and then can sign up to be interviewed for work-study jobs. Although some work-study jobs are relatively menial, the best options provide experience related to your academic studies while allowing you to earn money for college. Your salary is based on the skills required for a particular position and the hours involved. Keep in mind that you will be expected to accomplish specific tasks while on duty, although some supervisors might permit you to study during any down-time.

Cooperative (co-op) education allows you to alternate a term of study (a semester or quarter) with a term of paid work. Co-op opportunities are very common in the field of engineering, and the number of co-op programs in health care fields is growing. Colleges make information about co-ops available through the admissions office and individual academic departments.

Navigating Financial Aid

Financial aid seems complex because it can come from so many different sources. Each source may have a different set of rules about how to receive the money and how not to lose it. Your college's financial aid office and its Web site can help you find the way to get the largest amount of money that doesn't need to be repaid, the lowest interest rate on loans, and work opportunities that fit your academic program. Do not overlook this valuable campus resource, even if you dread having to fill out lots of forms that ask for personal financial information. In order to get the assistance you need and deserve, you'll have to be resilient and overcome any negative feelings you might have about asking for money.

Other organizations that can help students find the right college and the money to help them attend are located throughout the United States. Many of these organizations are members of the National College Access Network (which helps manage the National College Access Program Directory at **collegeaccess.org/Our_Members**) or participate in a national effort called KnowHow2Go (**knowhow2go.acenet.edu**). You might also be able to obtain funds from your employer, a local organization, or a private group.

The majority of students pay for college through a combination of various types of financial assistance: scholarships, grants, loans, and paid employment. Financial aid professionals refer to this combination as a *package*.

Qualifying for Aid

Most financial assistance requires you to fill out some kind of application form. The application used most often is the Free Application for Federal Student Aid (FAFSA). Every student should complete the FAFSA by the earliest deadline of the colleges you are applying to. Be sure to log on to the FAFSA Web site at **fafsa.ed.gov;** you will find it very informative. If additional forms are also required, such as the College Board's PROFILE form (**student.collegeboard.org/css-financial-aid-profile**) or individual scholarship applications, they will be listed in colleges' financial aid or

Show Me the Money
Don't let the paperwork scare you away. If you're not already receiving financial aid, be sure to investigate all the available options. Remember that your institution may also offer scholarships or grants that you don't have to repay.
AP Photo/Jon Elswick

admissions materials or by the organizations that offer scholarships. The box on this page outlines the steps you must take to qualify for most scholarships and grants, especially those sponsored by the federal government or state governments.

The amount of financial aid that you receive will depend on the cost of your academic program and what you or your family can pay as determined by the FAFSA. The cost includes average expenses for tuition and fees, books and supplies, room and board, transportation, and personal expenses. The financial aid office will subtract from the cost the amount that you and your family are expected to pay. In some cases, that amount can be as little as zero. Financial aid is designed to make up as much of the balance or "need" as possible.

Steps to Qualifying for Financial Aid

1. Enroll half-time or more in a certificate or degree program at one of the more than 4,500 colleges and universities certified to distribute federal financial aid. A few aid programs are available for less than half-time study; check with your department or college.

2. Complete the FAFSA. The first FAFSA you file is intimidating, especially if you rush to complete it right before the deadline. Completing the FAFSA in subsequent years is easier because you only need to update items that have changed. To make the process easier, get your personal identification number (PIN) a few weeks before the deadline. This PIN will be the same one you'll use throughout your college career. Try to do the form in sections rather than tackling all of it at once. Most of the information is basic: name, address, driver's license number, and things you will know or have in your personal files and records. For many undergraduates, the financial section will require your own and your parents' information from tax materials. However, if you are at least twenty-four, are a veteran, or have dependents, you do not need to submit your parents' tax information. If you are

married, your spouse's tax information will be needed.

3. Complete the College Board PROFILE form if your school or award-granting organization requires it. Review your college's admission information, or ask a financial aid adviser to determine whether this form is required.

4. Identify any additional applications that are required. These are usually scholarship applications with personal statements or short essays. The organizations, including the colleges that are giving the money, will provide instructions about what is required. Most have Web sites with complete information.

5. Follow instructions carefully, and submit each application on time. Financial aid is awarded from a fixed pool of funds. Once money is awarded, there is usually none left for those who file late.

6. Complete the classes for which you were given financial aid with at least a minimum grade point average as defined by your academic department or college, or by the organization that provided you the scholarship.

How to Keep Your Funding

If you earn average or better grades, complete your courses each term, and finish your program or degree on time, you should have no trouble maintaining your financial aid. It's a good idea to check with the financial aid office before you drop classes to make sure that you will not lose any aid.

Some types of aid, especially scholarships, require that you maintain full-time enrollment and make satisfactory academic progress. Dropping or failing a class might jeopardize all or part of your financial aid unless you are enrolled in more credits than the minimum required for financial aid. Full-time financial aid is often defined as twelve credit hours per term. If you initially enrolled in fifteen credit hours and dropped one three-hour course, your aid should not change. Even so, talk with a financial aid counselor before making the decision to drop a course, just to be sure.

Remember that although the financial aid office is there to serve you, you must be your own advocate. These tips should help:

- **File for financial aid every year.** Even if you don't think that you will receive aid for a certain year, you must file annually in case you become eligible in the future.
- **Meet all filing deadlines.** Students who do not meet filing deadlines risk losing aid from one year to the next.
- **Talk with a financial aid officer immediately if you or your family experiences a significant loss** (e.g., loss of a job, death of a parent or spouse). Don't wait for the next filing period; you might be eligible for funds for the current year.
- **Inquire every year about criteria-based aid.** Many colleges and universities have grants and scholarships for students who meet specific criteria. These might include grants for minority students, grants for students in specific academic majors, and grants for students of single-parent families.
- **Inquire about campus jobs throughout the year,** as these jobs might be available at any time, not just at the beginning of the term. If you do not have a job and want or need to work, keep asking.
- **Consider asking for a reassessment of your eligibility for aid.** If you have reviewed your financial aid package and think that your circumstances deserve additional consideration, you can ask the financial aid office to reassess your eligibility. The office is not always required to do so, but the request might be worth your effort.

ACHIEVING A BALANCE BETWEEN WORKING AND BORROWING

RETENTION STRATEGY > Even though it may sound counterintuitive to you and your students, explain the positive correlation between degree attainment and borrowing money for tuition to enable full-time enrollment versus not borrowing money, working more hours, and attending part-time.

After you have determined your budget, decided what (if anything) you can pay from savings, and taken your scholarships and grants into consideration, you might find that you still need additional income. Each term or year, you should decide how much you can work while maintaining good grades, and how much you should borrow from student loans.

Advantages and Disadvantages of Working

The majority of students today find that a combination of working and borrowing is the best way to gain experience, finance college, and complete their educational goals on time. Paid employment while you are in college has benefits beyond the money you can earn. Having a job in a field related to your major can help you develop a credential for graduate school and make you more employable later because it shows that you have the capability to manage several priorities at the same time. Working while you are in college can help you determine whether a particular career is what you will really want after you complete your education. And students who work a moderate amount (fifteen to twenty hours per week) typically get better grades than students who do not work at all.

PEER LEADERS > Attempting to work too many hours while maintaining a full-time course load often results in poor grades or even academic failure. Students will be more willing to listen to this message if it comes from you. Identify some options for students who are trying to work too many hours—such as borrowing money or reducing their overall course load—but be sensitive to students' reluctance to take on debt for any reason.

On the other hand, it's almost impossible to get great grades if you work full time while also trying to be a full-time student. Some students prefer not to take a job during their first year in college while they're making adjustments to a new academic environment. You might find that you're able to work some terms but not others, as family obligations or challenging classes can sometimes make the added burden of work impractical or impossible.

Part-time off-campus jobs that relate to your major or career plan are hard to come by. You'll likely find that most part-time employment has little or no connection to your career objectives. A better option may be to seek a job on campus. Students who work on campus develop relationships with instructors and staff members who can help them make plans for the future and negotiate the academic and social sides of campus life. While off-campus employers are often unwilling to allow their student employees time off for study and exam preparation, college employers will want you to put your studies and exam preparation first. The downside to on-campus employment is that you'll likely earn less than you would in an off-campus job, but if success in college is your top priority, the upside of working on campus outweighs the downside.

Student Loans

Although you should be careful not to borrow yourself into a lifetime of debt, avoiding loans altogether could delay your graduation and your progress up the career ladder. For most students, some level of borrowing is both necessary and prudent.

The following list provides information about the most common types of student loans. The list reflects the order in which you should apply for and accept loans to get the lowest interest rates and the best repayment terms.

- **Subsidized federal student loans** are backed by the government, which pays the loan interest on your behalf while you are enrolled in undergraduate, graduate, or professional school. These loans require at least half-time enrollment and a submitted FAFSA application.
- **Unsubsidized federal student loans** may require that you make interest payments while you are enrolled. If not, the interest is added to the amount you owe; this is called *capitalization*.

- **Parent Loan for Undergraduate Students (called PLUS loans)** are applied for and owed by parents but disbursed directly to students. The interest on PLUS loans is usually higher than the interest on federal student loans but lower than that on private loans. Parents who apply must provide information on the FAFSA.
- **Private student loans** are offered through banks and credit unions. Private loans often have stricter credit requirements and higher interest rates than federal loans do, and interest payments on private loans begin immediately.

Student loans are a very important source of money for college, but like paid employment, loans should be considered carefully. Loans for costs such as books and tuition are good investments. Loans for a more lavish lifestyle are likely to weigh you down in the future. As one wise person put it, if by borrowing you live like a wealthy graduate while you're a student, you'll live like a student after you graduate. Student loans can be a good way to begin using credit wisely, a skill you are likely to need throughout your life.

MANAGING CREDIT WISELY

RETENTION STRATEGY ❯ Evidence suggests that some students drop out of college because they abuse credit cards and accumulate unsustainable debt, especially for purposes unrelated to education. One of the financial-literacy skills students must therefore acquire is credit card management.

When you graduate, you will leave your institution with two significant numbers. The first is your grade point average (GPA), which represents the level of academic success you attained while in college. The second, your credit score, is a numerical representation of your fiscal responsibility. Although this second number might be less familiar to you than the first, it could be a factor that determines whether you get your dream job, regardless of your GPA. In addition, years from now you're likely to have forgotten your GPA, while your credit score will be more important than ever.

Your credit score is derived from a credit report that contains information about accounts in your name. These accounts include credit cards, student loans, utility bills, cell phones, and car loans, to name a few. This credit score can determine whether or not you will qualify for a loan (car, home, student, etc.), what interest rates you will pay, how much your car insurance will cost, and your chances of being hired by certain organizations. Even if none of these things are in your immediate future, now is the time to start thinking about your credit score.

Although using credit cards responsibly is a good way to build credit, acquiring a credit card has become much more difficult for college students. In May 2009, President Barack Obama signed legislation that prohibits college students under the age of twenty-one from obtaining a credit card unless they can prove that they are able to make the payments, or unless the credit card application is cosigned by a parent or guardian.

Understanding Credit

IN CLASS ❯ Ask students to share their opinions about the 2009 credit card legislation and its effect on college students. Do they think that the government was justified in changing the way that credit cards are made available? Consider organizing an in-class debate on the pros and cons of this legislation.

Even if you can prove that you have the means to repay credit card debt, it is important for you to thoroughly understand how credit cards work and how they can both help and hurt you. Several frequently asked

MASTER BUDGETING, VERSION 2.0!

Technology can really help you when it comes to keeping track of your money—knowing how much you have, how much you need, and whether there are any problems with transactions moving through your accounts.

The Problem

You want to keep track of your finances, but you are afraid of making mistakes and you don't know where to begin.

The Fix

Start with the financial institutions you already work with and see what technology tools they offer.

How to Do It

1. *Create a budget.* As you learned earlier in this chapter, a budget is a spending plan that tracks all of your sources of income and expenses during a set period of time. Working within a budget helps you meet your goals and obligations.

2. *Check with your banking institution.* See what apps and online services they offer. Many banks offer free online access to your accounts so that you can deposit funds, make purchases, transfer funds, and receive deposit or withdrawal notifications via your cell phone or e-mail. Many banks will also send you electronic notifications of these transactions so you are always aware of how much money is currently in your account and when activity occurs that will affect your account. These services allow you to review your account information and help you make better decisions about when you use your money.

3. *Use your bank's apps and online tools to help you with your budget.* Check out some of these cool apps:

    Mint mint.com
   This Web site and phone app allows you to combine information from all of your financial accounts in one place, so you can see how much money you have in investments, income, loans, and payments. While it is not a bank, it does allow you to see your whole financial picture at once.

    PayPal Mobile paypal.com
   This app allows you to spend money and allows other people to give you money, including money you earn from part-time jobs,

    Pocket Budget mapeapps.com
   This is a simple way to keep track of your budget that installs on your phone.

4. *Beware of scams.* As you improve how you track your finances, remember to exercise caution in dealing with banks, credit card companies, and all financial institutions:

   - Do not transmit personal information (social security number, bank details, credit or debit card numbers, passwords, etc.) through e-mail. Doing so could put you at risk of identity theft. (Read more about identity theft in the box later in this chapter.) If you need to contact a financial institution by phone, place the call yourself, and deal only with banks or other financial institutions you trust.

   - Do not answer questions about vital personal information over the phone if you didn't originate the call.

   - Do not reply to e-mail, pop-ups, or text messages that ask you to reveal personal information.

   - Never click on links in unsolicited e-mails or paste URLs or lines of code into your browser bar.

   - Use good judgment. If an offer sounds too good to be true—like a huge line of credit with 0% annual percentage rate—it probably is.

EXTRA STYLE POINTS: Keep tabs on your credit report. Regularly reviewing your credit history pays off in major ways. It alerts you to any new accounts that might have been opened in your name. It also lets you catch unauthorized activity on accounts that questions about credit cards are answered in the box later in this chapter. Simply put, a credit card allows you to buy something now and pay for it later. Each month, you will receive a statement listing all the purchases you made using your credit card during the previous thirty days. The statement will request a payment toward your balance and will set a payment due date. Your payment options will vary: You can pay your entire balance, pay a specified amount of the balance, or pay only a minimum payment, which may be as low as $10.

But beware: If you make only a minimum payment, the remaining balance on your card will be charged a finance fee, or interest charge, causing your balance to increase before your next bill arrives, even if you don't make any more purchases. Paying the minimum payment is almost never a good strategy and can add years to your repayment time. In fact, assuming an 18 percent interest rate, if you continually pay only $10 per month toward a $500 credit card balance, it will take you more than seven years to pay it off, and you'll pay an extra $431 in interest, almost doubling the amount you originally charged.

Avoid making late payments. Paying your bill even one day late can result in a finance charge of $30 or more; it can also raise the interest rate not only on that card, but also on any other credit accounts you have. If you decide to use a credit card to build credit, you might want to set up online, automatic payments to avoid incurring expensive late fees. Remember that the payment due date is the date that the credit card lender should receive your payment, not the date that you should send it.

If you decide to apply for a credit card while you're in college, remember that it should be used to build credit and for emergencies. Credit cards should not be used to fund a lifestyle that you cannot otherwise

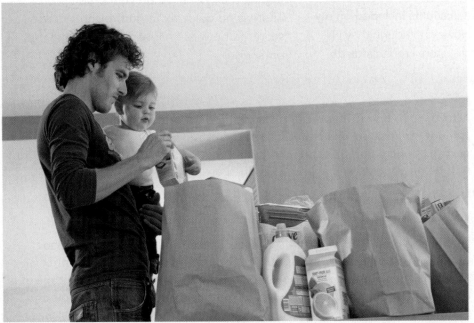

In Case of Emergency
Having a credit card for emergencies is a good practice. Circumstances that might warrant the use of credit include paying critical expenses to care for yourself or your family, dealing with an auto accident or an unforeseen medical expense, or traveling on short notice to handle a crisis. Spring break is *not* an emergency.
© Britt Erlanson/cultura/Corbis

Frequently Asked Questions about Credit Cards and Identity Theft

- **I have a credit card with my name on it, but it is actually my parents' account number. Is this card building credit for me?** No. You are considered an authorized user on the account, but your parents are the primary account holders. To build credit, you must be the primary account holder, or at least a joint account holder.

- **I have a credit card and am the primary account holder. How can I resist abusing it?** Use your credit card to help you build credit by making small charges and paying them off in full each month. Stick to two expense categories only, such as gas and groceries, and don't make any exceptions unless you have a serious emergency.

- **I choose the "credit" option every time I use my debit card. Is this building credit for me?** No. Using the credit function of your debit card is more like writing an electronic check because you are still taking money directly out of your checking account. Even if your debit card has a major credit card (Visa, MasterCard, etc.) logo on it, it is not building credit for you.

- **I have a few store credit cards (Target, Best Buy, etc.). Are these accounts included on my credit report?** Yes. However, though they will affect your credit score, store credit cards do not carry as much weight as major credit cards such as Visa or MasterCard. It is OK to have a few store credit cards, but a major credit card will do more to help you build credit.

- **Where can I apply for a major credit card?** A good place to begin is your bank or credit union. Remember that you might have to prove your ability to make payments in order to obtain a card.

- **If one credit card will help me build credit, will several build my credit even more?** Research shows that there is no benefit to having more than two major credit cards. And even if you're able to pay the required monthly amounts, having too many accounts open can make you appear risky to the credit bureaus determining your credit score.

- **What if I forget and make a late payment? Is my credit score ruined?** Your credit report reflects at least the past seven years of activity, but it puts the most emphasis on the most recent two years. In other words, the farther you get from your mistakes, the less impact they will have on your credit score. There is no quick fix for improving a credit score, so beware of advertisements that say otherwise.

afford, or to buy things that you want but don't need (see the "Living on a Budget" section in this chapter). On the other hand, if you use your credit card just once a month and pay the balance as soon as the bill arrives, you will be on your way to a strong credit score in just a few years.

Debit Cards

Although you might want to use a credit card for emergencies and to establish a good credit rating, you might also look into the possibility of applying for a debit card (also called a checkcard). The big advantage of a debit card is that you don't always have to carry cash, and thus you don't run the risk of losing your money. Because the amount of your purchases will be limited to the funds in your bank account, a debit card is also a good way to constrain your spending.

- **If building credit is a wise decision, what's so bad about using credit cards to buy some things that I really want but can't afford right now?** It is not wise to use credit cards to purchase things that you cannot afford. Living within your means is always the way to go.

- **What is identity theft?** In this insidious and increasingly common crime, someone assumes your identity, secretly opens up accounts in your name, and has the bills sent to another address.

- **How can I protect myself from identity theft?** *Be password savvy.* The more sensitive the information, the stronger your password should be. Aim for passwords with eight to fourteen characters, including numbers, both uppercase and lowercase letters, and, if allowed, a few special characters like @ and #. Never use an obvious number like your birthday or wedding anniversary. Don't use the same username and password for every site. Change the password to your online credit card or bank account at least once a year. If you must keep a written record of your usernames and passwords, keep the list in a secure place at home, not in your wallet. *Beware of scams.* Don't make yourself vulnerable. A few tips: Research a company or

organization before submitting your résumé. Don't e-mail any personal information (social security number, bank details, credit or debit card numbers, passwords, etc.) that could put you at risk of identity theft. Don't answer questions about vital personal information over the phone if you didn't originate the call. Don't reply to e-mails, pop-ups, or text messages that ask you to reveal sensitive information. Don't send sensitive data by e-mail. Call instead, and deal only with businesses you trust. Never click on links in unsolicited e-mails or paste URLs or lines of code into your browser bar. If an offer sounds too good to be true, it probably is.

- **Where can I get my credit report?** You can keep an eye on your credit report by visiting the free (and safe) Web site **annualcreditreport.com** at least once a year. Regularly reviewing your credit history pays off in major ways. It alerts you to any new accounts that might have been opened in your name. It also lets you catch unauthorized activity on accounts that you've closed or haven't used lately. Everyone is entitled to one free credit report a year from each of the three major credit bureaus.

The only real disadvantage is that a debit card provides direct access to your checking account, so it's very important to keep your card in a safe place and away from your personal identification number (PIN). The safest way to protect your account is to commit your PIN to memory. If you lose your debit card—or your credit card—notify your bank immediately.

your turn Work Together

Credit or Debit: Which Works Better for You?

With a small group, discuss your use of credit or debit cards. Which of these do you have, and which do you prefer? Make a list of the advantages and disadvantages of each, and share your list with the whole class.

high-impact practice 3

HIGH-IMPACT PRACTICE > This Your Turn exercise will enable your students to collaborate and share valuable information about how they choose to manage their money. By working together, they can also recognize the pros and cons of each method.

Don't Let This Happen to You

The 2013 comedy *Identity Thief* tells the story of an identity theft victim, played by Jason Bateman, who confronts the thief, played by Melissa McCarthy. In the movie, the victim answers questions about vital personal information in a phone call that he did not initiate—a big no-no—and his life is turned upside down. If identity theft happens to you, it's not so funny.

Bob Mahoney/© Universal/courtesy Everett Collection

 high-impact practice 2

HIGH-IMPACT PRACTICE > This short exercise will introduce students to persuasive writing about a topic that is critical to their success: managing money wisely. This individual writing can also be shared in a small group, where students can work collaboratively to build a list of the common ways college students are tempted to waste money.

your turn Write and Reflect

Beware: It's Easy to Waste Money in College

Write a "warning letter" to a younger sibling (real or imaginary) about ways that students are tempted to waste money in college and what can happen as a result. In your letter, include strategies from this chapter for carefully managing money.

PLANNING FOR THE FUTURE

It's never too early to begin thinking about how you will finance your life after graduation and whether you will begin working immediately or pursue a graduate or professional degree. Your work, whether on or off campus, will help you make that decision. Here are some tips that will help you plan now for your future:

- **Figure out your next step—more education or work?** If you are working on campus, get to know faculty or staff members and seek their advice about your future plans. If you are working off campus, think carefully about whether your current job is one that you would want to continue after you graduate. If not, keep your options open and look for part-time work in a field that more closely aligns with your career plans or long-term educational objectives.
- **Keep your address current with the registrar.** Even when you have finished your degree or program, and especially if you stop classes for a term, alert the registrar of any changes in address. This is doubly important if you have a student loan; you don't want to get a negative report on your credit rating because you missed information about your loan.
- **Establish a savings account.** Add to it regularly, even if you can manage to deposit only a few dollars a month. The sooner you start, the greater your returns will be.

Your education is the most productive investment that you can make for your future and the future of your family. Research shows that completion of programs or degrees after high school increases earnings, opens up career options, leads to greater satisfaction in work, results in more engaged citizenship such as voting and community service, and greatly increases the probability that your children will go to college. Although college is a big investment of time and money, it's an investment you'll be glad you made.

checklist for success

Money

■ **Make learning financial-literacy skills a key college success skill.** Understanding how to manage money has life-long benefits.

■ **Create a budget and then live on it.** Remember that it's your budget, tailor-made by and for you.

■ **Act on some of the suggestions offered in this chapter for cutting your costs.** For most college students, cutting costs is even more important than increasing their income.

■ **Learn as much as you can about the different types of financial aid.** Find out what is offered to U.S. college students by the government and by your particular college, even though the term has already started. It's never too late to take advantage of these opportunities.

■ **Consider the pros and cons of working while in college.** If you do work, consider how much and where you will work. Realize that students who borrow money and attend college full time are more likely to attain their degrees than those who use a different strategy.

■ **Remember that you will finish college with two key numbers: your GPA and your credit score.** Potential employers will check both your transcript and your credit report.

■ **Learn the strategies in this chapter for wise credit card management.** College is a time to learn how to use credit wisely.

■ **Take advantage of help offered on your campus to learn financial-management skills.** You can't help it if you didn't learn these skills before; you may not have had any money to manage!

REFLECT ON CHOICES

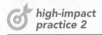 high-impact practice 2 | Successful college students learn to manage their money. They are careful to manage their income and their expenditures. Write about the choices you have already made about how to spend your money? This chapter offers lots of good strategies for handling your finances. Which of them will you practice this term?

APPLY WHAT YOU'VE LEARNED

Now that you have read and discussed this chapter, consider how you can apply what you have learned to your academic life and your personal life. The following prompts will help you reflect on chapter material and its relevance to you both now and in the future.

1. Sometimes it's hard to plan for the future. Describe two ways that you can save money each week, such as using public transportation to reduce the expense of owning a car.

2. Money is a difficult subject to talk about, and sometimes it seems easier not to worry about it. Ask yourself hard questions. Do you spend money without much thought? Do you have a lot of debt? Describe your ideal financial picture.

USE YOUR RESOURCES

> **Your Institution's Financial Aid Office** Be sure to visit your institution's financial aid office to take advantage of financial aid opportunities and to learn how to apply for scholarships.

> **Special Scholarships** If you are a veteran, an under-represented student, or an adult student, your institution may have special scholarship opportunities designed for you. Check with the financial aid office for leads on special scholarship opportunities.

> **Local United Way Office** If your college or university doesn't offer credit counseling, look online or in the telephone book for credit counseling agencies within the local United Way office.

> **Campus Programs** Be on the lookout for special campus programs on money management. These programs are often offered in residence halls or through the division of student affairs.

> **Business School or College** Faculty or staff members within a school or college of business or a division of continuing education sometimes offer a course in personal finance. Check your college catalog or Web site, or call the school, college, or division office to see if there are options that you can take advantage of either this term or next.

> **Counseling Center** If money problems are related to compulsive shopping or gambling, be sure to seek counseling at your institution's counseling center.

> **Budget Wizard: cashcourse.org.** The National Endowment for Financial Education (NEFE) offers this free, secure, budgeting tool.

> **Free Application for Federal Student Aid: fafsa.ed.gov.** The online form allows you to set up an account, complete the application electronically, save your work, and monitor the progress of your application.

> **FastWeb: FastWeb.com.** Register for this free scholarship-search service and discover sources of educational funding you never knew existed.

> **Bankrate: bankrate.com.** This free site provides unbiased information about the interest rates, fees, and penalties associated with major credit cards and private loans. It also provides calculators that let you determine the long-term costs of different kinds of borrowing.

> **Susan Knox, *Financial Basics: A Money-Management Guide for Students.*** (Columbus: Ohio State University Press, 2004.) The author blends money-management experience with her desire to inform and help students master their finances, sharing experiences about money lessons learned in college, and offering sound solutions and advice for students and their families.

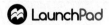 LaunchPad

LaunchPad is a great resource! For *Your College Experience*, go to macmillanhighered.com/gardner12e. For the Concise edition, go to macmillanhighered.com/collegesuccessmedia.

glossary

abstract   A paragraph-length summary of the methods and major findings of an article in a scholarly journal.

abstract conceptualization   A learner's ability to integrate observations into logically sound theories. One of the four stages of the Kolb Inventory of Learning Styles.

academic adviser   A faculty or staff member who provides official advice to students on course selection and academic planning.

academic calendar   A calendar that shows all the important dates specific to your campus: financial aid, registration, and add/drop deadlines; midterm and final exam dates; holidays; graduation deadlines; and so forth.

academic integrity   Intellectual honesty; the avoidance of cheating and plagiarism.

academic plan/map   A list of the courses you need to take and complete in a program of study to graduate with a degree.

academic planning   Creating a plan of coursework that leads to a college degree.

accommodators   Individuals who prefer hands-on learning. They are skilled at making things happen, rely on their intuition, and might use trial and error rather than logic to solve problems. Accommodators often major in business. One of the learner groups of the Kolb Inventory of Learning Styles.

acronym   A memory device created by forming new words from the first letters of several words.

acrostic   A verse in which certain letters of each word or line form a message.

active experimentation   A learner's ability to make decisions, solve problems, and test what he or she has learned in new situations. One of the four stages of the Kolb Inventory of Learning Styles.

active learning   Learning by participation, such as listening critically, discussing what you are learning, and writing about it.

active reading   A four-step process to reading that involves using strategies, such as highlighting and taking notes, to help you stay focused. The steps in the active reading process are previewing, marking, reading with concentration, and reviewing.

adaptability   The ability to adjust your thinking and behavior when faced with new or unexpected situations.

analysis   The process of breaking down material into its parts so that you can understand its structure. Includes categorizing, comparing, contrasting, and questioning. One of the six levels of Bloom's Taxonomy.

annotate   To add critical or explanatory margin notes on a page as you read.

annotation   Note or remark written in the margin about a piece of writing.

application   The process of using what you have learned, such as rules and methods, in new situations. Application includes choosing, illustrating, practicing, and interpreting. One of the six levels of Bloom's Taxonomy.

argument   Reason and evidence brought together in logical support of a claim.

assertiveness   Standing up for yourself when you need to, without being too aggressive.

assimilators   Individuals who like to develop theories and think about abstract concepts. Assimilators often major in math, physics, or chemistry. One of the learner groups of the Kolb Inventory of Learning Styles.

attention deficit hyperactivity disorder (ADHD)   A disorder characterized by difficulty organizing tasks, completing work, and listening to and following directions.

aural learner   A person who prefers to learn by listening to information. One of the preferences described by the VARK Learning Styles Inventory.

autonomy   Self-direction or independence. College students usually have more autonomy than high school students.

behavioral interview   An interview in which the interviewer questions the candidate about past experiences and how they helped the candidate learn and grow. This type of interview helps assess skills and behaviors.

bias   A tendency against or in favor of certain groups or value systems.

biorhythms   The internal mechanisms that drive our daily patterns of physical, emotional, and mental activity.

bodily/kinesthetic learner   An individual who prefers learning by moving around and is good at sports, dance, and acting. One of the eight intelligences described by the theory of multiple intelligences.

Campus SAVE Act   A federal law passed in 2013 mandating that all colleges and universities provide sexual assault, violence, and harassment education to students.

campus wide common intellectual experience   A program in which students take required "common-core" courses, participate in a required learning community, or engage in other shared experiences such as a "common reading" (a high-impact practice).

capstone course or project   A course or experience taken during the senior year that requires students to reflect on what they learned in all their courses and create a project of some sort that integrates and applies that knowledge (a high-impact practice).

cheating   Dishonesty in academic work. Each campus has its own definition, which could include looking over a classmate's shoulder for an answer, using a calculator when it is not permitted, obtaining or discussing an exam or individual questions from an exam without permission, copying someone else's lab notes, purchasing term papers over the Internet, watching the video instead of reading the book, and copying computer files.

chunking   A previewing method that involves making a list of terms and definitions from the reading and then dividing the terms into smaller clusters of five, seven, or nine to learn the material more effectively.

citation   A source or author of certain material. When browsing the Internet for sources, use only material that has citations crediting the author, where it came from, and who posted it.

cloud computing   A term that describes using the Internet as a storage device and sharing files and folders with others.

co-curricular experience   Learning that occurs outside the classroom through on-campus clubs and groups, co-op programs, internships, or other means.

cognitive restructuring   A technique of applying positive thinking and giving oneself encouraging messages rather than self-defeating, negative ones.

collaborative assignment   A learning activity in which you work and solve problems with your classmates (a high-impact practice).

comprehension   Understanding the meaning of material. Comprehension includes classifying, describing, explaining, and translating. One of the six levels of Bloom's Taxonomy.

computerized test   A test that is often taken in a computer lab or testing center and is usually not administered online.

computer literacy   Facility with electronic tools, both for conducting searches and for presenting to others what you have found and analyzed.

concrete experience   Abilities that allow learners to be receptive to others and open to their feelings and specific experiences. One of the four stages of the Kolb Inventory of Learning Styles.

convergers   People who enjoy the world of ideas and theories and are good at thinking about how to apply those theories to real-world, practical situations. Convergers tend to choose health-related and engineering majors. One of the learner groups of the Kolb Inventory of Learning Styles.

Cornell format   A method for organizing notes in which one side of the notebook page is designated for note taking during class, and the other serves as a "recall" column where main ideas and important details for tests are jotted down as soon as possible after class.

credit hours   A representation of the number of clock hours you spend in each class every week during a term, and the number of credits you will earn if you satisfactorily complete a course. A one-credit course generally meets for 50 to 60 minutes once a week.

credit score   A numerical representation of your level of fiscal responsibility, derived from a credit report that contains information about all the accounts in your name. This score can determine your ability to qualify for loans, the interest rates and insurance rates you pay, and can sometimes affect your employability.

critical thinking   Thoughtful consideration of the information, ideas, observations, and arguments that you encounter; in essence, a search for truth.

cultural literacy   Knowing what is going on around you and what has happened in the past.

culture   The aspects of a group of people that are passed on or learned. Traditions, food, language, clothing styles, artistic expression, and beliefs are all part of culture.

cyberbullying   Any behavior performed through electronic or digital media by individuals or groups who repeatedly communicate hostile or aggressive messages intended to inflict harm or discomfort on others.

database   An organized and searchable set of information. Like a special search engine, a database is often classified by a certain subject area, such as chemistry or U.S. history.

deep learning   Understanding the "why" and "how" behind the details.

degree   The type of diploma students receive after graduation.

delayed gratification   The ability to resist the temptation for an immediate reward and wait for a later reward.

digital footprint   How you represent yourself—and how others represent you—online on Facebook, Instagram, Twitter, and other social media sites.

digital persona/profile   The version of yourself that you present online on Facebook, Instagram, Twitter, and other social media sites.

discipline   An area of academic study, such as sociology, anthropology, or engineering.

discrimination   The act of treating people differently because of their race, ethnicity, gender, socioeconomic class, or other identifying characteristics, rather than on their merits.

divergers   Individuals who are adept at reflecting on situations from many viewpoints. They excel at brainstorming

visualization   A memory technique used to associate words, concepts, or stories with visual images.

visual learner   A person who prefers to learn by reading words on a printed page or by looking at pictures, charts, graphs, symbols, video, and other visual means. One of the preferences described by the VARK Learning Styles Inventory.

visual/spatial learner   An individual who likes to draw and play with machines and is good at puzzles and reading maps and charts. One of the eight intelligences described by the theory of multiple intelligences.

work-study award   A form of federal financial aid that covers a portion of college costs in return for on-campus employment.

writing-intensive courses   Courses across the curriculum that engage students in multiple forms of writing for different audiences. This textbook offers various writing activities that make your first-year seminar a writing-intensive course (a high-impact practice).

index